EATER NOT!

ATSUSHI OHKUBO

3

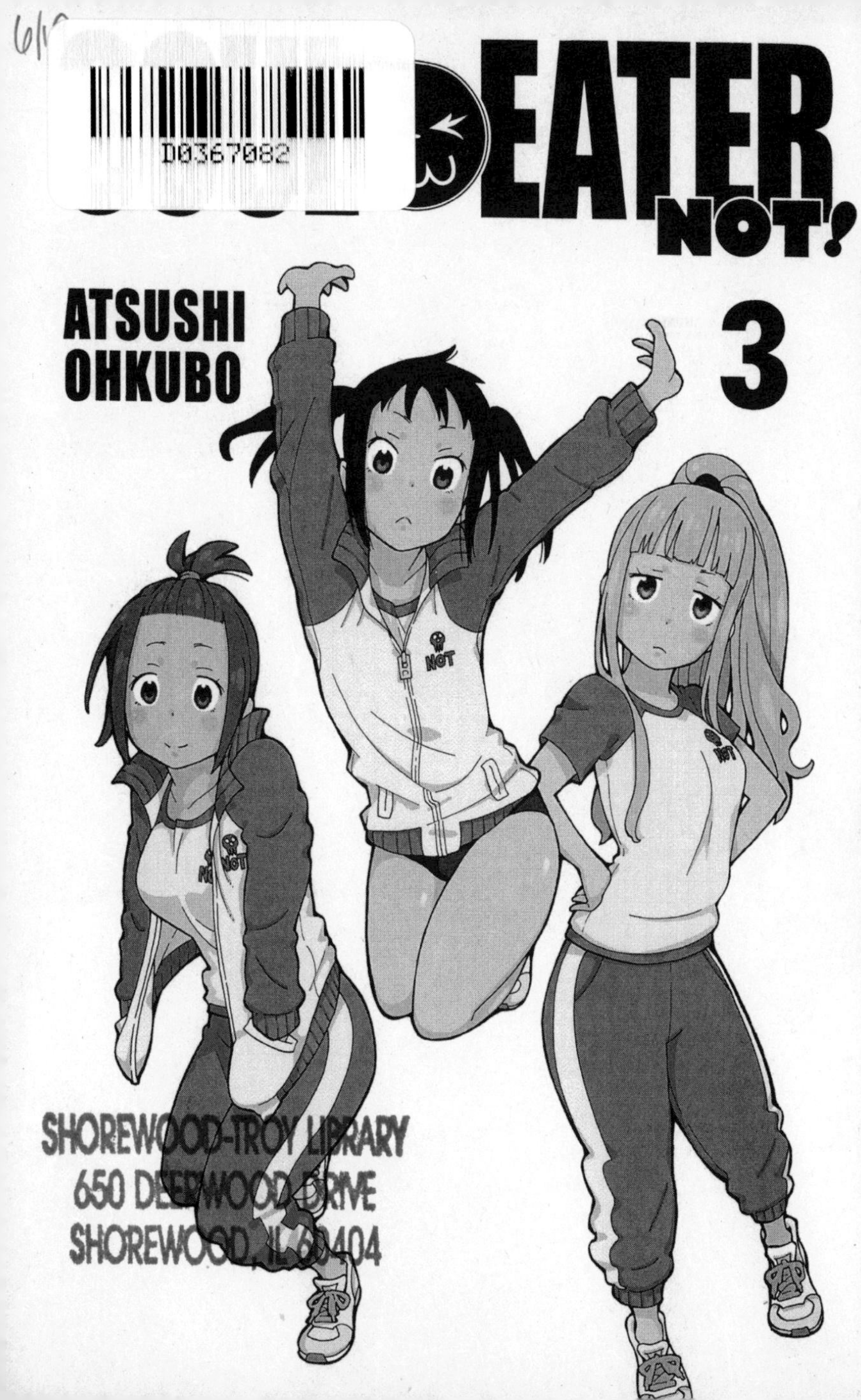
NOT
NOT
NOT
NOT

EATER

ATSUSHI OHKUBO

SOUL

03

NO

SOUL EATER NOT! 03

CONTENTS

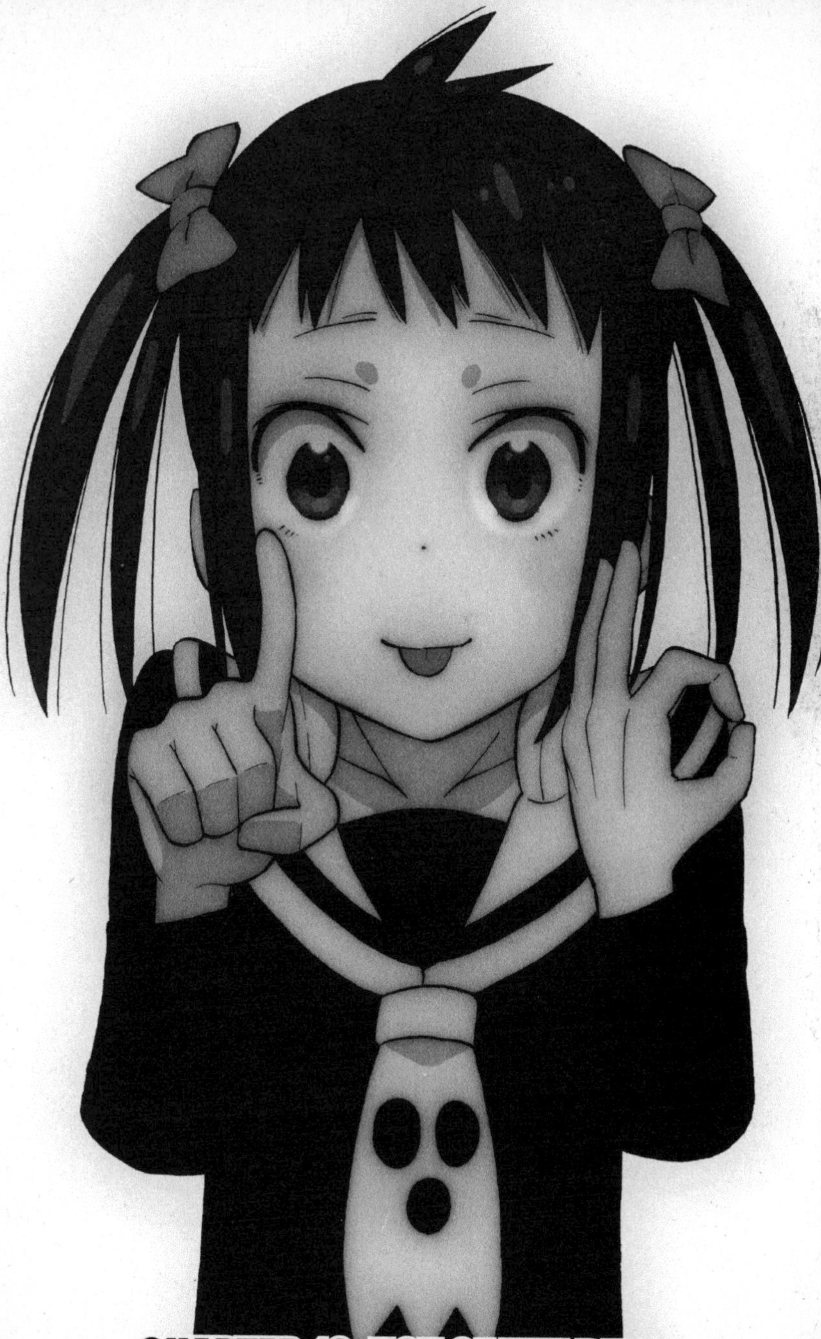

CHAPTER 16: NOT OF THE DEAD!

SOUL EATER NOT!

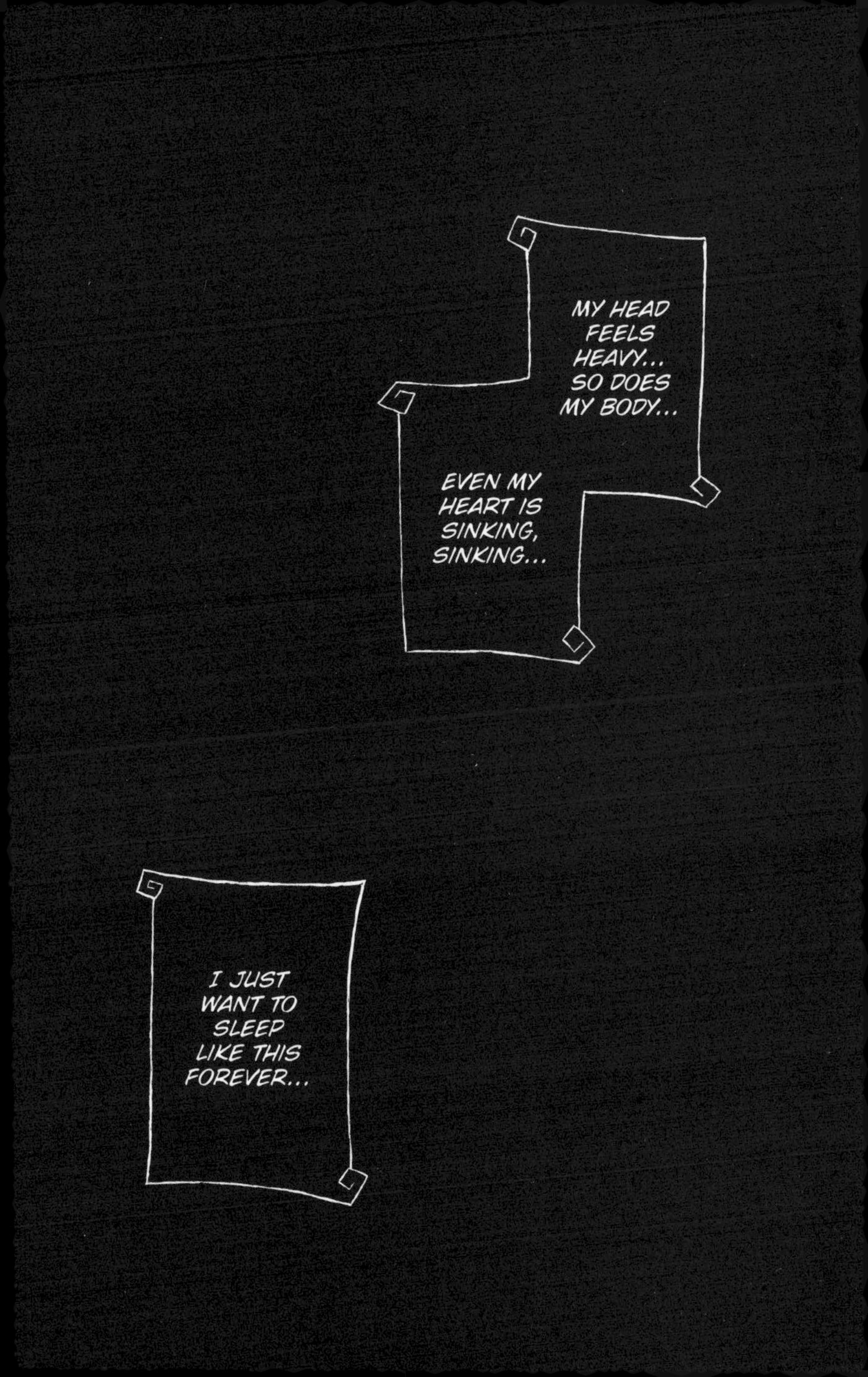
MY HEAD FEELS HEAVY... SO DOES MY BODY...
EVEN MY HEART IS SINKING, SINKING...
I JUST WANT TO SLEEP LIKE THIS FOREVER...

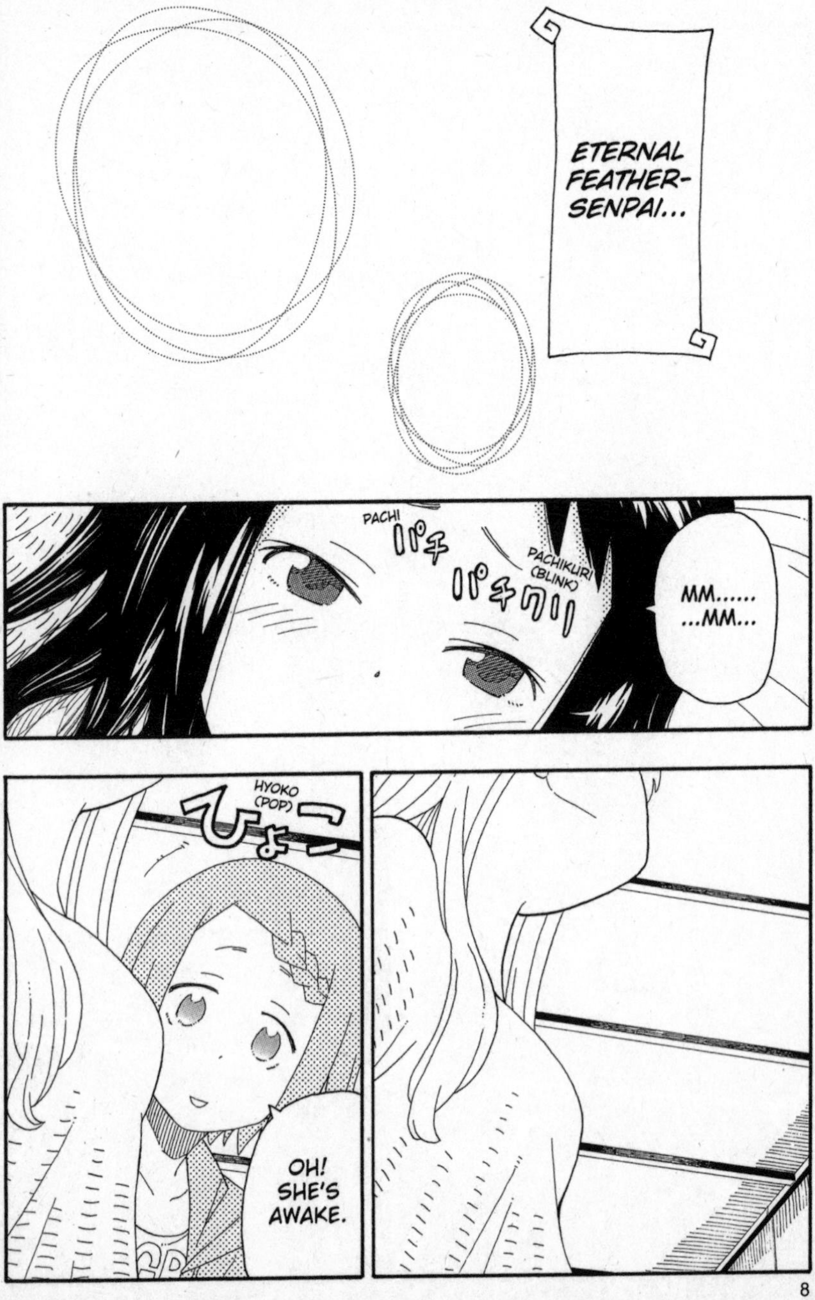
ETERNAL FEATHER-SENPAI...
MM...... ...MM...
PACHIKURI (BLINK)
パチクリ
PACHI
パチ
HYOKO (POP)
ひょこ
OH! SHE'S AWAKE.

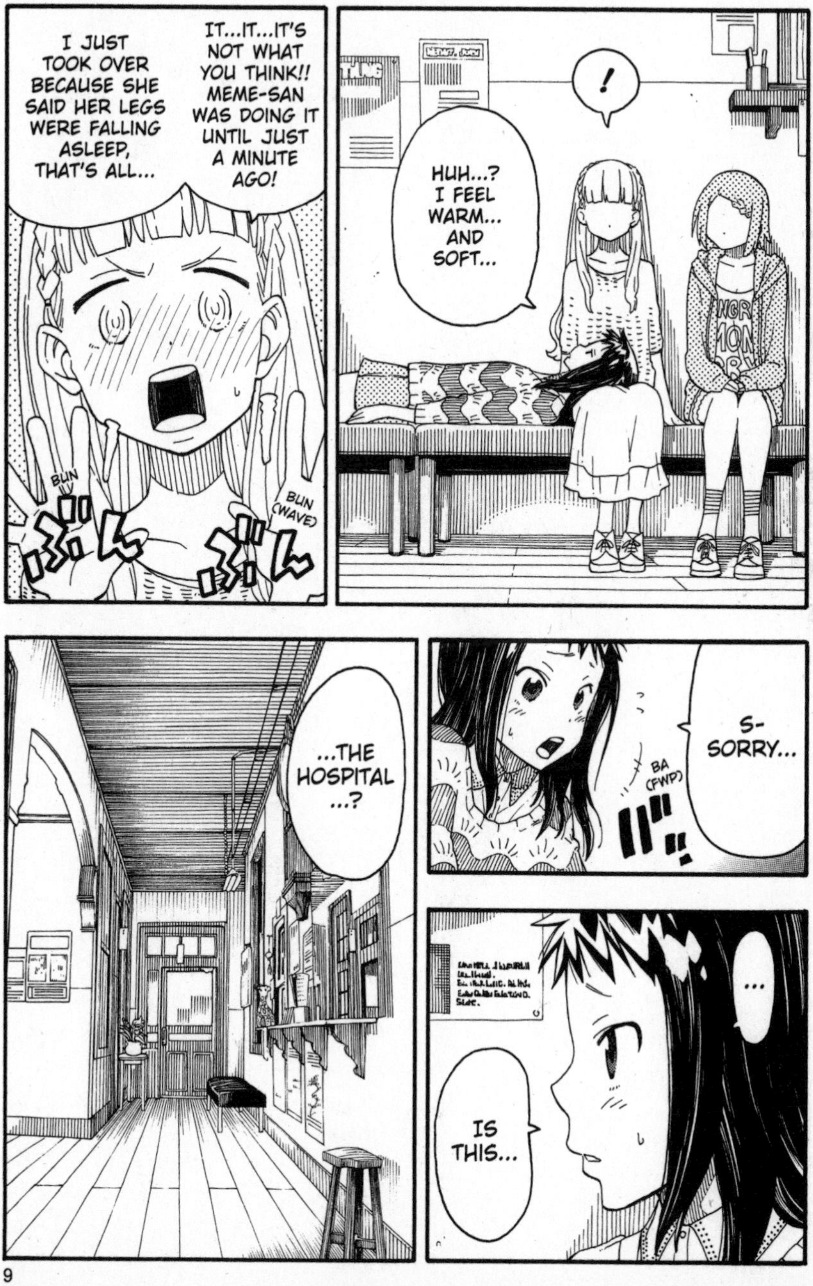
!
HUH...? I FEEL WARM... AND SOFT...
IT...IT...IT'S NOT WHAT YOU THINK!! MEME-SAN WAS DOING IT UNTIL JUST A MINUTE AGO!
I JUST TOOK OVER BECAUSE SHE SAID HER LEGS WERE FALLING ASLEEP, THAT'S ALL...
BUN (WAVE)
ぶん
BUN
ぶん
S-SORRY...
BA (FWP)
バッ
...
IS THIS...
...THE HOSPITAL ...?

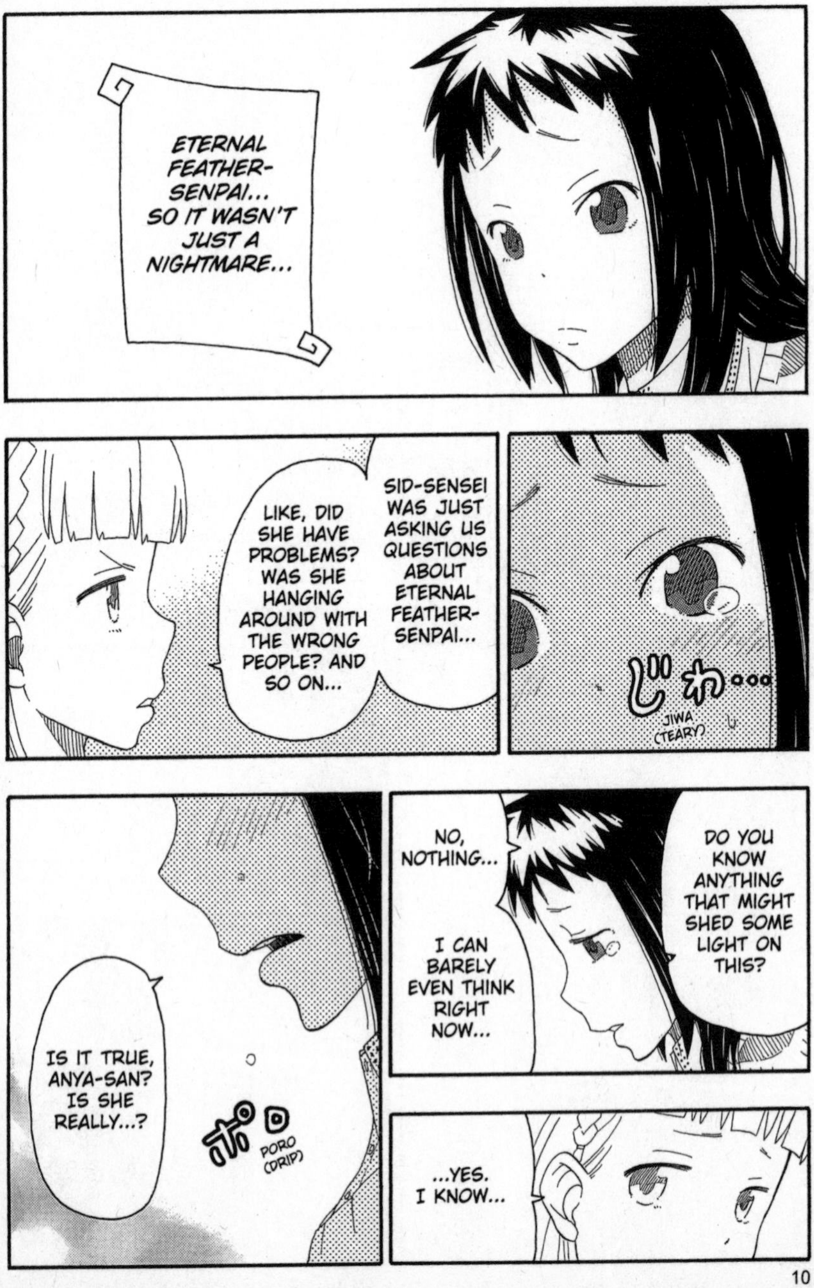
ETERNAL FEATHER-SENPAI... SO IT WASN'T JUST A NIGHTMARE...
じわ...
JIWA (TEARY)
SID-SENSEI WAS JUST ASKING US QUESTIONS ABOUT ETERNAL FEATHER-SENPAI...
LIKE, DID SHE HAVE PROBLEMS? WAS SHE HANGING AROUND WITH THE WRONG PEOPLE? AND SO ON...
DO YOU KNOW ANYTHING THAT MIGHT SHED SOME LIGHT ON THIS?
NO, NOTHING...
I CAN BARELY EVEN THINK RIGHT NOW...
...YES. I KNOW...
IS IT TRUE, ANYA-SAN? IS SHE REALLY...?
ポロ
PORO (DRIP)

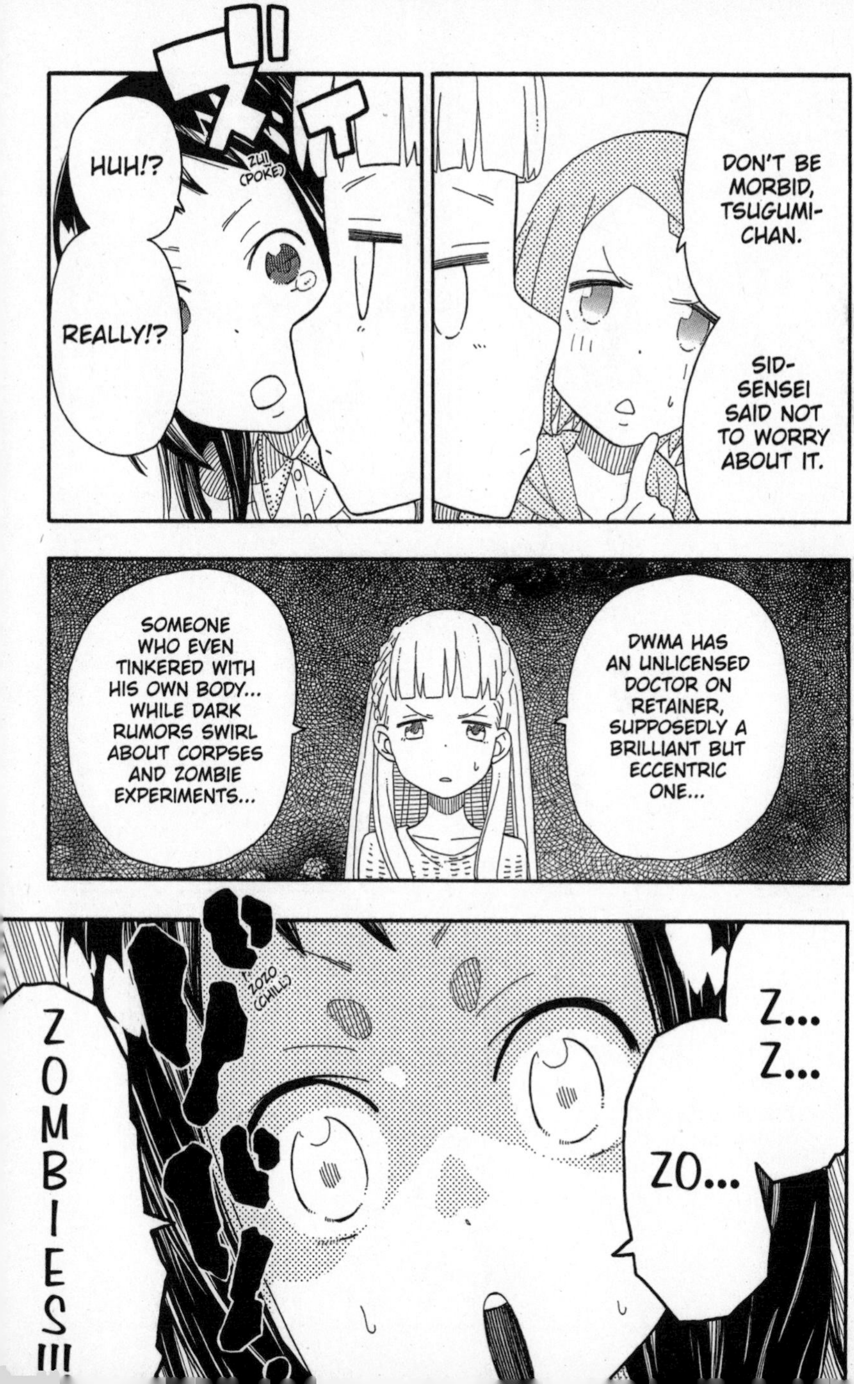
DON'T BE MORBID, TSUGUMI-CHAN.
SID-SENSEI SAID NOT TO WORRY ABOUT IT.
ZUI (POKE)
HUH!?
REALLY!?
DWMA HAS AN UNLICENSED DOCTOR ON RETAINER, SUPPOSEDLY A BRILLIANT BUT ECCENTRIC ONE...
SOMEONE WHO EVEN TINKERED WITH HIS OWN BODY... WHILE DARK RUMORS SWIRL ABOUT CORPSES AND ZOMBIE EXPERIMENTS...
Z... Z...
ZO...
ZOZO (CHILL)
ZOMBIES!!!

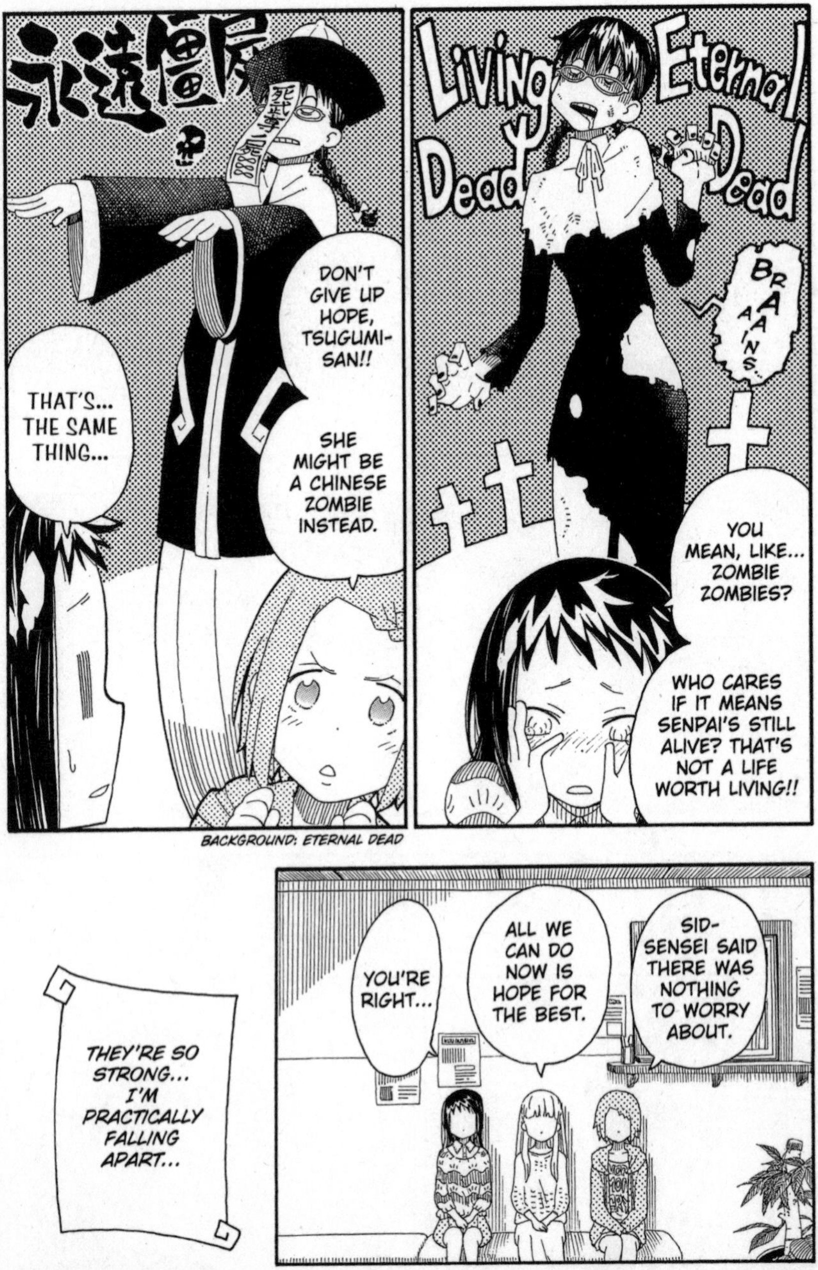
Living Dead
Eternal Dead
BRAAAINS..
YOU MEAN, LIKE... ZOMBIE ZOMBIES?
WHO CARES IF IT MEANS SENPAI'S STILL ALIVE? THAT'S NOT A LIFE WORTH LIVING!!
永遠僵屍
DON'T GIVE UP HOPE, TSUGUMI-SAN!!
SHE MIGHT BE A CHINESE ZOMBIE INSTEAD.
THAT'S... THE SAME THING...
BACKGROUND: ETERNAL DEAD
SID-SENSEI SAID THERE WAS NOTHING TO WORRY ABOUT.
ALL WE CAN DO NOW IS HOPE FOR THE BEST.
YOU'RE RIGHT...
THEY'RE SO STRONG... I'M PRACTICALLY FALLING APART...

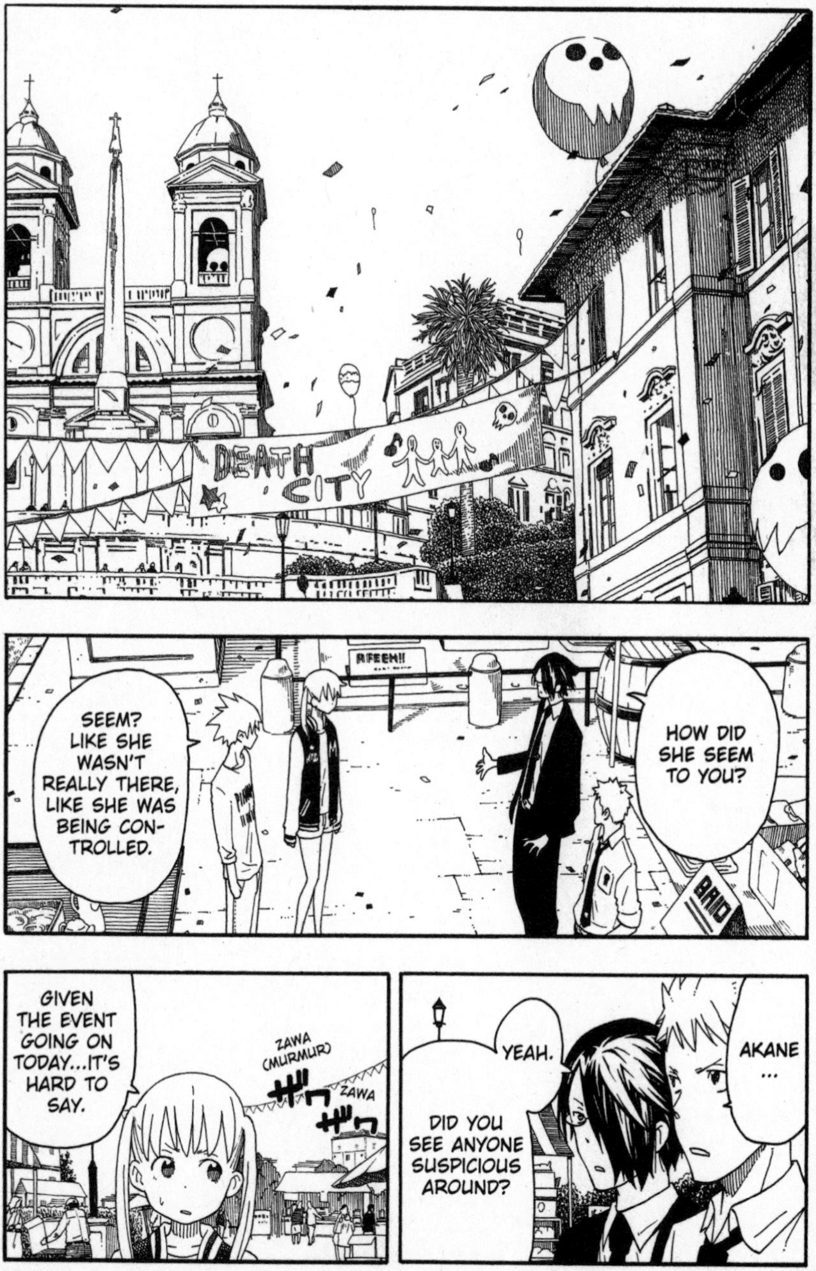
DEATH CITY
HOW DID SHE SEEM TO YOU?
SEEM? LIKE SHE WASN'T REALLY THERE, LIKE SHE WAS BEING CON-TROLLED.
AKANE ...
YEAH.
DID YOU SEE ANYONE SUSPICIOUS AROUND?
GIVEN THE EVENT GOING ON TODAY...IT'S HARD TO SAY.
ZAWA (MURMUR)
ZAWA

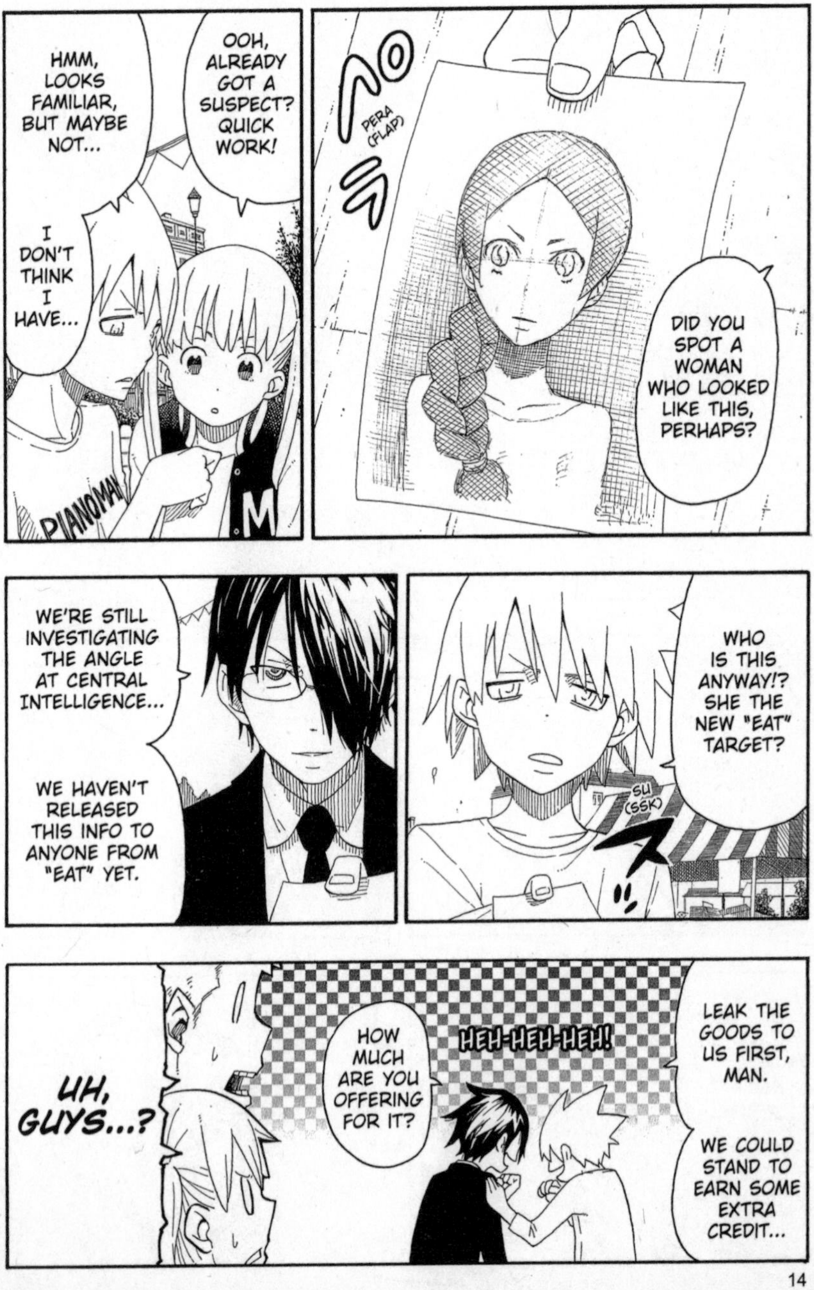
PERA (FLAP)
DID YOU SPOT A WOMAN WHO LOOKED LIKE THIS, PERHAPS?
OOH, ALREADY GOT A SUSPECT? QUICK WORK!
HMM, LOOKS FAMILIAR, BUT MAYBE NOT...
I DON'T THINK I HAVE...
WHO IS THIS ANYWAY!? SHE THE NEW "EAT" TARGET?
SU (SSK)
WE'RE STILL INVESTIGATING THE ANGLE AT CENTRAL INTELLIGENCE...
WE HAVEN'T RELEASED THIS INFO TO ANYONE FROM "EAT" YET.
LEAK THE GOODS TO US FIRST, MAN.
WE COULD STAND TO EARN SOME EXTRA CREDIT...
HEH-HEH-HEH!
HOW MUCH ARE YOU OFFERING FOR IT?
UH, GUYS...?

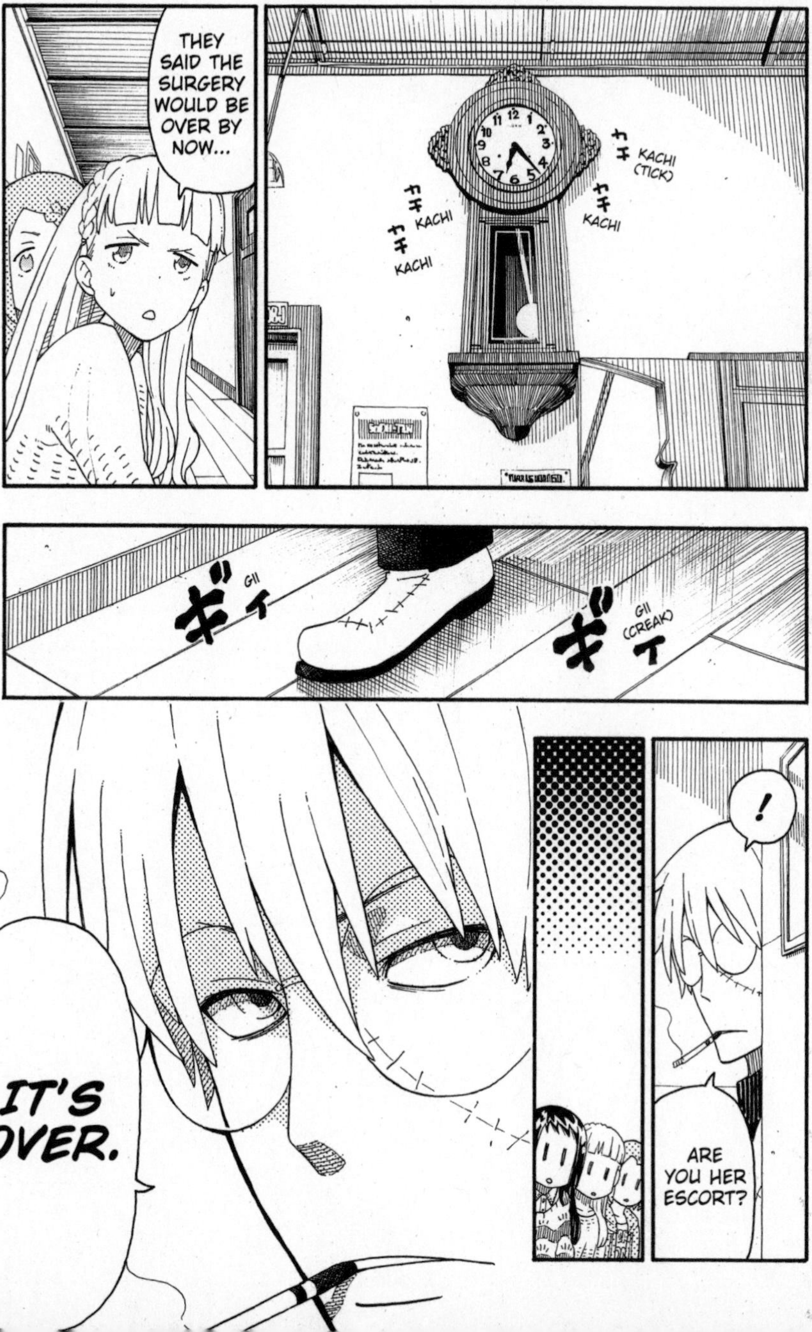
カチ KACHI (TICK)
カチ KACHI
カチ KACHI
カチ KACHI
THEY SAID THE SURGERY WOULD BE OVER BY NOW...
ギィ GII (CREAK)
ギィ GII
!
ARE YOU HER ESCORT?
IT'S OVER.

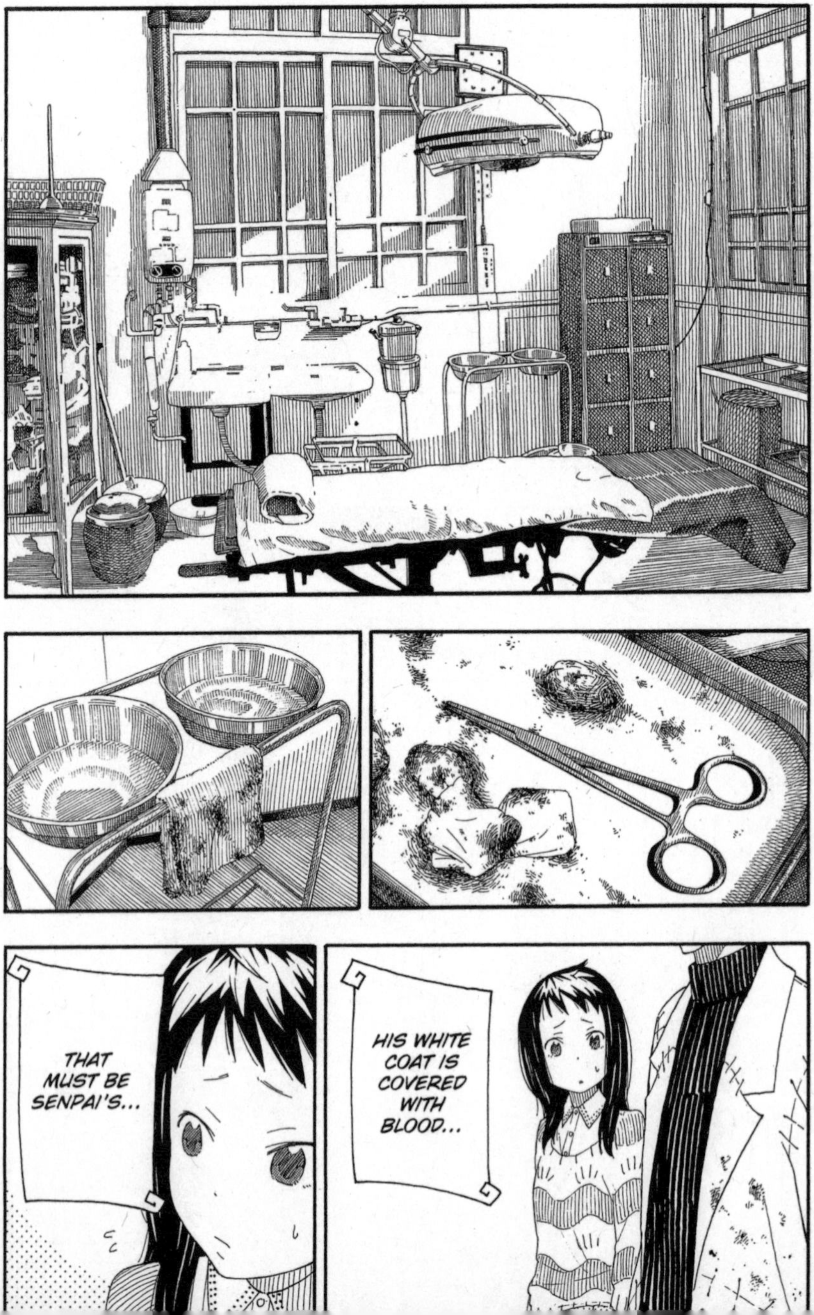
HIS WHITE COAT IS COVERED WITH BLOOD...
THAT MUST BE SENPAI'S...

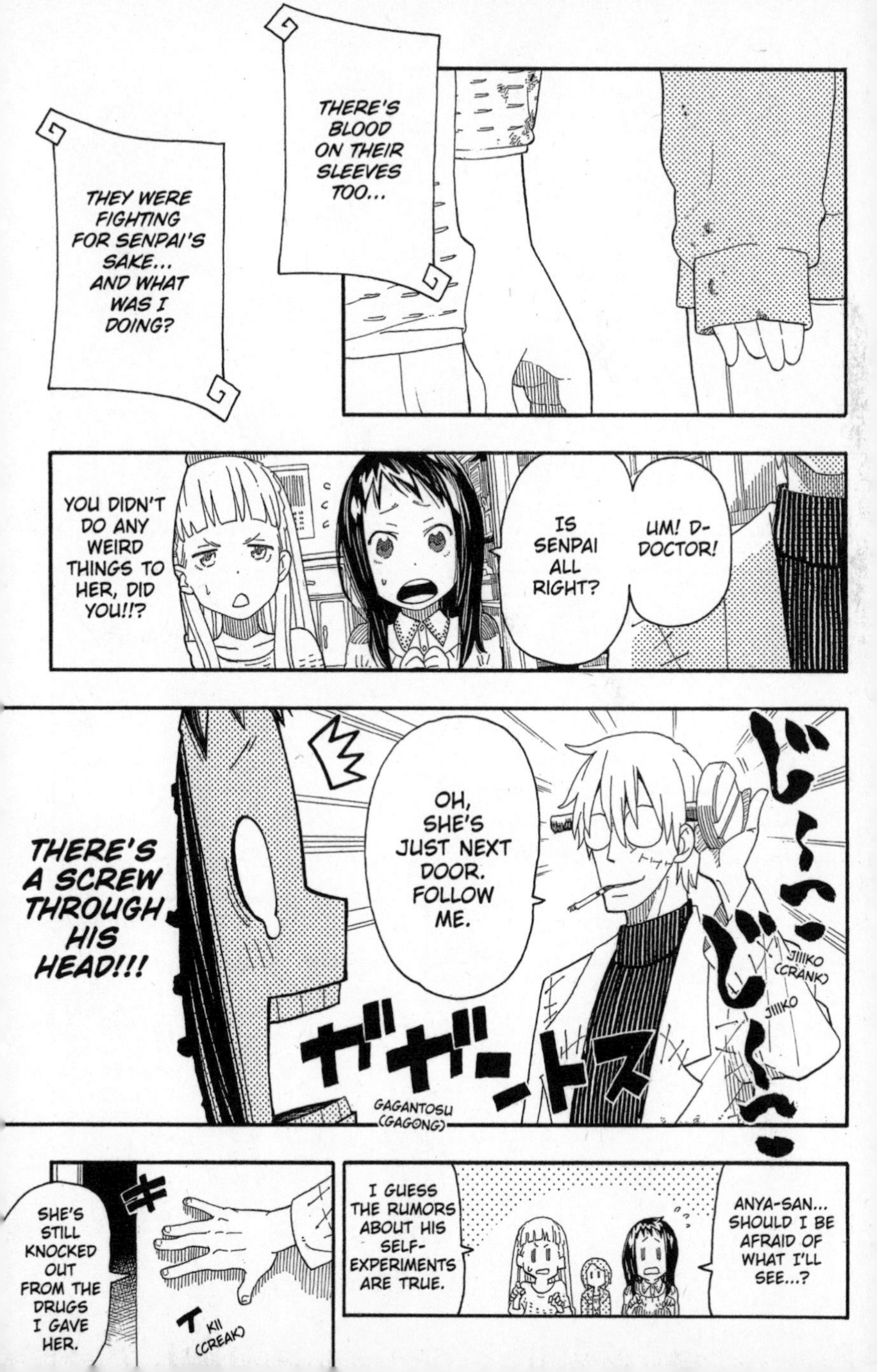
THERE'S BLOOD ON THEIR SLEEVES TOO...
THEY WERE FIGHTING FOR SENPAI'S SAKE... AND WHAT WAS I DOING?
UM! D-DOCTOR!
IS SENPAI ALL RIGHT?
YOU DIDN'T DO ANY WEIRD THINGS TO HER, DID YOU!!?
JIIIKO (CRANK)
JIIIKO
OH, SHE'S JUST NEXT DOOR. FOLLOW ME.
GAGANTOSU (GAGONG)
THERE'S A SCREW THROUGH HIS HEAD!!!
ANYA-SAN... SHOULD I BE AFRAID OF WHAT I'LL SEE...?
I GUESS THE RUMORS ABOUT HIS SELF-EXPERIMENTS ARE TRUE.
KII (CREAK)
SHE'S STILL KNOCKED OUT FROM THE DRUGS I GAVE HER.

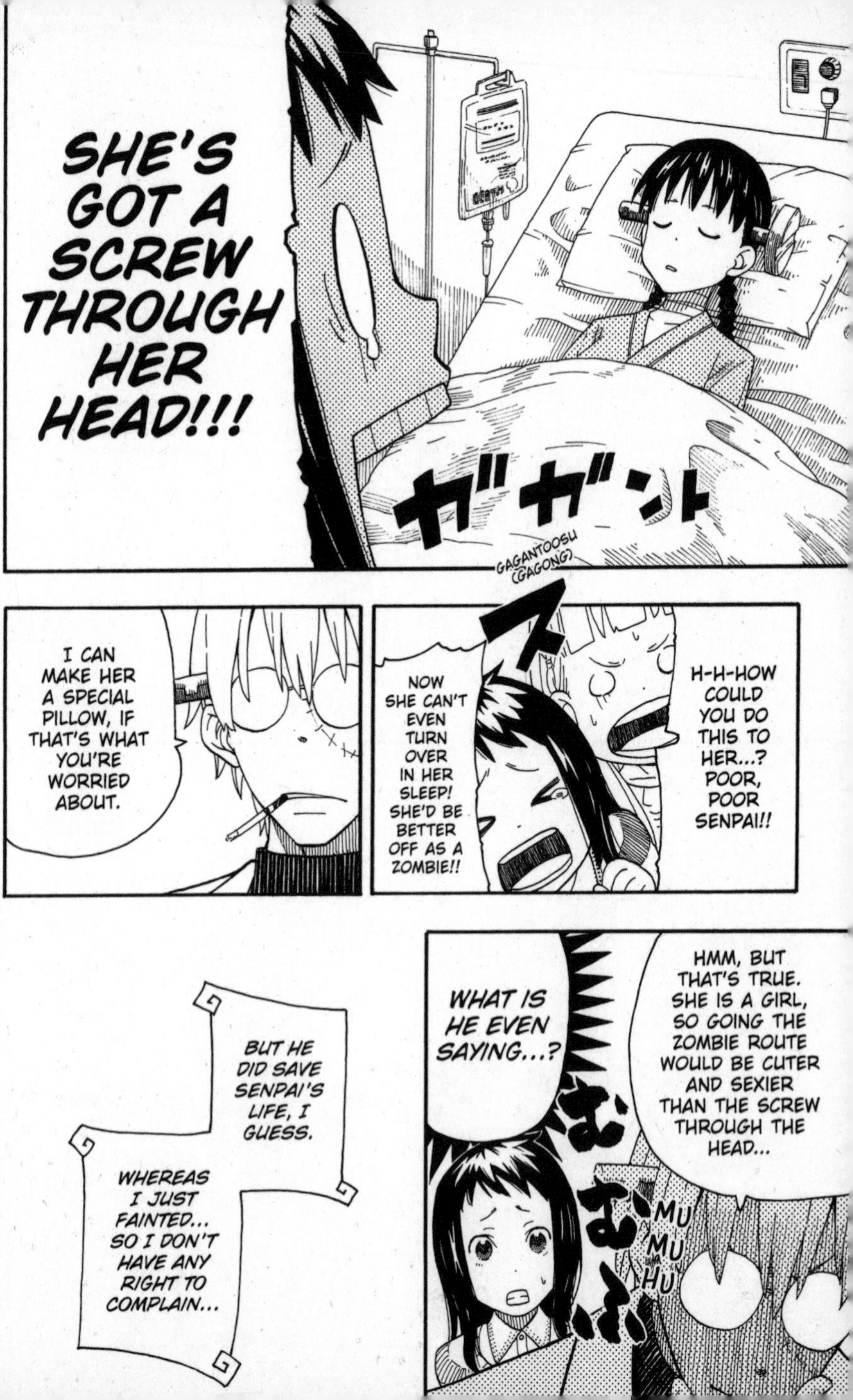
SHE'S GOT A SCREW THROUGH HER HEAD!!!
GAGANTOOSU (GAGONG)
H-H-HOW COULD YOU DO THIS TO HER...? POOR, POOR SENPAI!!
NOW SHE CAN'T EVEN TURN OVER IN HER SLEEP! SHE'D BE BETTER OFF AS A ZOMBIE!!
I CAN MAKE HER A SPECIAL PILLOW, IF THAT'S WHAT YOU'RE WORRIED ABOUT.
HMM, BUT THAT'S TRUE. SHE IS A GIRL, SO GOING THE ZOMBIE ROUTE WOULD BE CUTER AND SEXIER THAN THE SCREW THROUGH THE HEAD...
MU MU HU
WHAT IS HE EVEN SAYING...?
BUT HE DID SAVE SENPAI'S LIFE, I GUESS.
WHEREAS I JUST FAINTED... SO I DON'T HAVE ANY RIGHT TO COMPLAIN...

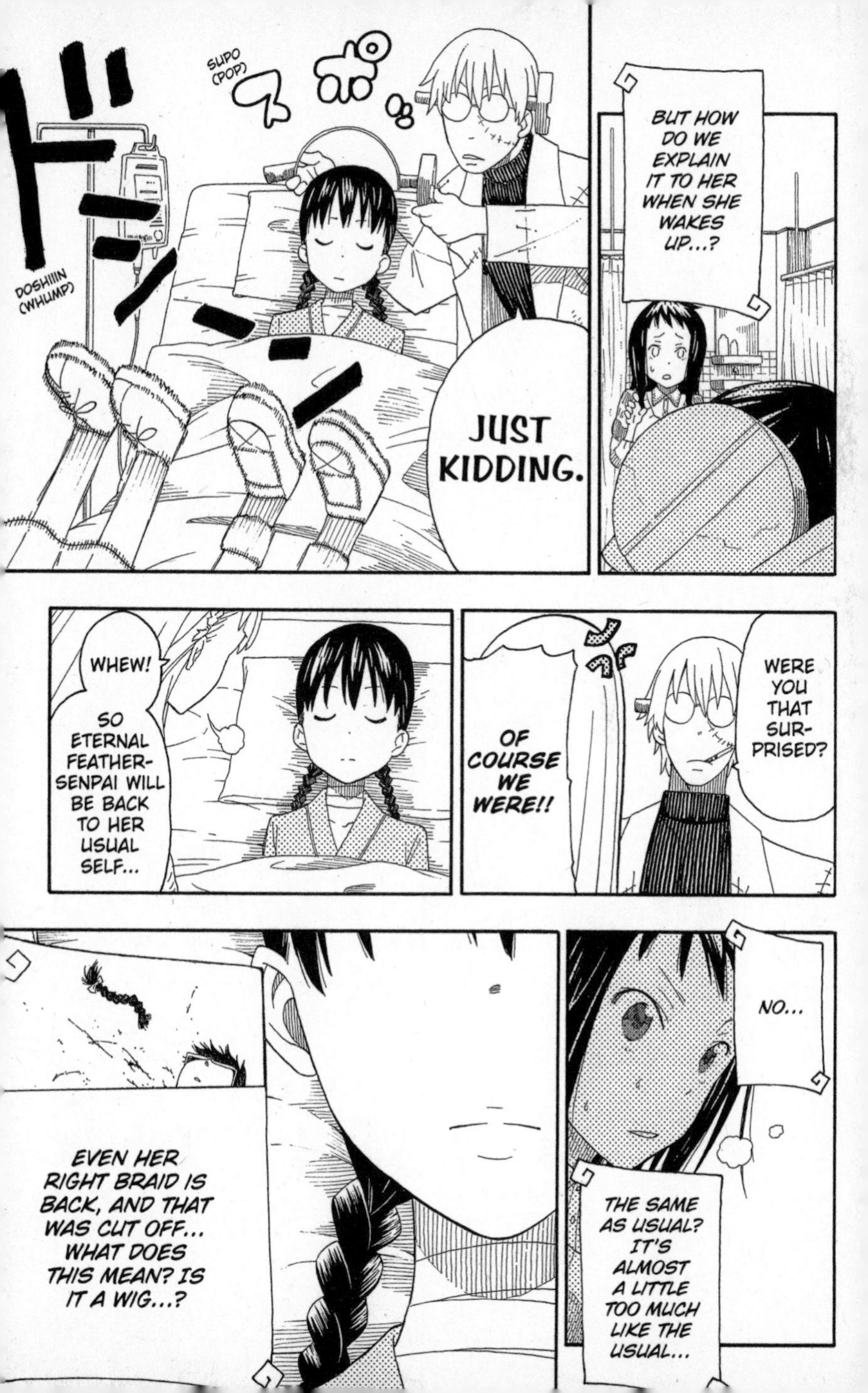
BUT HOW DO WE EXPLAIN IT TO HER WHEN SHE WAKES UP...?
SUPO (POP)
DOSHIIIN (WHUMP)
JUST KIDDING.
WERE YOU THAT SUR-PRISED?
OF COURSE WE WERE!!
WHEW!
SO ETERNAL FEATHER-SENPAI WILL BE BACK TO HER USUAL SELF...
NO...
THE SAME AS USUAL? IT'S ALMOST A LITTLE TOO MUCH LIKE THE USUAL...
EVEN HER RIGHT BRAID IS BACK, AND THAT WAS CUT OFF... WHAT DOES THIS MEAN? IS IT A WIG...?

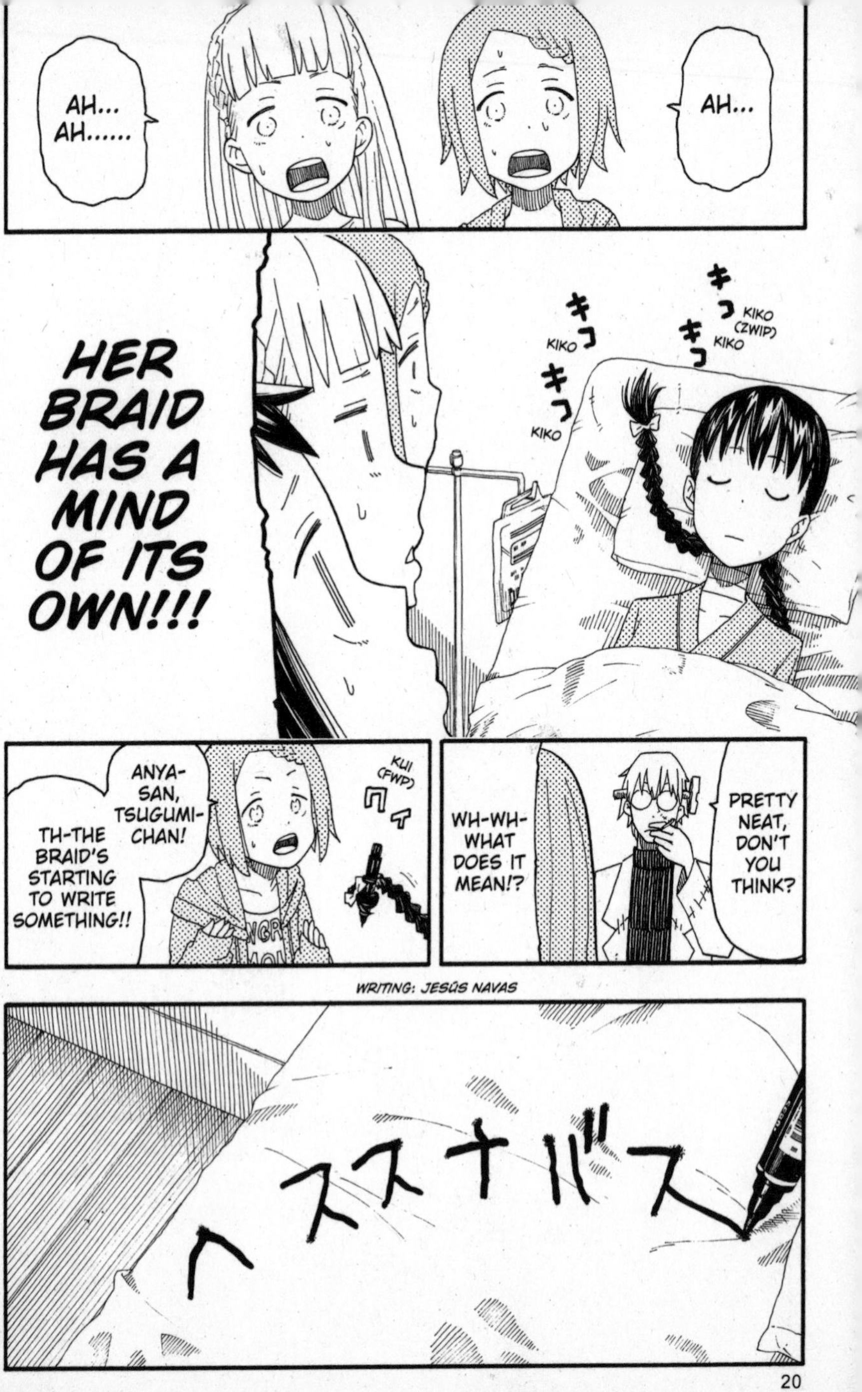
AH...
AH... AH......
キコ KIKO (ZWIP)
キコ KIKO
キコ KIKO
キコ KIKO
HER BRAID HAS A MIND OF ITS OWN!!!
PRETTY NEAT, DON'T YOU THINK?
WH-WH-WHAT DOES IT MEAN!?
クイ KUI (FWP)
ANYA-SAN, TSUGUMI-CHAN!
TH-THE BRAID'S STARTING TO WRITE SOMETHING!!
WRITING: JESÚS NAVAS
ヘススナバス

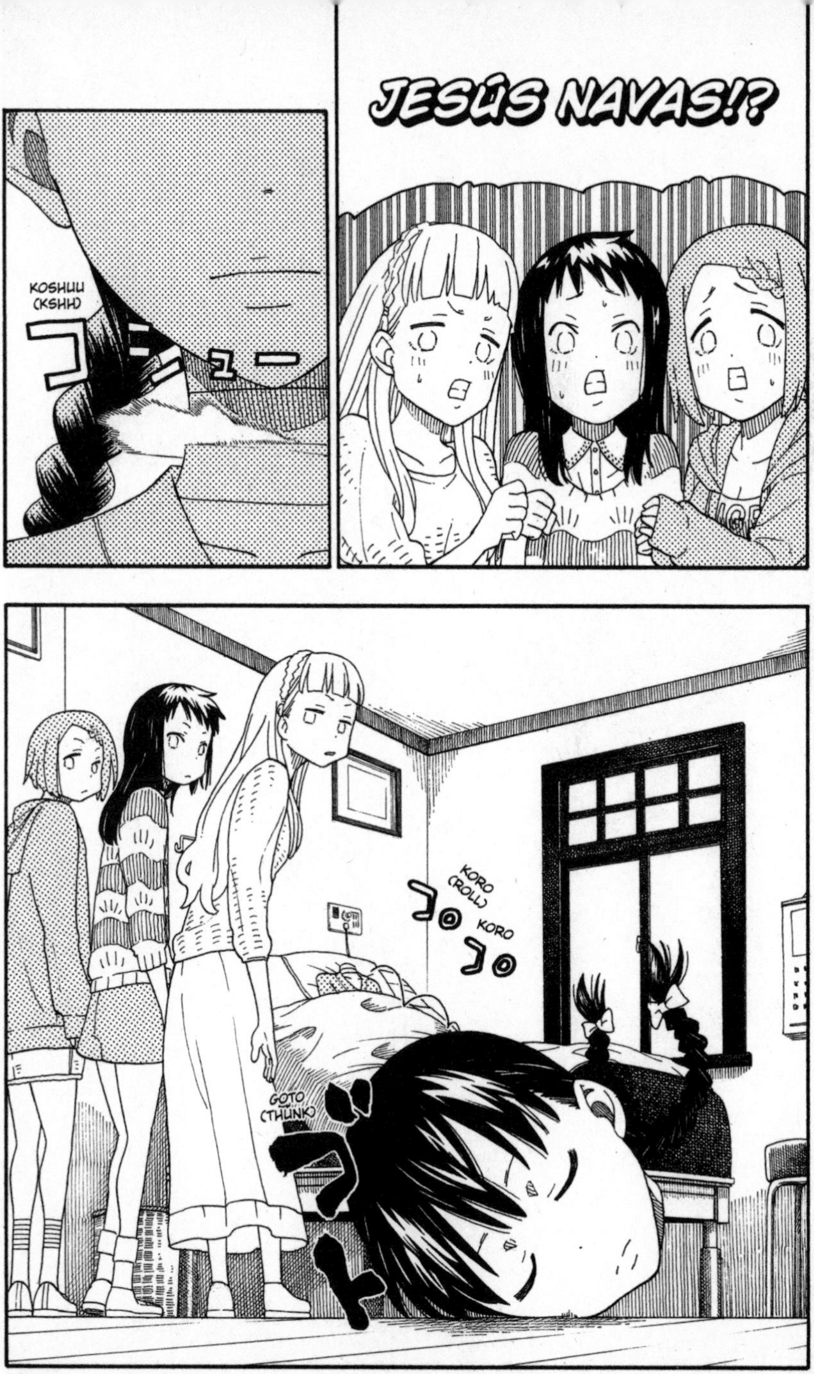
JESÚS NAVAS!?
KOSHUU (KSHH)
KORO (ROLL)
KORO
GOTO (THUNK)

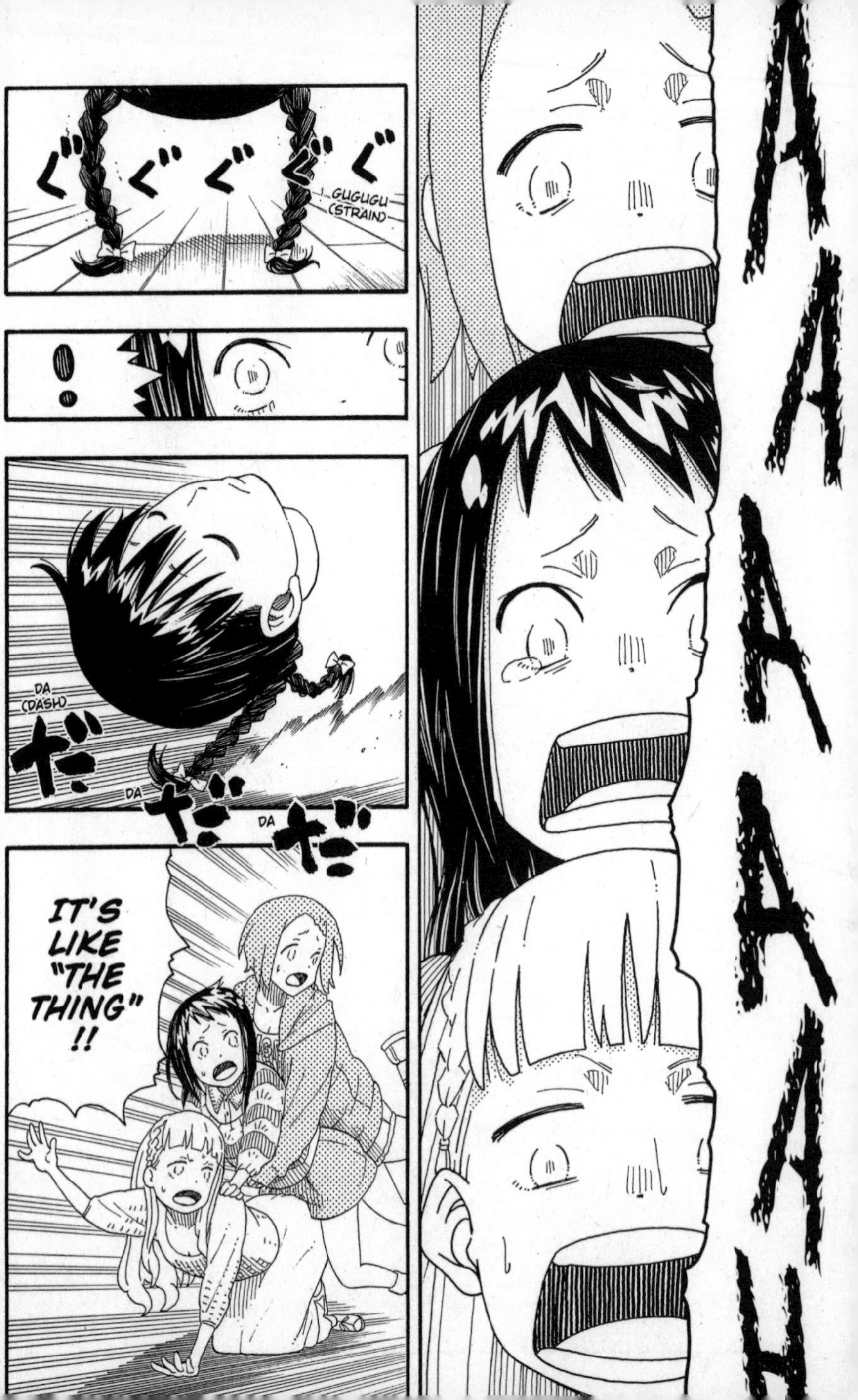
AAAAAH
ぐぐぐぐぐ
GUGUGU (STRAIN)
!
DA (DASH)
だ
DA
だ
DA
だ
IT'S LIKE "THE THING"!!

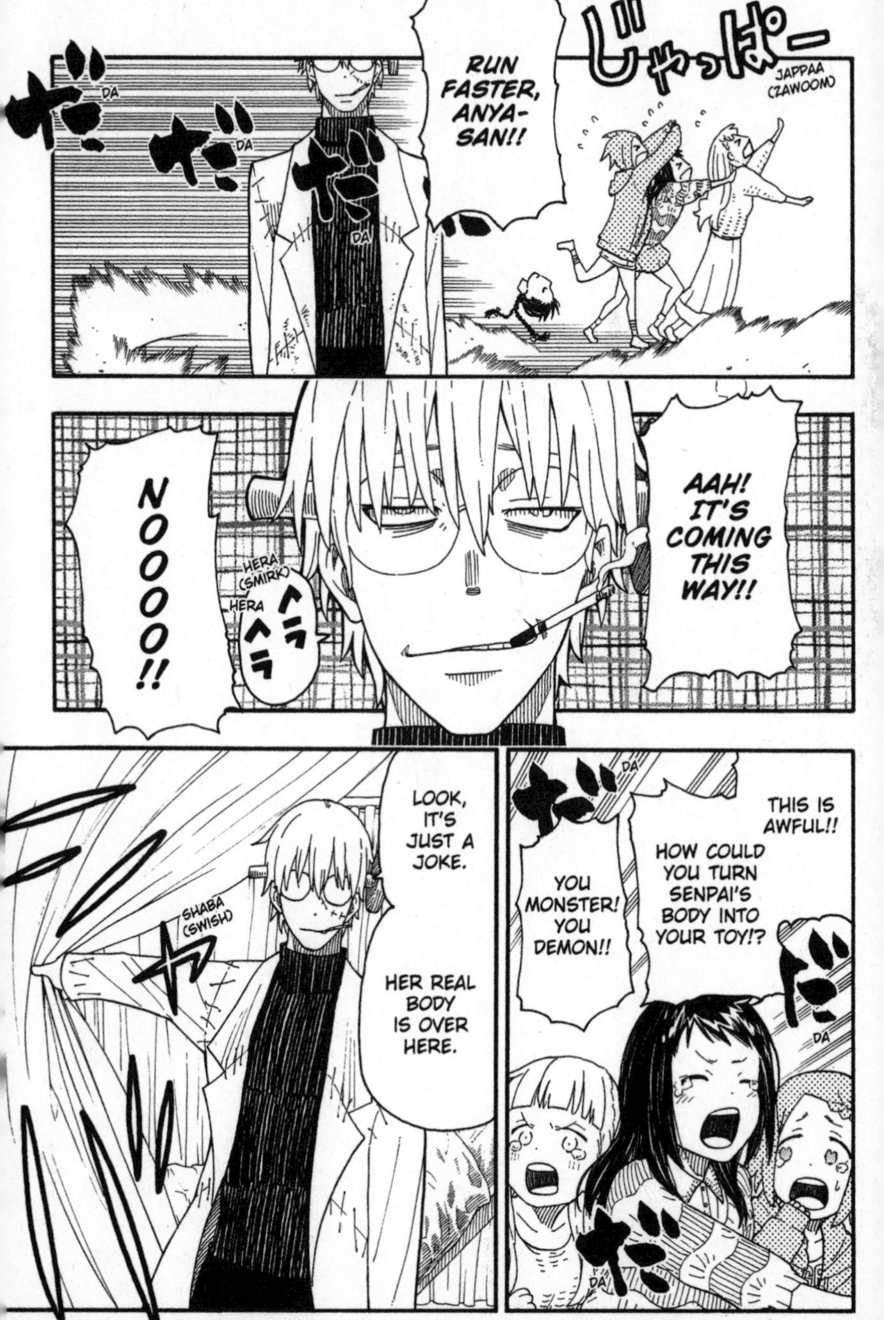
じゃっぱー
JAPPAA (ZAWOOM)
RUN FASTER, ANYA-SAN!!
DA
DA
DA
AAH! IT'S COMING THIS WAY!!
HERA HERA (SMIRK)
ヘラヘラ
NOOOOO!!
DA
THIS IS AWFUL!!
HOW COULD YOU TURN SENPAI'S BODY INTO YOUR TOY!?
YOU MONSTER! YOU DEMON!!
DA
DA
LOOK, IT'S JUST A JOKE.
HER REAL BODY IS OVER HERE.
SHABA (SWISH)

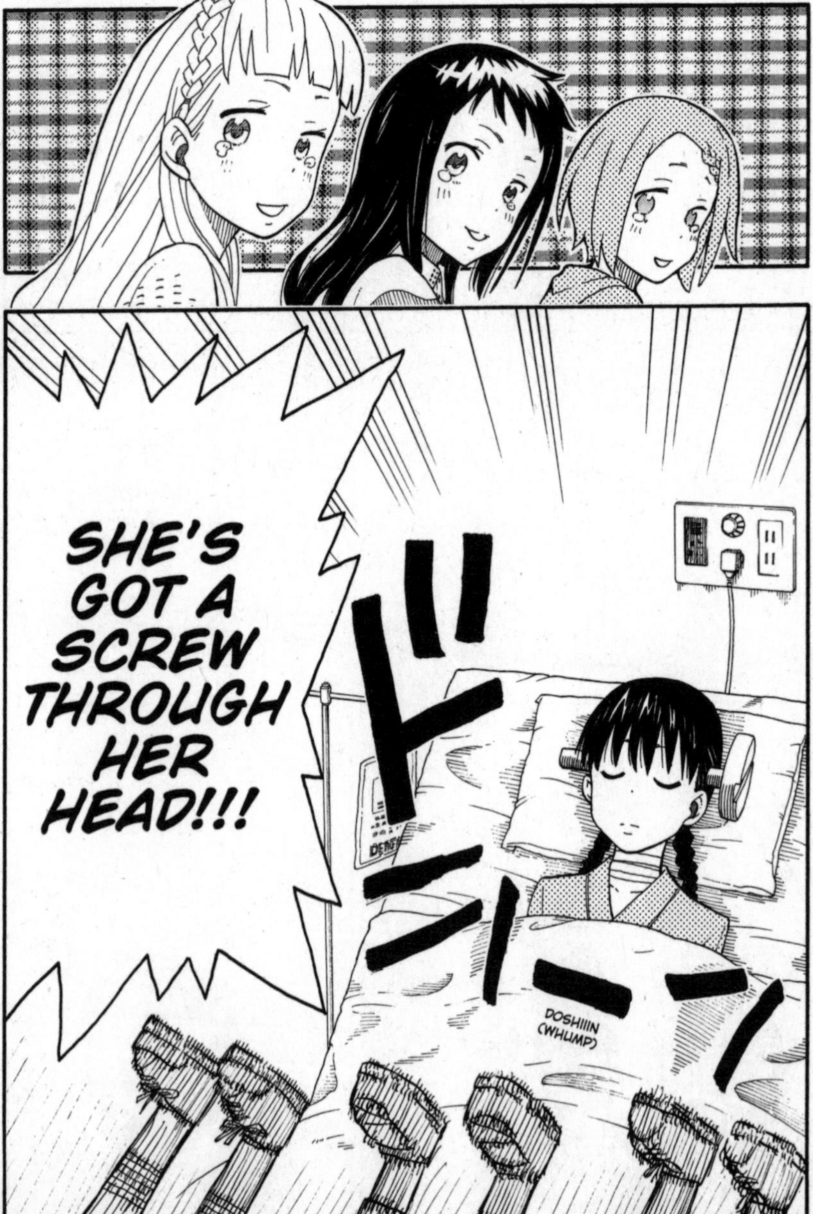
SHE'S GOT A SCREW THROUGH HER HEAD!!!
DOSHIIIN (WHUMP)

SOUL EATER NOT!

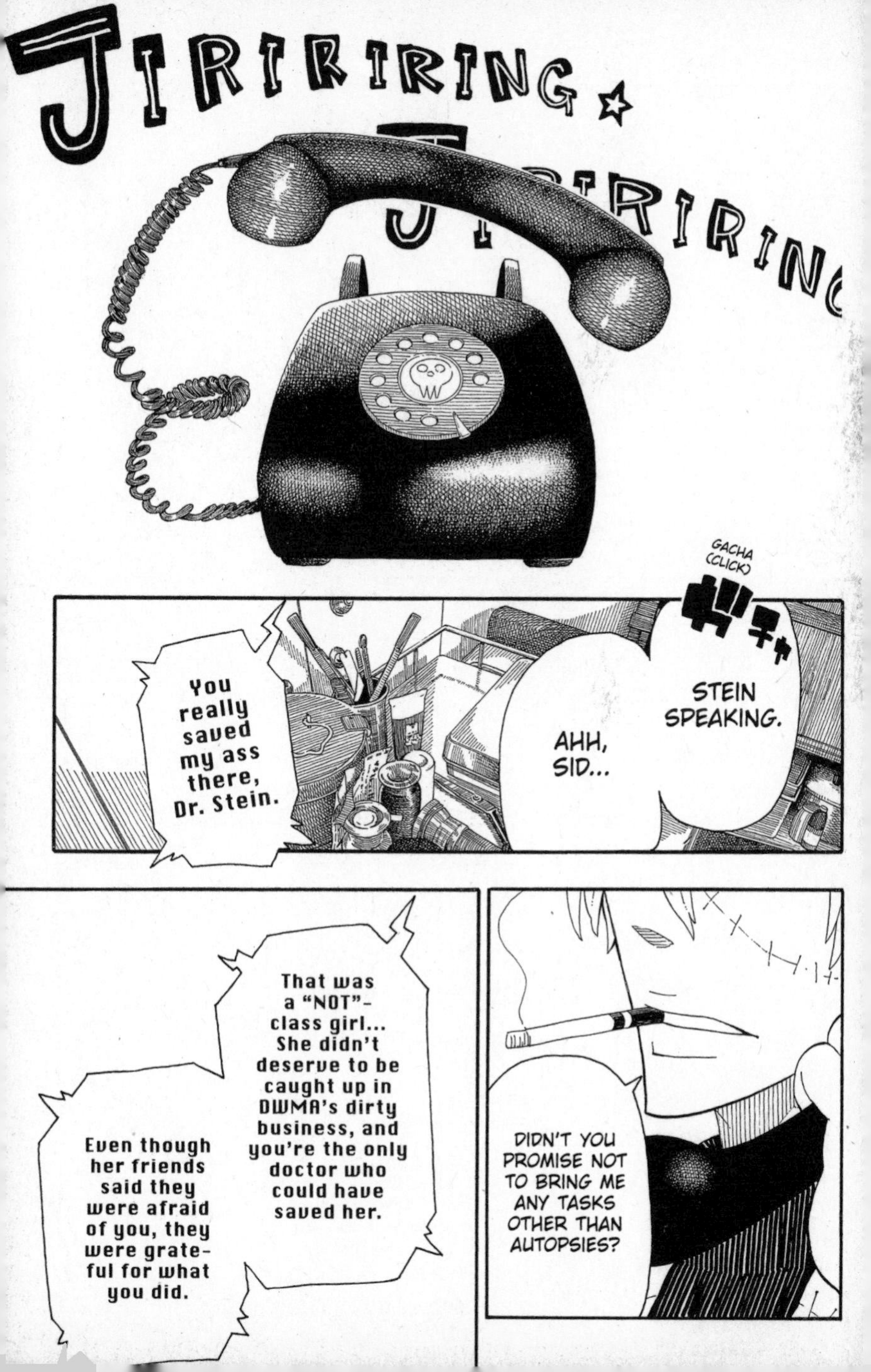
JIRIRIRING☆
JIRIRIRING
GACHA (CLICK)
STEIN SPEAKING.
AHH, SID...
You really saved my ass there, Dr. Stein.
DIDN'T YOU PROMISE NOT TO BRING ME ANY TASKS OTHER THAN AUTOPSIES?
That was a "NOT"-class girl... She didn't deserve to be caught up in DWMA's dirty business, and you're the only doctor who could have saved her.
Even though her friends said they were afraid of you, they were grateful for what you did.

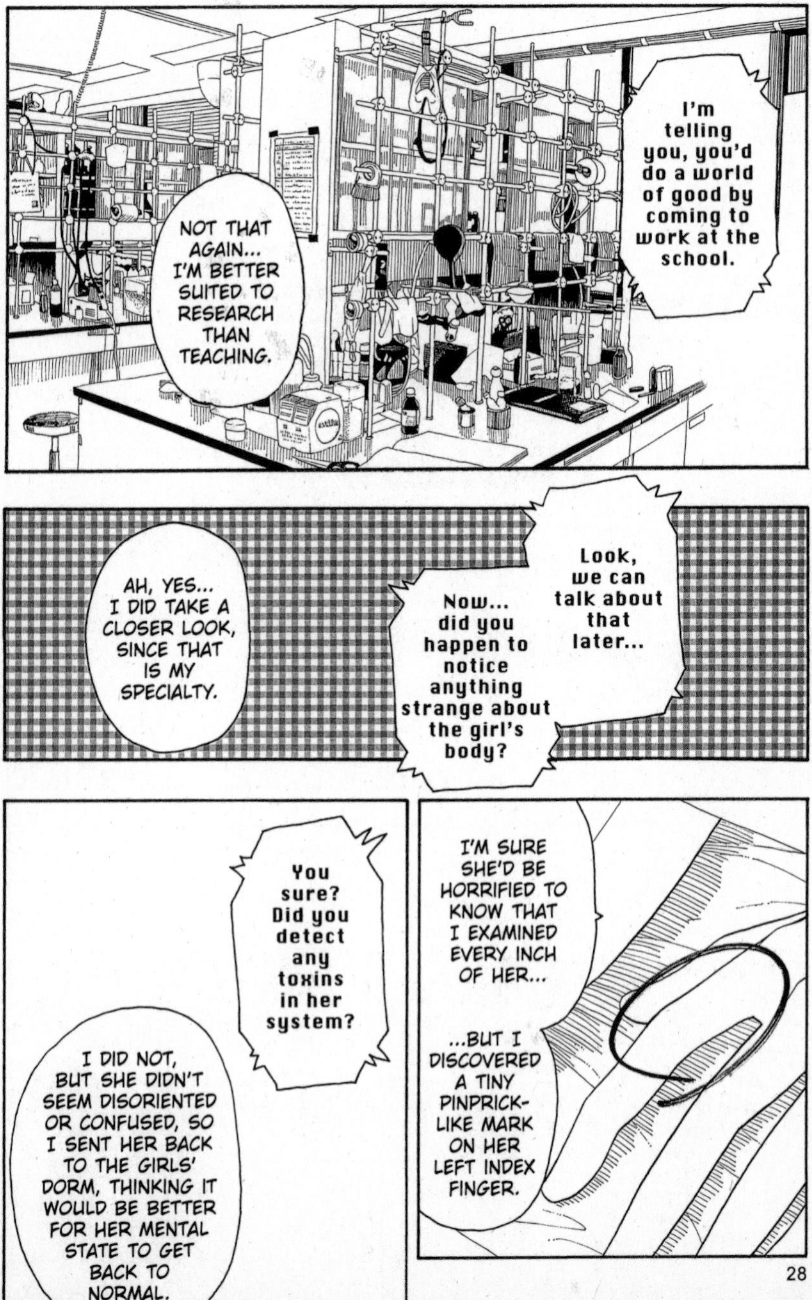
I'm telling you, you'd do a world of good by coming to work at the school.
NOT THAT AGAIN... I'M BETTER SUITED TO RESEARCH THAN TEACHING.
Look, we can talk about that later...
Now... did you happen to notice anything strange about the girl's body?
AH, YES... I DID TAKE A CLOSER LOOK, SINCE THAT IS MY SPECIALTY.
I'M SURE SHE'D BE HORRIFIED TO KNOW THAT I EXAMINED EVERY INCH OF HER...
...BUT I DISCOVERED A TINY PINPRICK-LIKE MARK ON HER LEFT INDEX FINGER.
You sure? Did you detect any toxins in her system?
I DID NOT, BUT SHE DIDN'T SEEM DISORIENTED OR CONFUSED, SO I SENT HER BACK TO THE GIRLS' DORM, THINKING IT WOULD BE BETTER FOR HER MENTAL STATE TO GET BACK TO NORMAL.

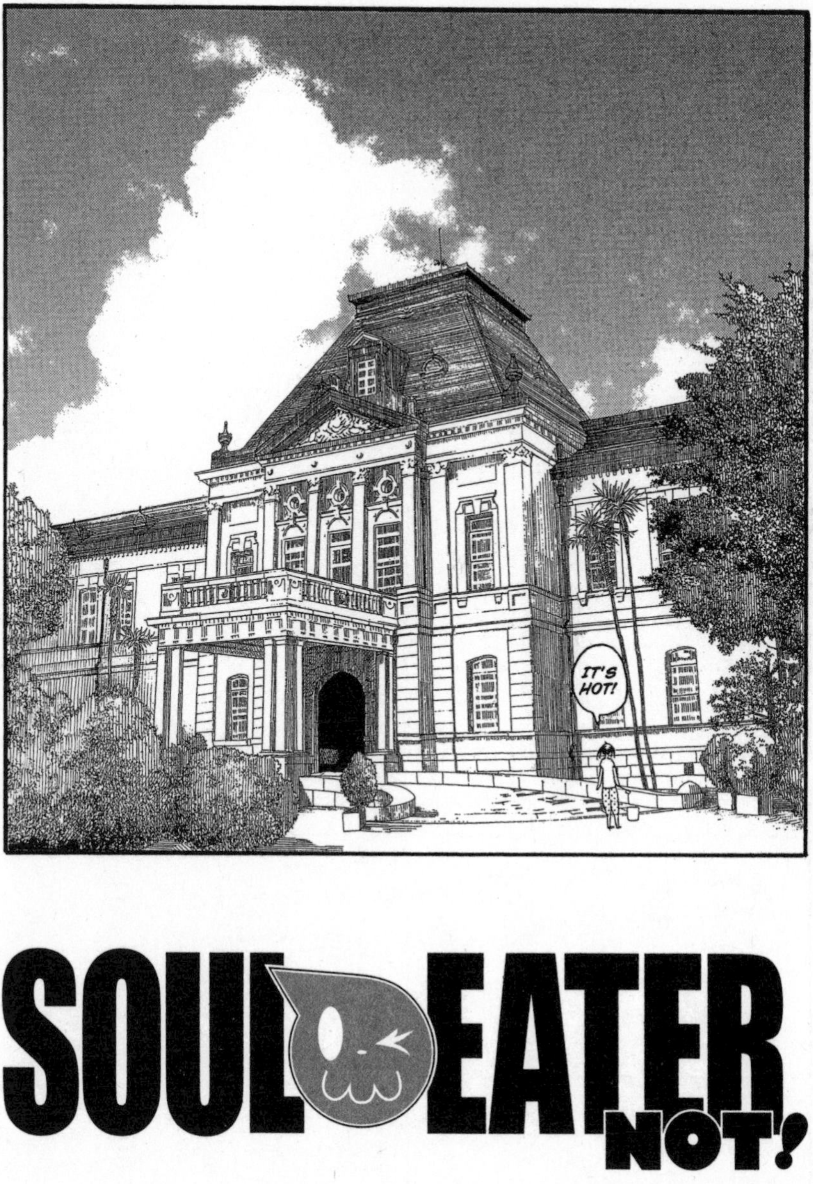
IT'S HOT!

SOUL EATER NOT!

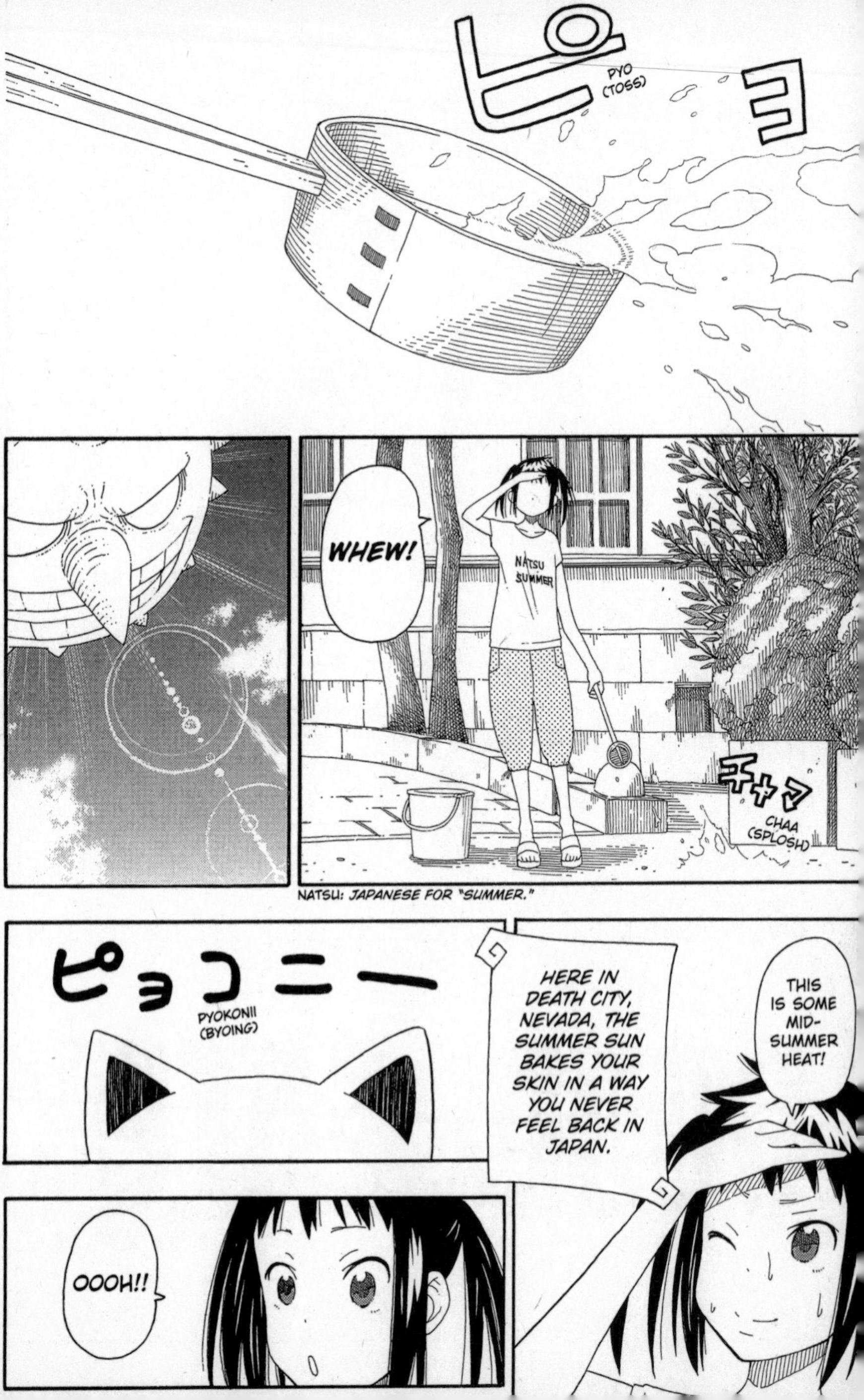
ピョ
PYO (TOSS)
WHEW!
チャ
CHAA (SPLOSH)
HERE IN DEATH CITY, NEVADA, THE SUMMER SUN BAKES YOUR SKIN IN A WAY YOU NEVER FEEL BACK IN JAPAN.
THIS IS SOME MID-SUMMER HEAT!
ピョコニー
PYOKONII (BYOING)
OOOH!!

NATSU: JAPANESE FOR "SUMMER."

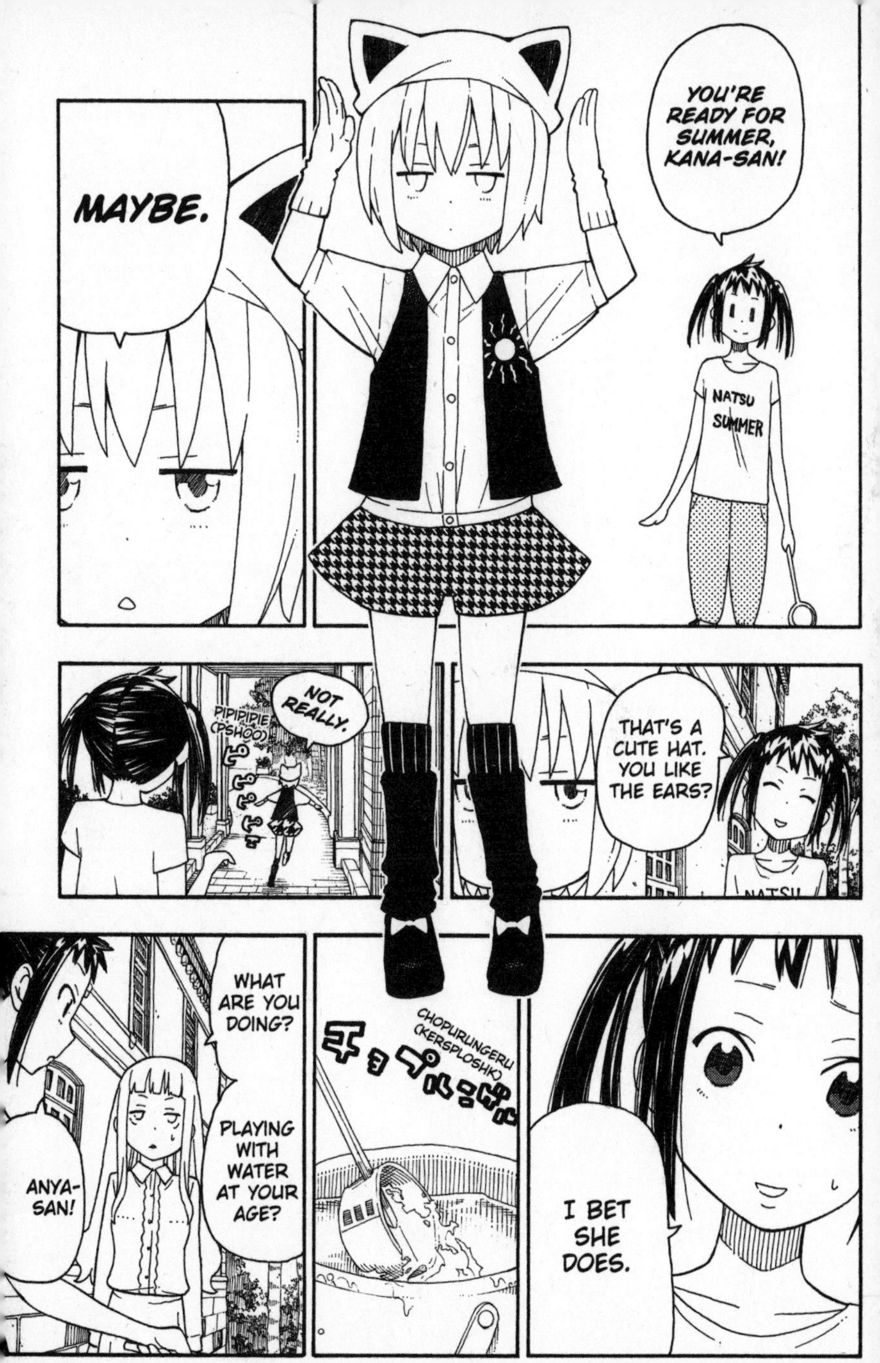

YOU'RE READY FOR SUMMER, KANA-SAN!
NATSU SUMMER
MAYBE.
THAT'S A CUTE HAT. YOU LIKE THE EARS?
NATSU
NOT REALLY.
PIPIPIPIE (PSHOO)
I BET SHE DOES.
CHOPURUNGERU (KERSPLOSHK)
WHAT ARE YOU DOING?
PLAYING WITH WATER AT YOUR AGE?
ANYA-SAN!

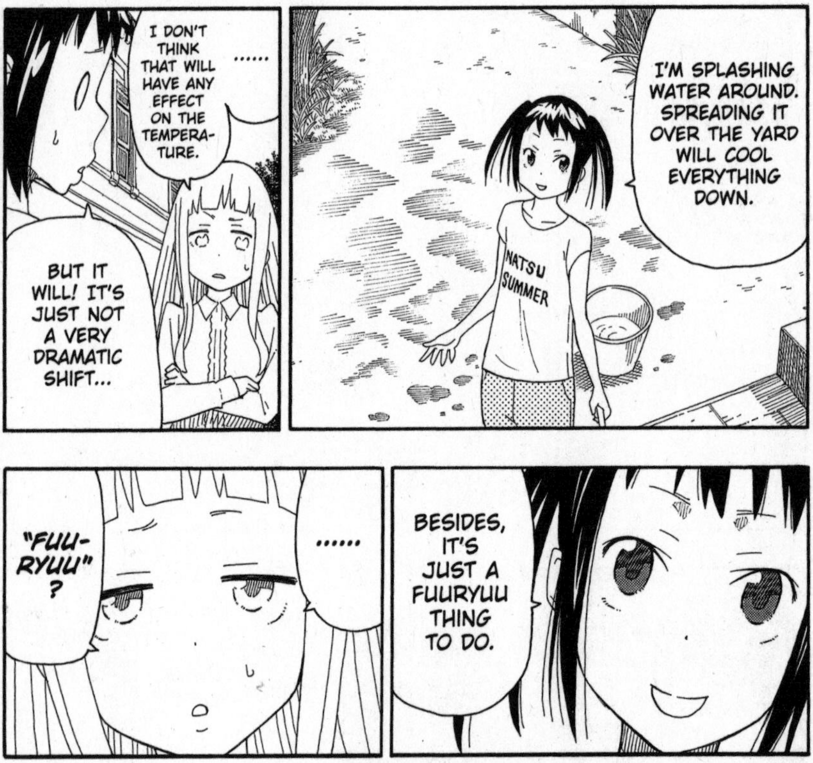
I'M SPLASHING WATER AROUND. SPREADING IT OVER THE YARD WILL COOL EVERYTHING DOWN.
NATSU SUMMER
......
I DON'T THINK THAT WILL HAVE ANY EFFECT ON THE TEMPERATURE.
BUT IT WILL! IT'S JUST NOT A VERY DRAMATIC SHIFT...
BESIDES, IT'S JUST A FUURYUU THING TO DO.
......
"FUURYUU"?

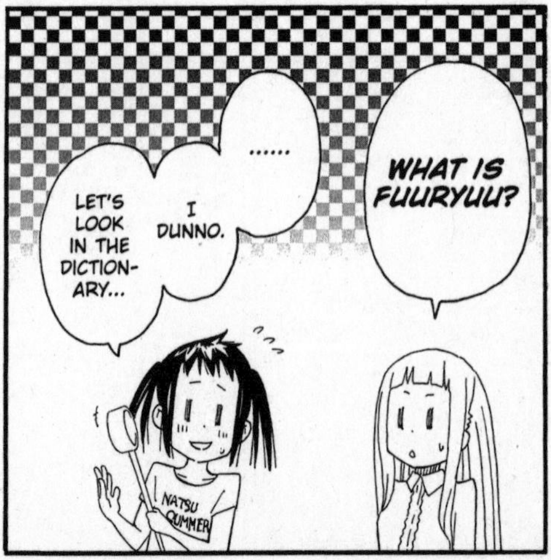
WHAT IS FUURYUU?
......
I DUNNO.
LET'S LOOK IN THE DICTIONARY...
NATSU SUMMER

fuuryuu *adj.*
1. having refined, elegant tastes. **2.** maintaining an air of gracefulness. **3.** being separate from the vulgar world and close to nature.

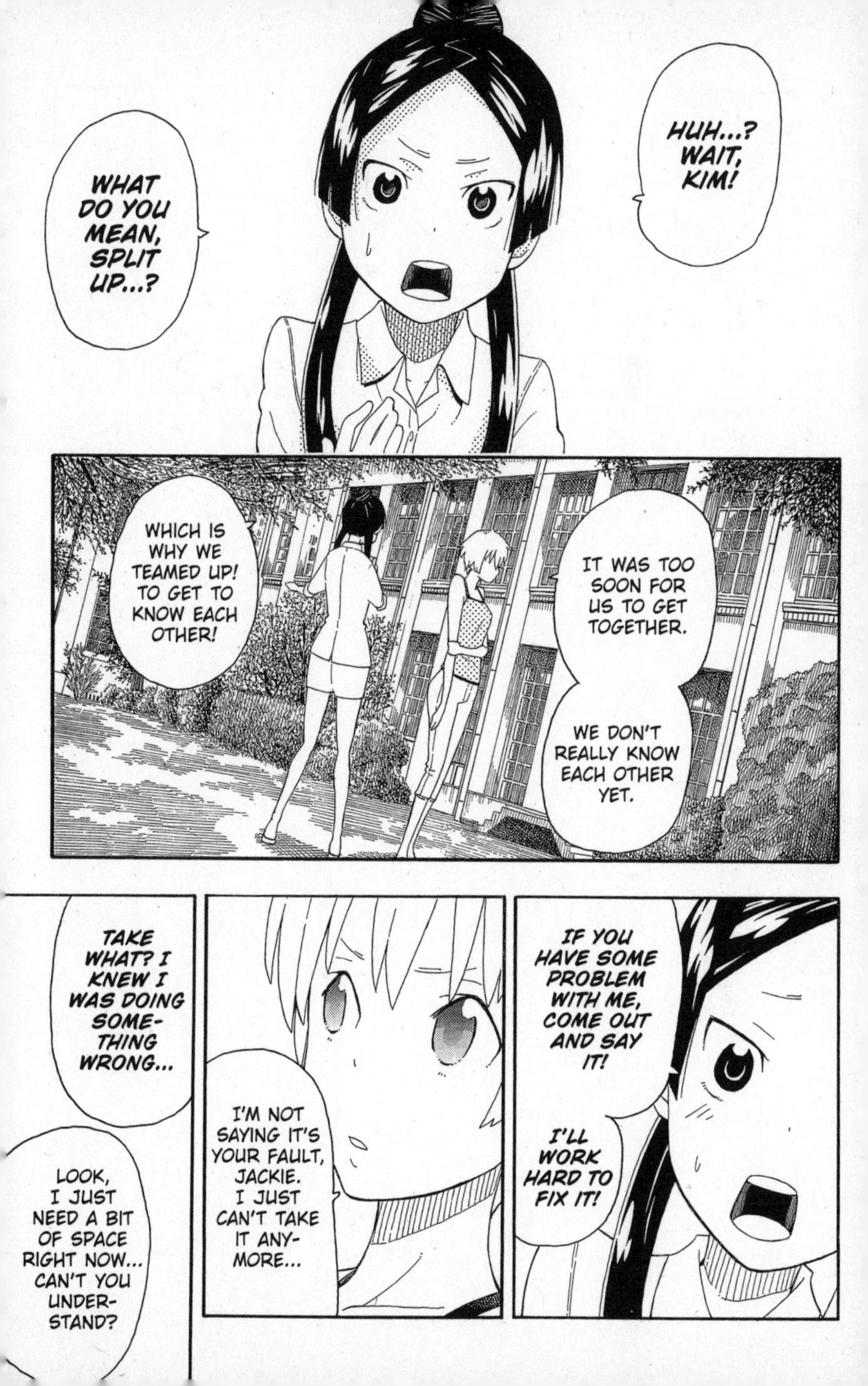
HUH...? WAIT, KIM!
WHAT DO YOU MEAN, SPLIT UP...?
IT WAS TOO SOON FOR US TO GET TOGETHER.
WE DON'T REALLY KNOW EACH OTHER YET.
WHICH IS WHY WE TEAMED UP! TO GET TO KNOW EACH OTHER!
IF YOU HAVE SOME PROBLEM WITH ME, COME OUT AND SAY IT!
I'LL WORK HARD TO FIX IT!
I'M NOT SAYING IT'S YOUR FAULT, JACKIE. I JUST CAN'T TAKE IT ANY-MORE...
TAKE WHAT? I KNEW I WAS DOING SOME-THING WRONG...
LOOK, I JUST NEED A BIT OF SPACE RIGHT NOW... CAN'T YOU UNDER-STAND?

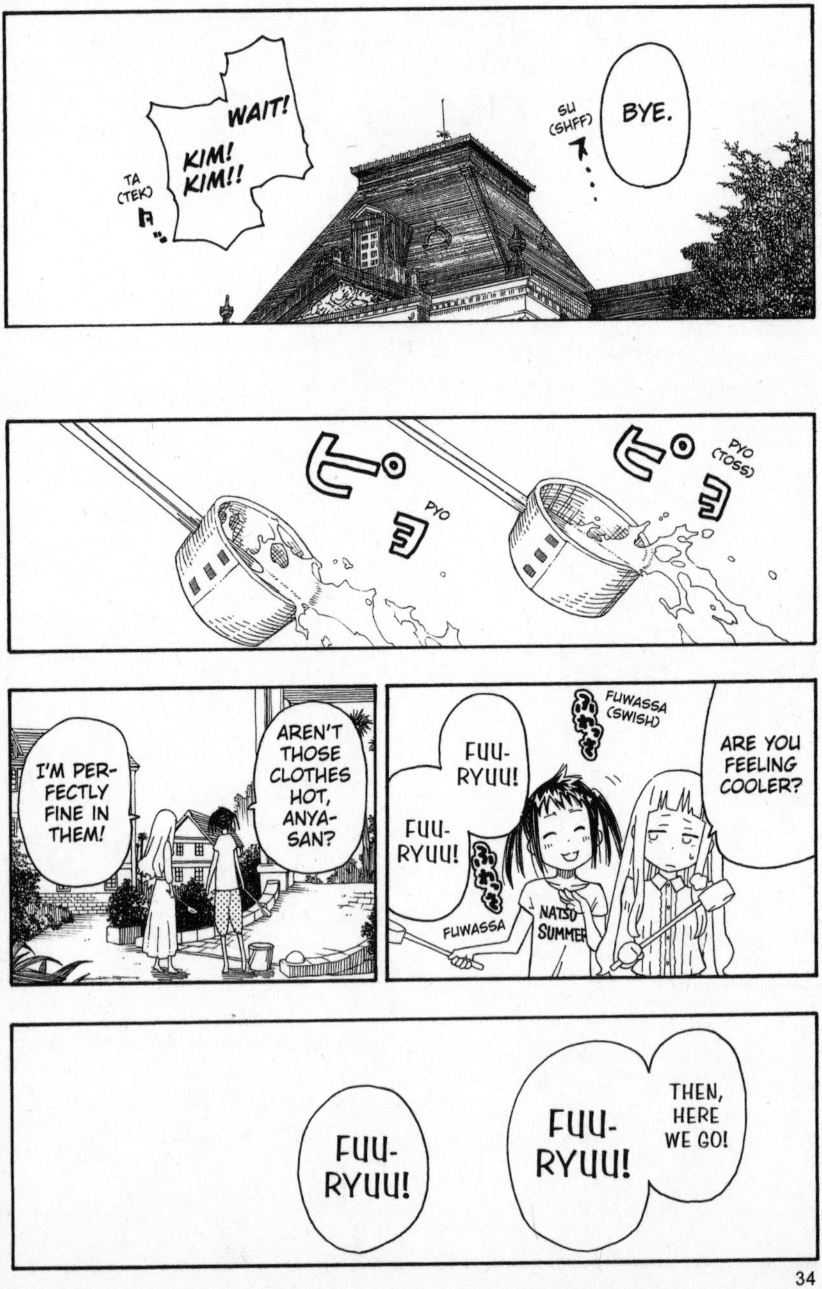

BYE.
SU (SHFF)
WAIT!
KIM! KIM!!
TA (TEK)
PYO (TOSS)
PYO
ARE YOU FEELING COOLER?
FUWASSA (SWISH)
FUU-RYUU!
FUU-RYUU!
FUWASSA
AREN'T THOSE CLOTHES HOT, ANYA-SAN?
I'M PERFECTLY FINE IN THEM!
THEN, HERE WE GO!
FUU-RYUU!
FUU-RYUU!

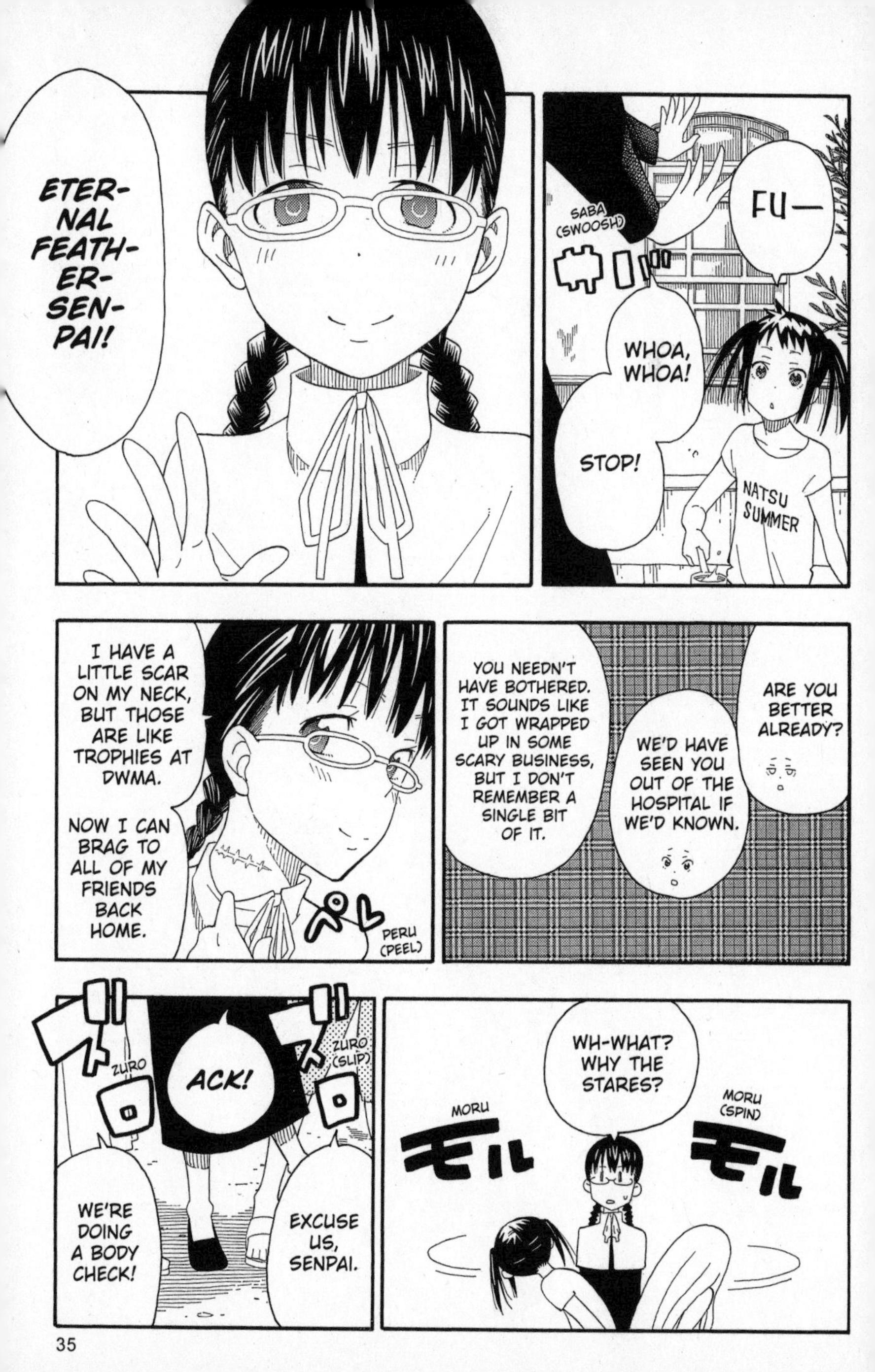
FU—
SABA (SWOOSH)
WHOA, WHOA!
STOP!
NATSU SUMMER
ETERNAL FEATHERER-SENPAI!
ARE YOU BETTER ALREADY?
WE'D HAVE SEEN YOU OUT OF THE HOSPITAL IF WE'D KNOWN.
YOU NEEDN'T HAVE BOTHERED. IT SOUNDS LIKE I GOT WRAPPED UP IN SOME SCARY BUSINESS, BUT I DON'T REMEMBER A SINGLE BIT OF IT.
I HAVE A LITTLE SCAR ON MY NECK, BUT THOSE ARE LIKE TROPHIES AT DWMA.
NOW I CAN BRAG TO ALL OF MY FRIENDS BACK HOME.
PERU (PEEL)
MORU (SPIN)
WH-WHAT? WHY THE STARES?
MORU
ZURO (SLIP)
ACK!
ZURO
EXCUSE US, SENPAI.
WE'RE DOING A BODY CHECK!

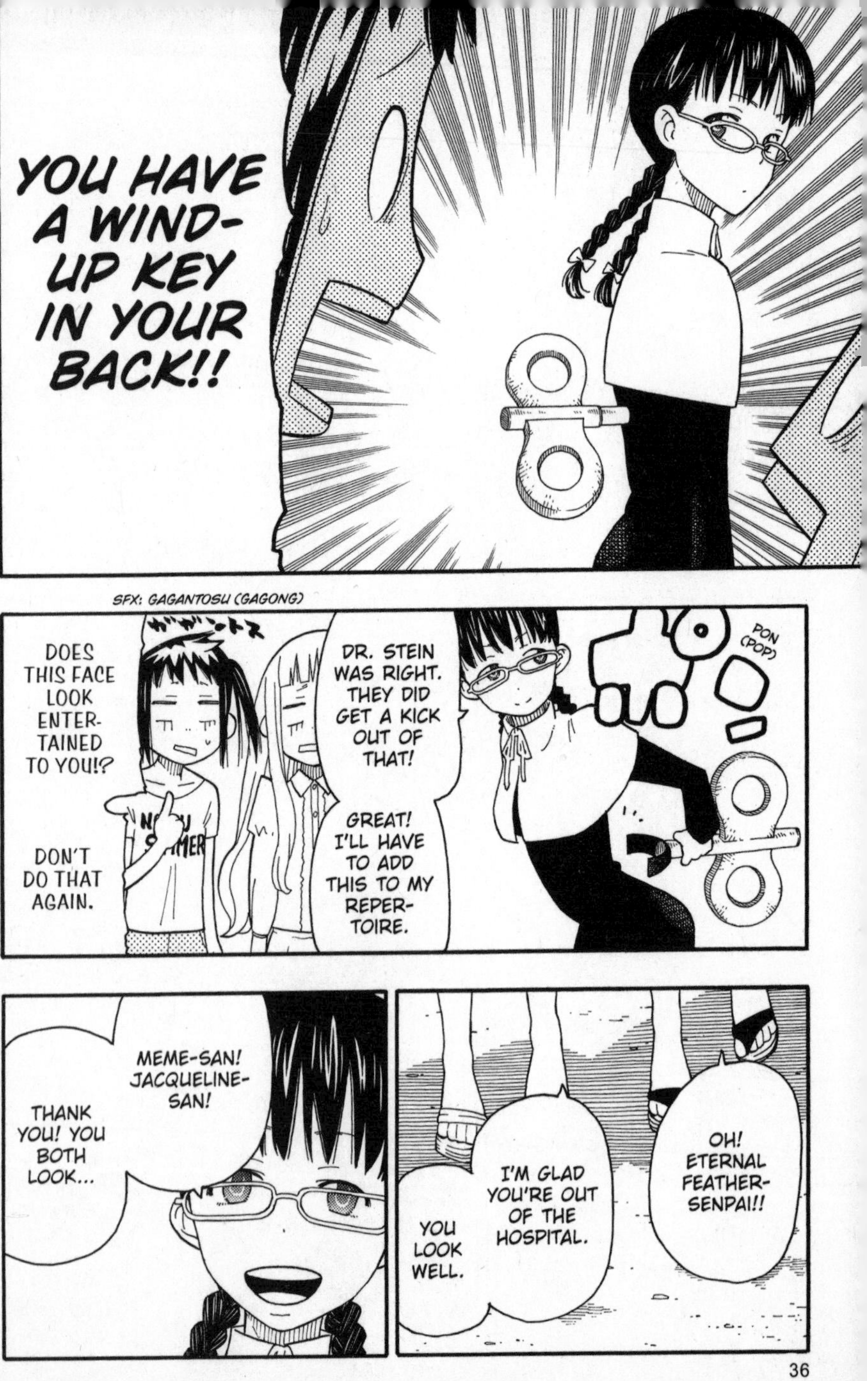
YOU HAVE A WIND-UP KEY IN YOUR BACK!!
SFX: GAGANTOSU (GAGONG)
PON (POP)
DR. STEIN WAS RIGHT. THEY DID GET A KICK OUT OF THAT!
DOES THIS FACE LOOK ENTERTAINED TO YOU!?
GREAT! I'LL HAVE TO ADD THIS TO MY REPERTOIRE.
DON'T DO THAT AGAIN.
OH! ETERNAL FEATHER-SENPAI!!
I'M GLAD YOU'RE OUT OF THE HOSPITAL.
YOU LOOK WELL.
MEME-SAN! JACQUELINE-SAN!
THANK YOU! YOU BOTH LOOK...

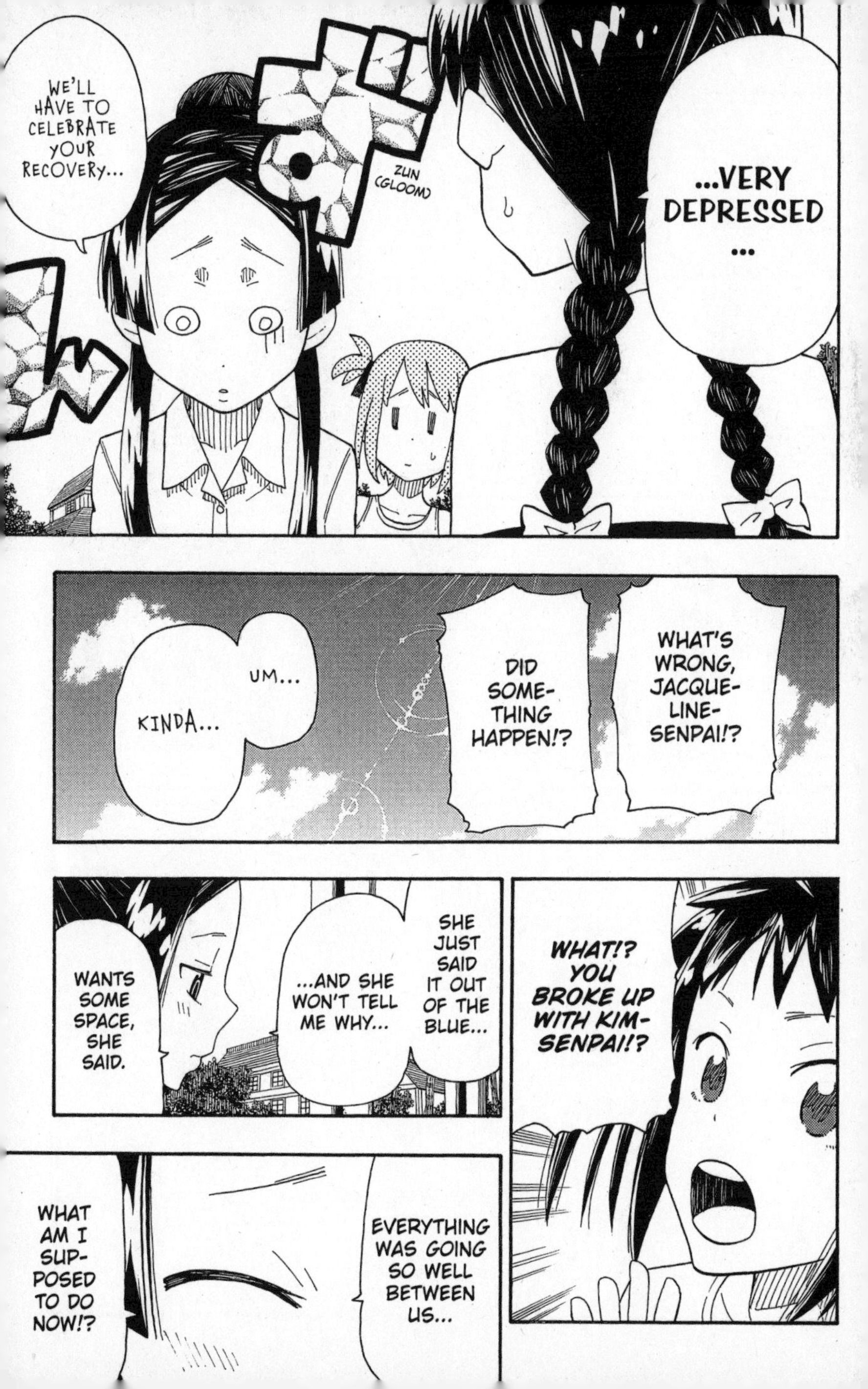

...VERY DEPRESSED ...
ZUN (GLOOM)
WE'LL HAVE TO CELEBRATE YOUR RECOVERY...
WHAT'S WRONG, JACQUE-LINE-SENPAI!?
DID SOME-THING HAPPEN!?
UM... KINDA...
WHAT!? YOU BROKE UP WITH KIM-SENPAI!?
SHE JUST SAID IT OUT OF THE BLUE...
...AND SHE WON'T TELL ME WHY...
WANTS SOME SPACE, SHE SAID.
EVERYTHING WAS GOING SO WELL BETWEEN US...
WHAT AM I SUP-POSED TO DO NOW!?

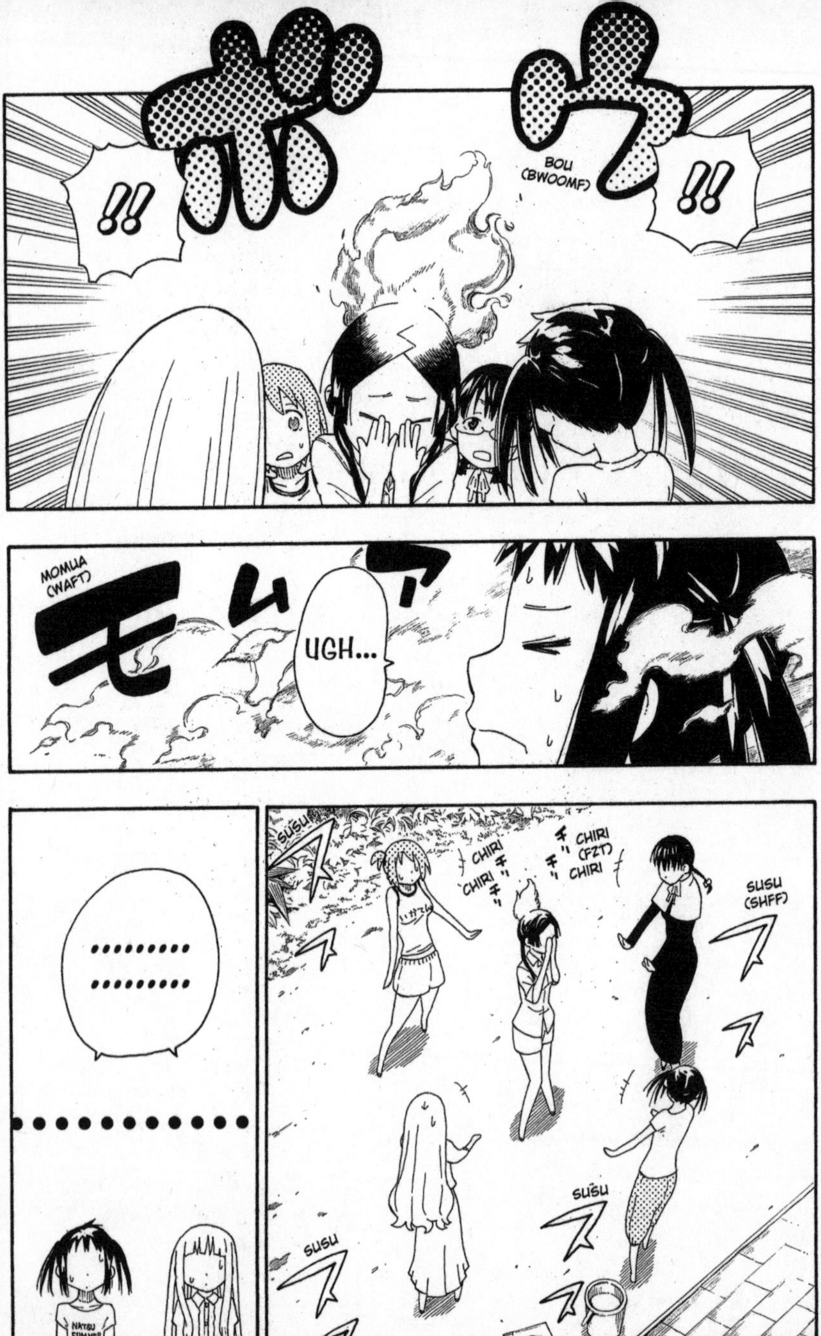
!!
BOU (BWOOMF)
ボウ
!!
UGH...
MOMUA (WAFT)
モムア
SUSU (SHFF)
チリ CHIRI (FZT)
チリ CHIRI
CHIRI チリ
CHIRI チリ
SUSU
SUSU
SUSU
....
....
....
NATSU SUMMER

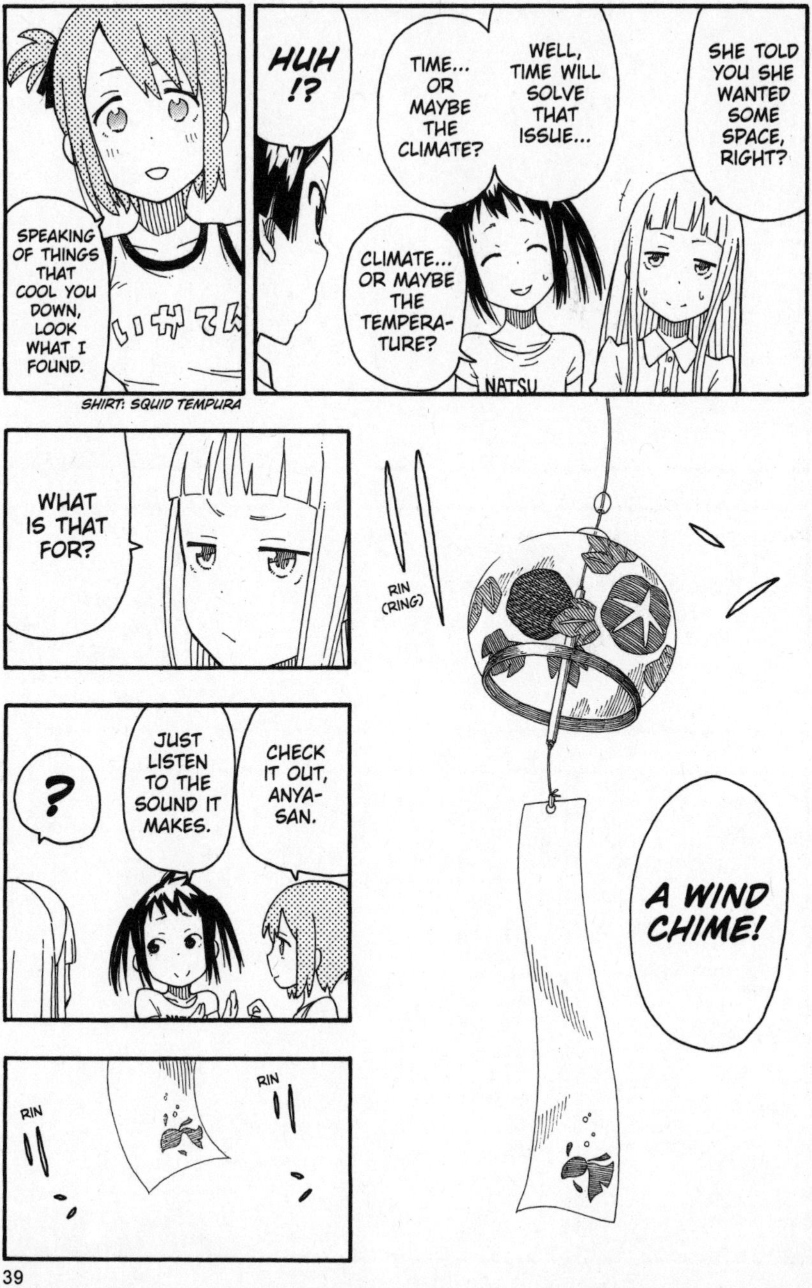
SHE TOLD YOU SHE WANTED SOME SPACE, RIGHT?
WELL, TIME WILL SOLVE THAT ISSUE...
TIME... OR MAYBE THE CLIMATE?
CLIMATE... OR MAYBE THE TEMPERATURE?
HUH!?
NATSU
SPEAKING OF THINGS THAT COOL YOU DOWN, LOOK WHAT I FOUND.
SHIRT: SQUID TEMPURA
A WIND CHIME!
RIN (RING)
WHAT IS THAT FOR?
CHECK IT OUT, ANYA-SAN.
JUST LISTEN TO THE SOUND IT MAKES.
?
RIN
RIN

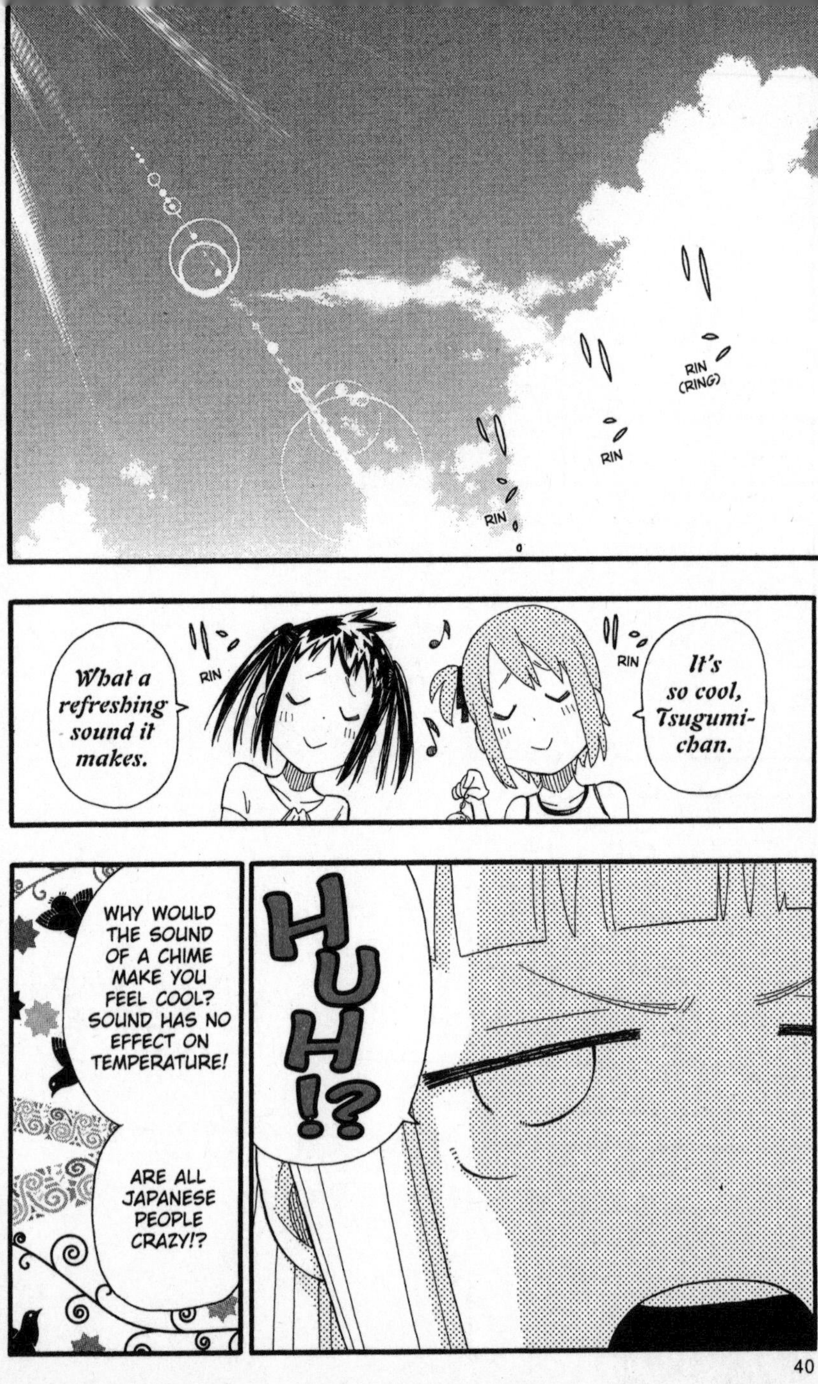
RIN (RING)
RIN
RIN
RIN
It's so cool, Tsugumi-chan.
RIN
What a refreshing sound it makes.
HUH!?
WHY WOULD THE SOUND OF A CHIME MAKE YOU FEEL COOL? SOUND HAS NO EFFECT ON TEMPERATURE!
ARE ALL JAPANESE PEOPLE CRAZY!?

SFX: FUWASSA (SWISH) FUWASSA

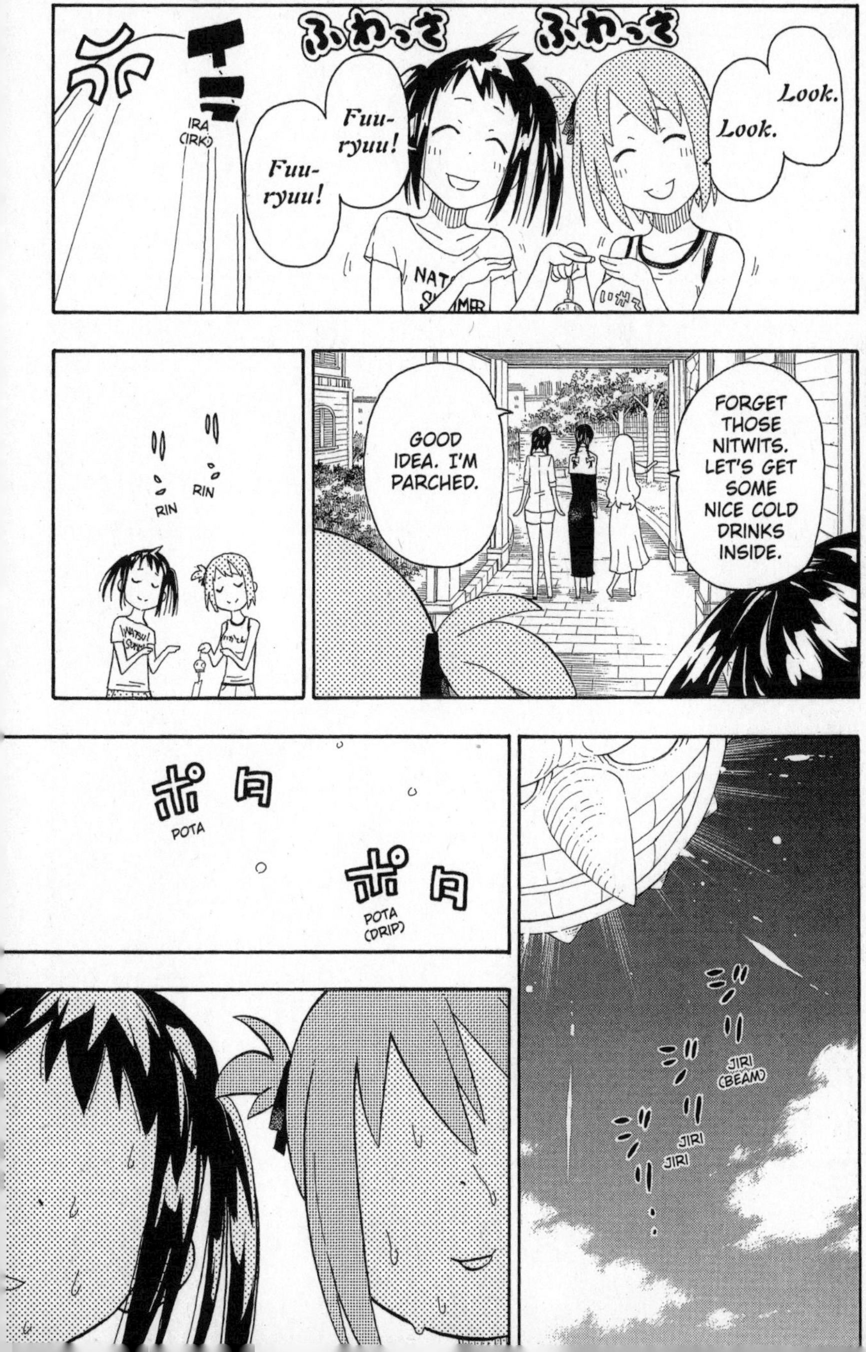

Look.
Look.
Fuu-ryuu!
Fuu-ryuu!
IRA (IRK)
FORGET THOSE NITWITS. LET'S GET SOME NICE COLD DRINKS INSIDE.
GOOD IDEA. I'M PARCHED.
RIN
RIN
JIRI (BEAM)
JIRI
JIRI
POTA
POTA (DRIP)

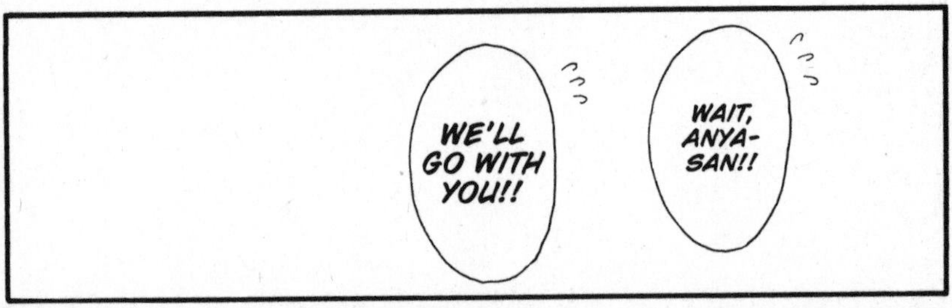
WAIT, ANYA-SAN!!
WE'LL GO WITH YOU!!

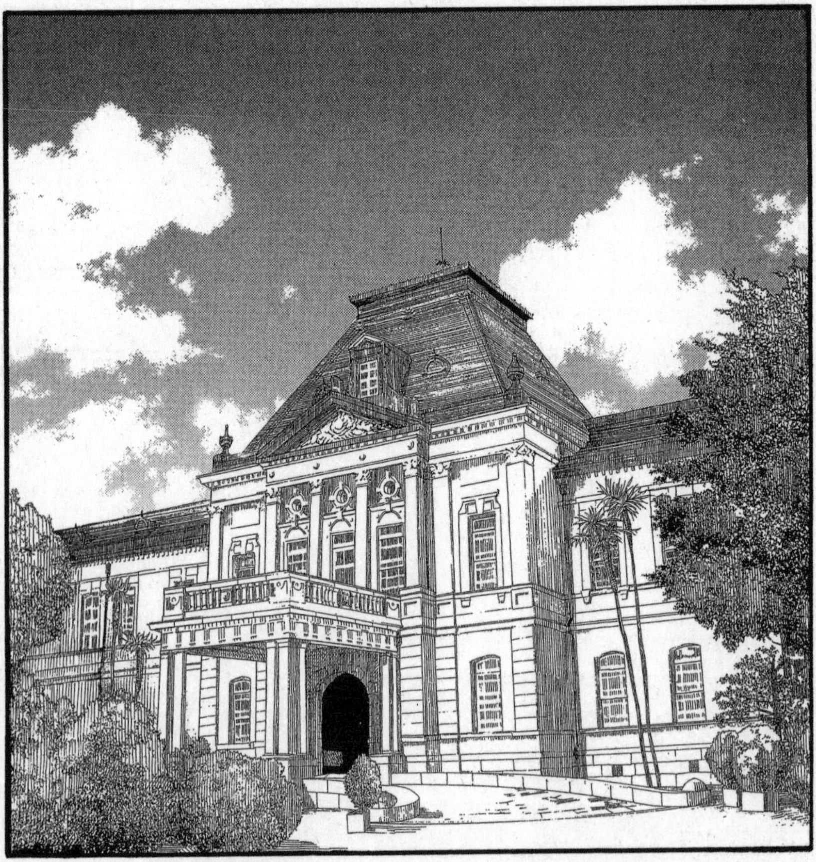

CHAPTER 17: COMING HOME!

SOUL EATER NOT!

SOUL EATER JOT

PART 1

ATSUSHI OHKUBO

SPECIALTY

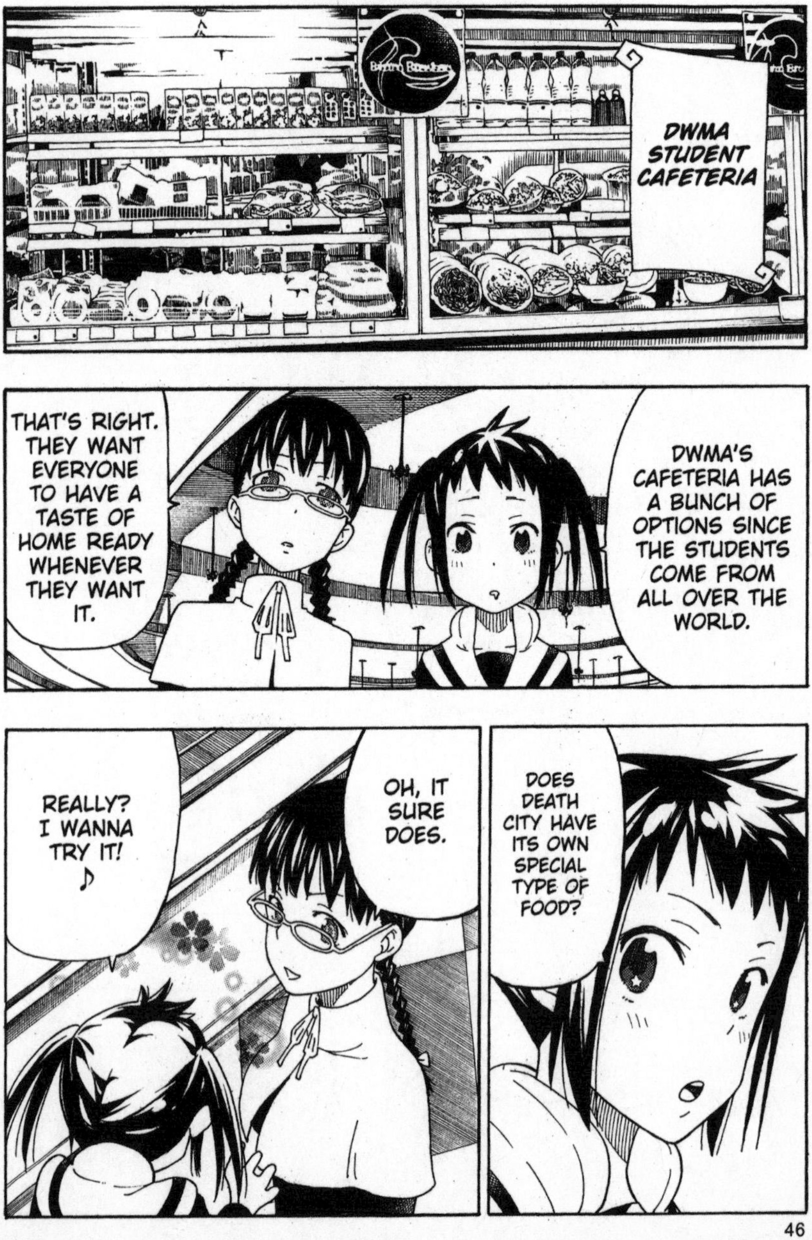
DWMA STUDENT CAFETERIA
DWMA'S CAFETERIA HAS A BUNCH OF OPTIONS SINCE THE STUDENTS COME FROM ALL OVER THE WORLD.
THAT'S RIGHT. THEY WANT EVERYONE TO HAVE A TASTE OF HOME READY WHENEVER THEY WANT IT.
DOES DEATH CITY HAVE ITS OWN SPECIAL TYPE OF FOOD?
OH, IT SURE DOES.
REALLY? I WANNA TRY IT! ♪

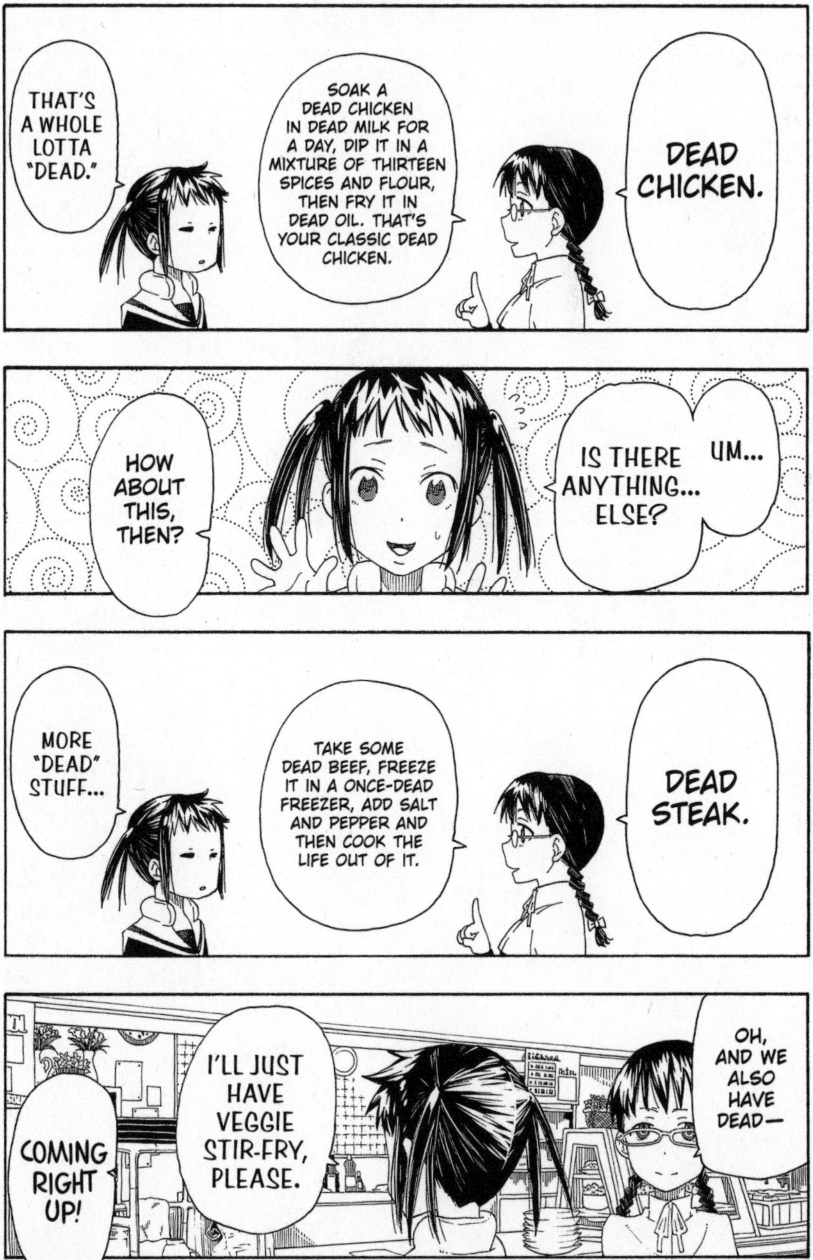
DEAD CHICKEN.
SOAK A DEAD CHICKEN IN DEAD MILK FOR A DAY, DIP IT IN A MIXTURE OF THIRTEEN SPICES AND FLOUR, THEN FRY IT IN DEAD OIL. THAT'S YOUR CLASSIC DEAD CHICKEN.
THAT'S A WHOLE LOTTA "DEAD."
UM...
IS THERE ANYTHING... ELSE?
HOW ABOUT THIS, THEN?
DEAD STEAK.
TAKE SOME DEAD BEEF, FREEZE IT IN A ONCE-DEAD FREEZER, ADD SALT AND PEPPER AND THEN COOK THE LIFE OUT OF IT.
MORE "DEAD" STUFF...
OH, AND WE ALSO HAVE DEAD—
I'LL JUST HAVE VEGGIE STIR-FRY, PLEASE.
COMING RIGHT UP!

AFTER THAT...

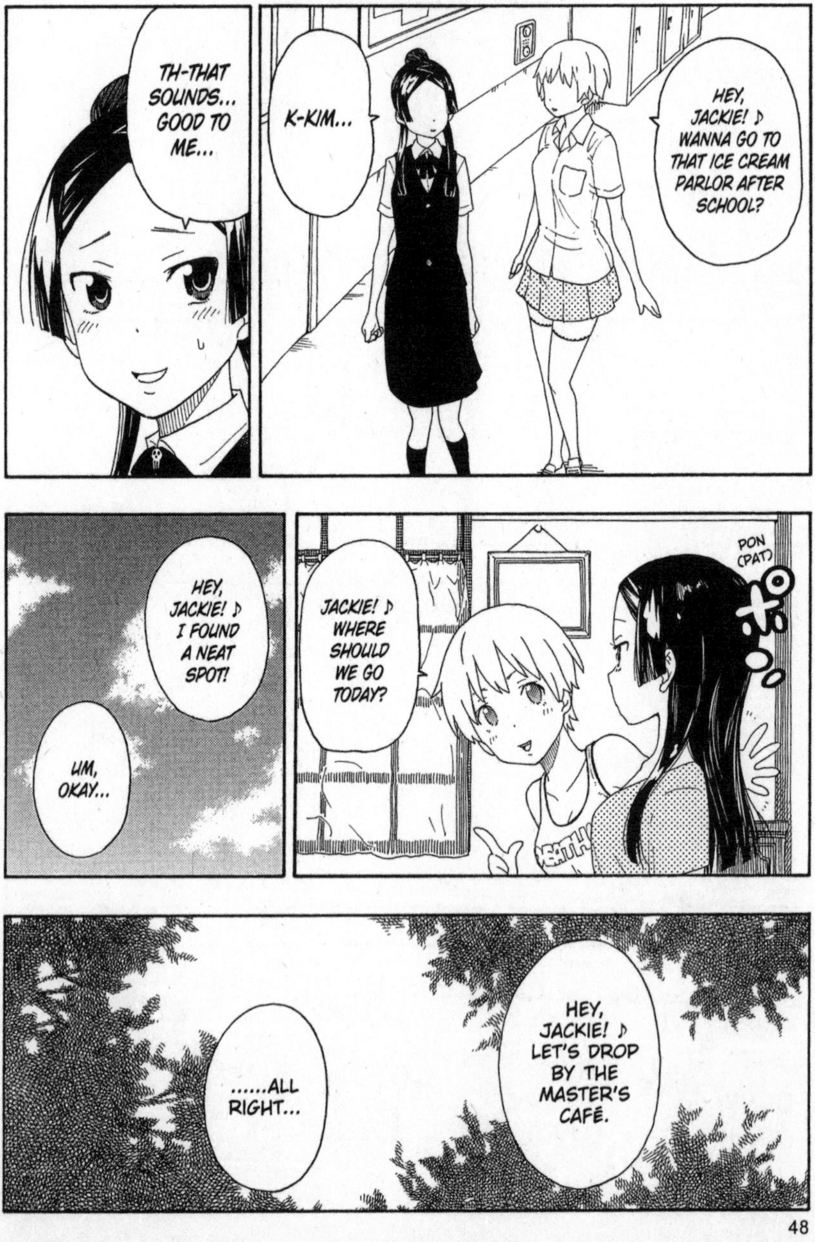
HEY, JACKIE! ♪ WANNA GO TO THAT ICE CREAM PARLOR AFTER SCHOOL?
K-KIM...
TH-THAT SOUNDS... GOOD TO ME...
PON (PAT)
JACKIE! ♪ WHERE SHOULD WE GO TODAY?
HEY, JACKIE! ♪ I FOUND A NEAT SPOT!
UM, OKAY...
HEY, JACKIE! ♪ LET'S DROP BY THE MASTER'S CAFÉ.
......ALL RIGHT...

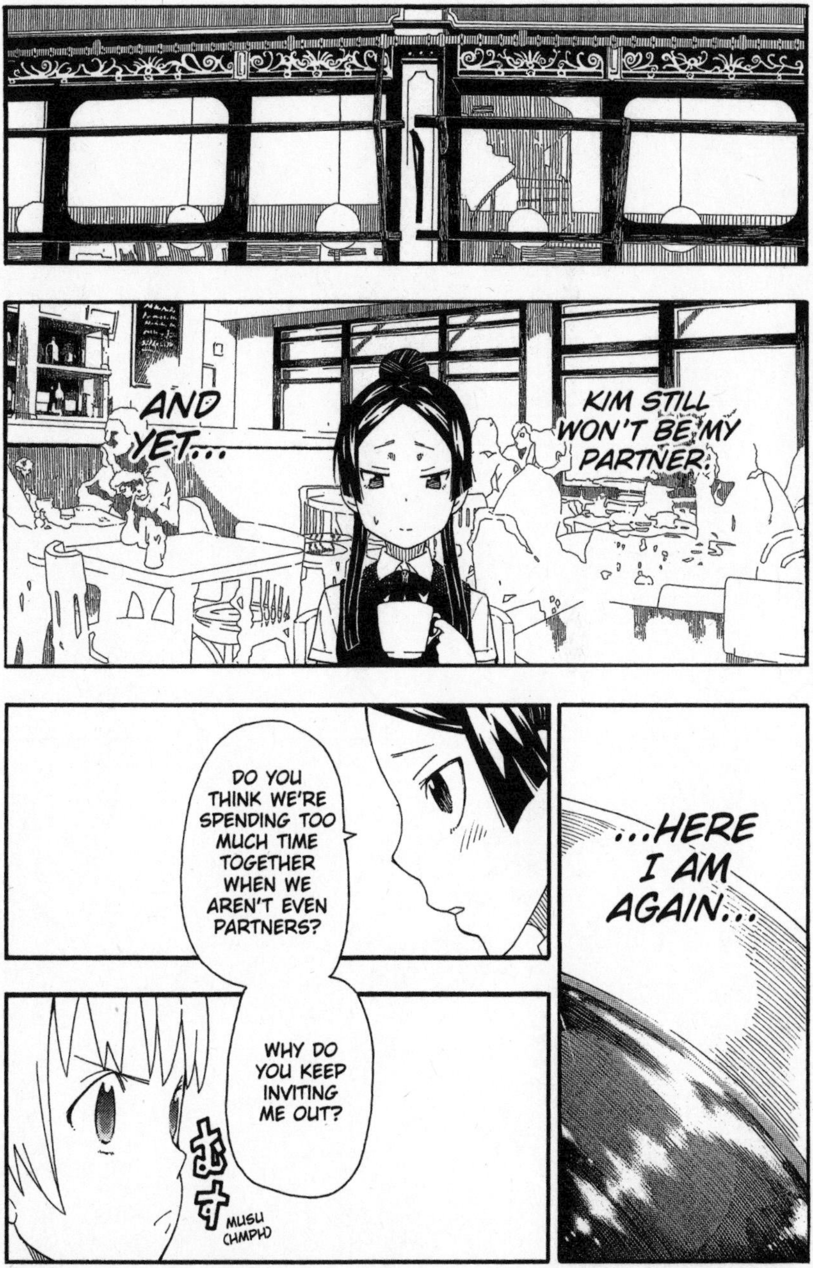
KIM STILL WON'T BE MY PARTNER.
AND YET...
...HERE I AM AGAIN...
DO YOU THINK WE'RE SPENDING TOO MUCH TIME TOGETHER WHEN WE AREN'T EVEN PARTNERS?
WHY DO YOU KEEP INVITING ME OUT?
MUSU
CHMPH

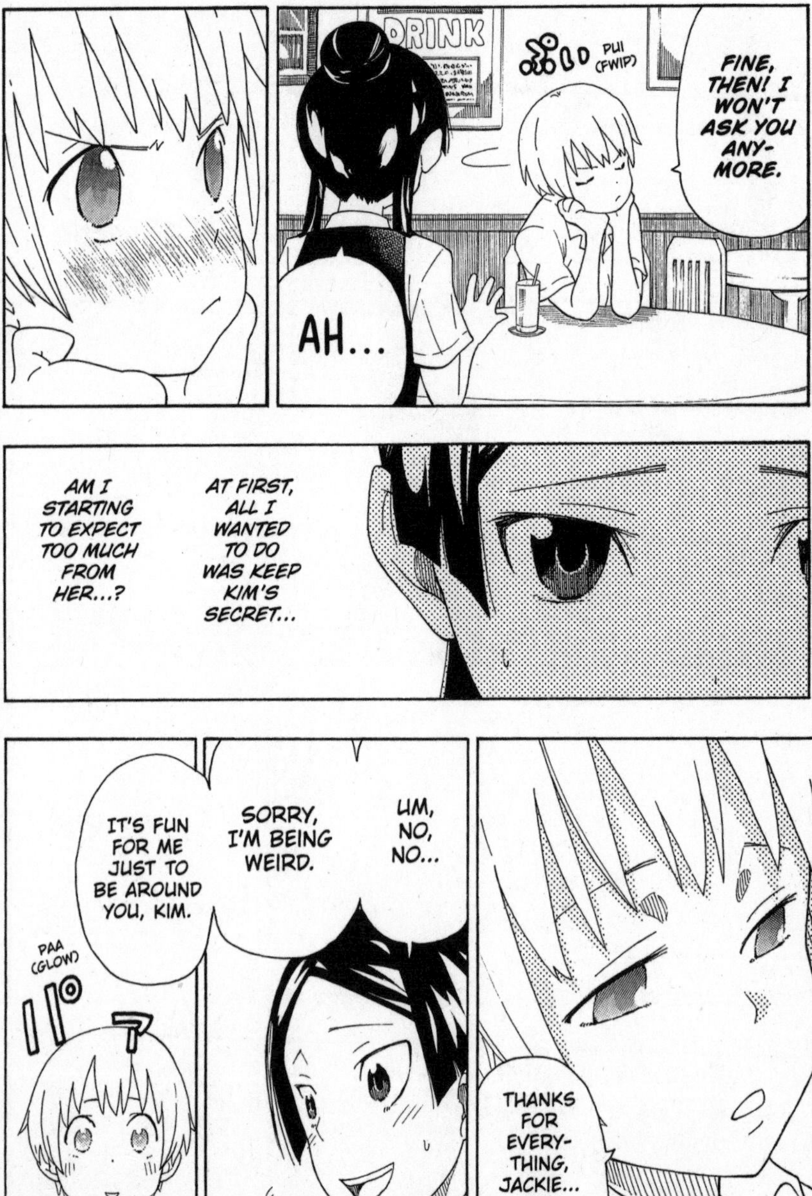
DRINK
FINE, THEN! I WON'T ASK YOU ANYMORE.
PUI (FWIP)
AH...
AT FIRST, ALL I WANTED TO DO WAS KEEP KIM'S SECRET...
AM I STARTING TO EXPECT TOO MUCH FROM HER...?
THANKS FOR EVERYTHING, JACKIE... I'M SORRY.
UM, NO, NO...
SORRY, I'M BEING WEIRD.
IT'S FUN FOR ME JUST TO BE AROUND YOU, KIM.
PAA (GLOW)

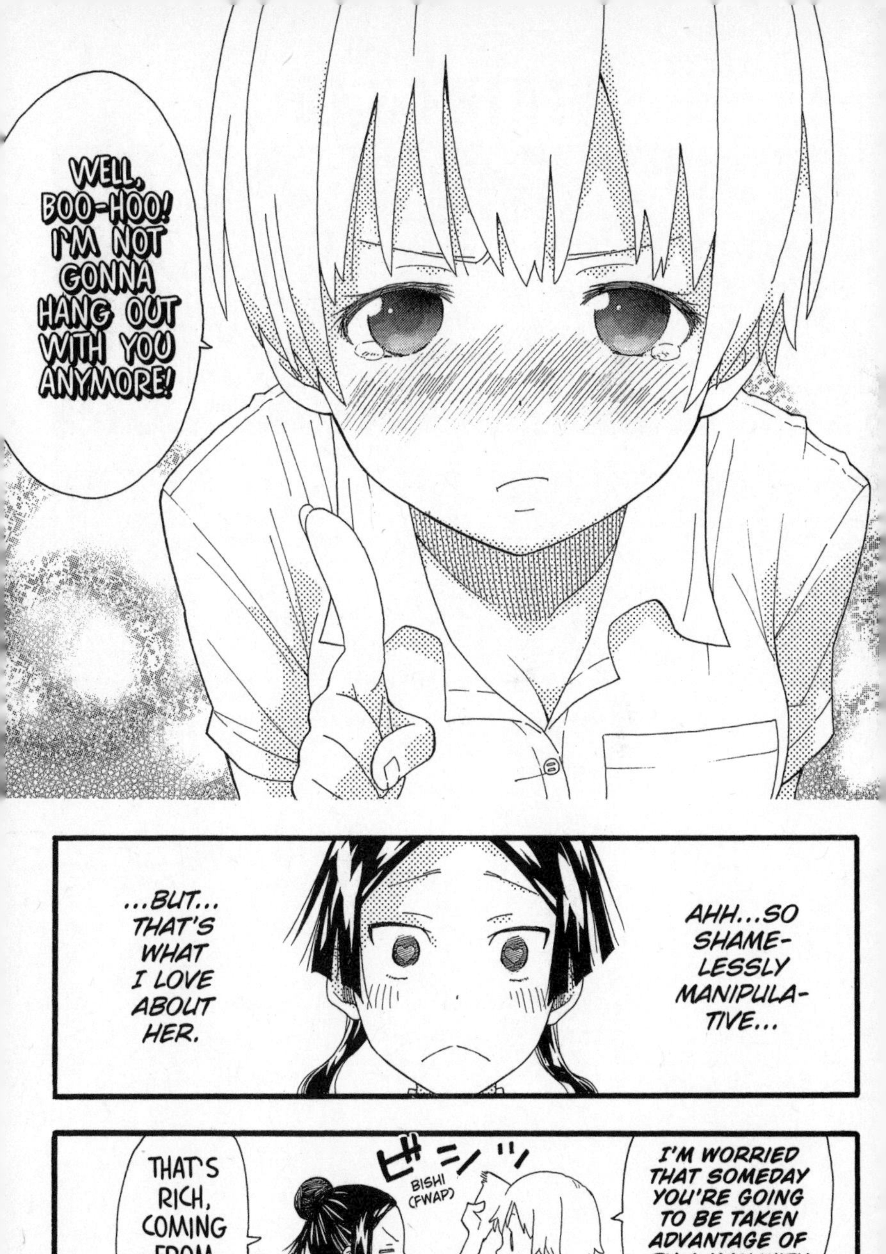
WELL, BOO-HOO! I'M NOT GONNA HANG OUT WITH YOU ANYMORE!
AHH...SO SHAMELESSLY MANIPULATIVE...
...BUT... THAT'S WHAT I LOVE ABOUT HER.
I'M WORRIED THAT SOMEDAY YOU'RE GOING TO BE TAKEN ADVANTAGE OF BY A MAN WITH BAD INTENTIONS.
BISHI (FWAP)
THAT'S RICH, COMING FROM YOU.

DEATH CHILD

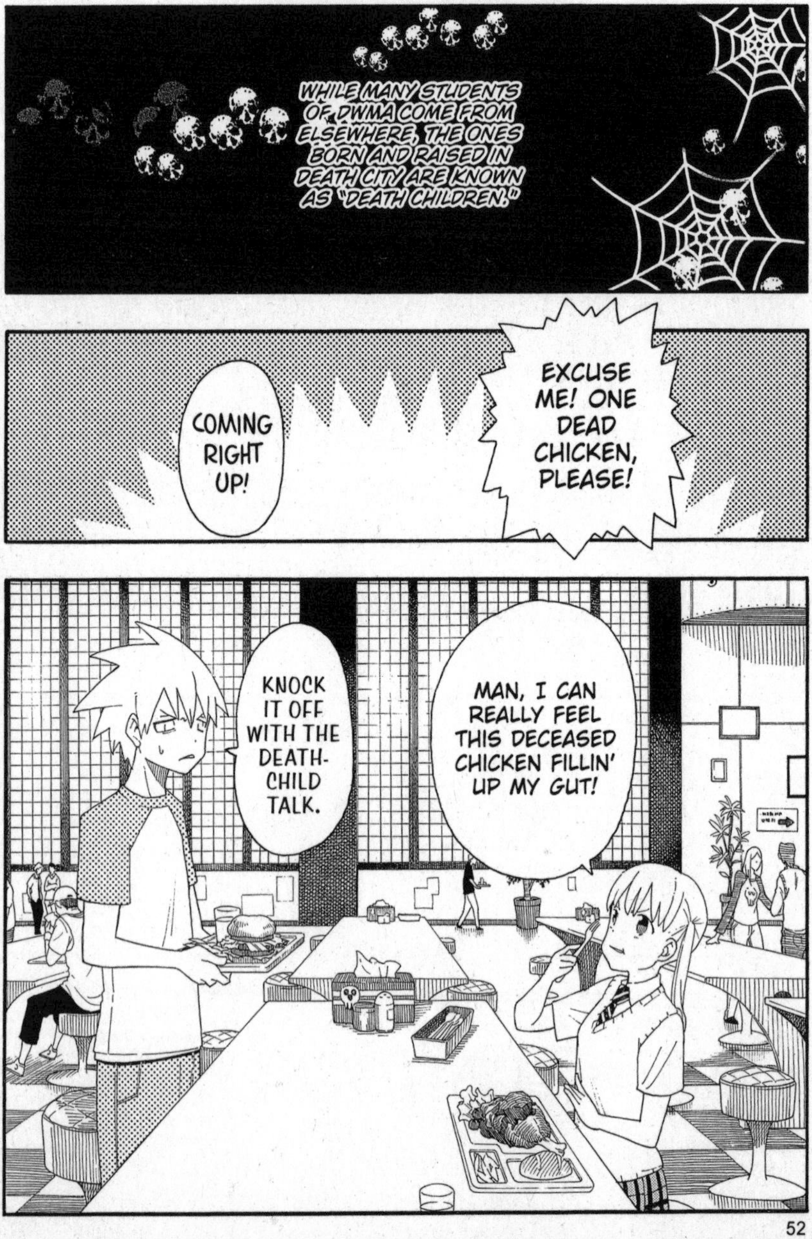
WHILE MANY STUDENTS OF DWMA COME FROM ELSEWHERE, THE ONES BORN AND RAISED IN DEATH CITY ARE KNOWN AS "DEATH CHILDREN."
EXCUSE ME! ONE DEAD CHICKEN, PLEASE!
COMING RIGHT UP!
MAN, I CAN REALLY FEEL THIS DECEASED CHICKEN FILLIN' UP MY GUT!
KNOCK IT OFF WITH THE DEATH-CHILD TALK.

SOUL EATER NOT!

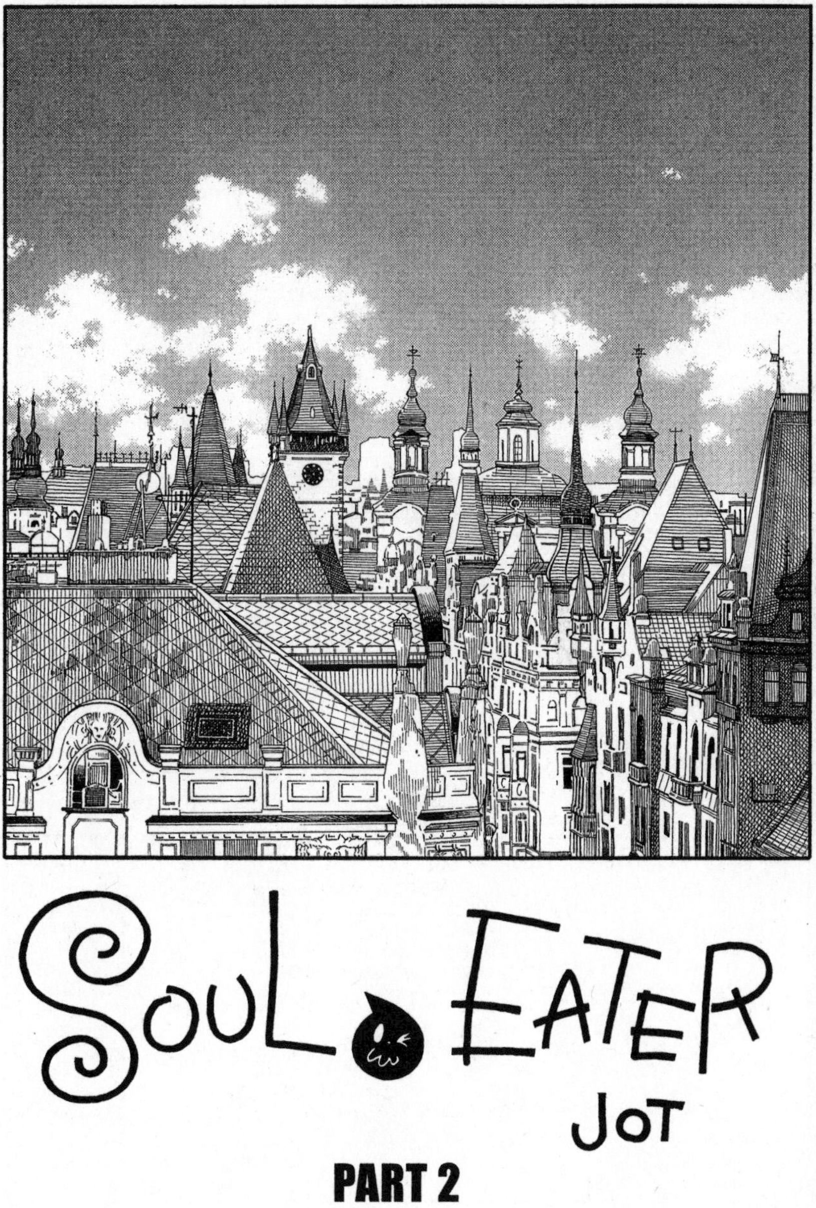

SOUL EATER

JOT

PART 2

A JOT OLDER

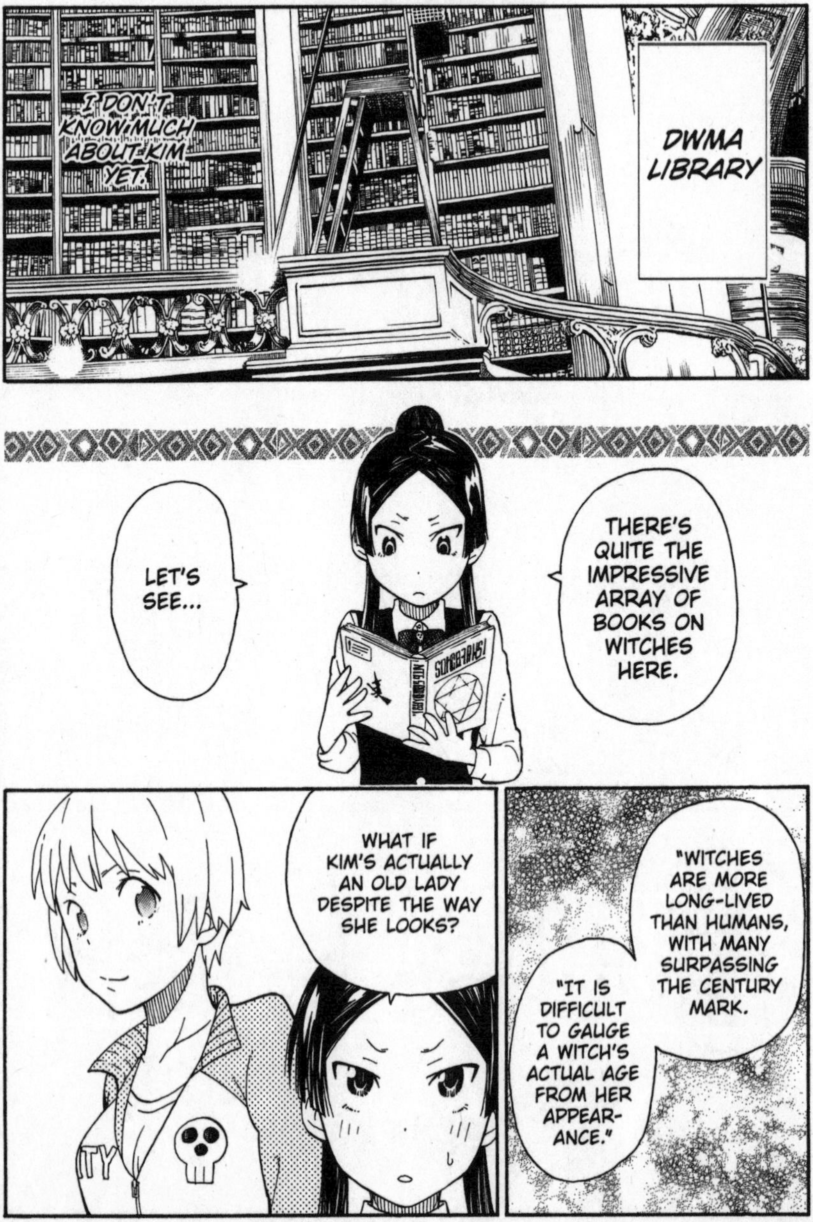
DWMA LIBRARY
I DON'T KNOW MUCH ABOUT KIM YET.
THERE'S QUITE THE IMPRESSIVE ARRAY OF BOOKS ON WITCHES HERE.
LET'S SEE...
"WITCHES ARE MORE LONG-LIVED THAN HUMANS, WITH MANY SURPASSING THE CENTURY MARK.
"IT IS DIFFICULT TO GAUGE A WITCH'S ACTUAL AGE FROM HER APPEARANCE."
WHAT IF KIM'S ACTUALLY AN OLD LADY DESPITE THE WAY SHE LOOKS?

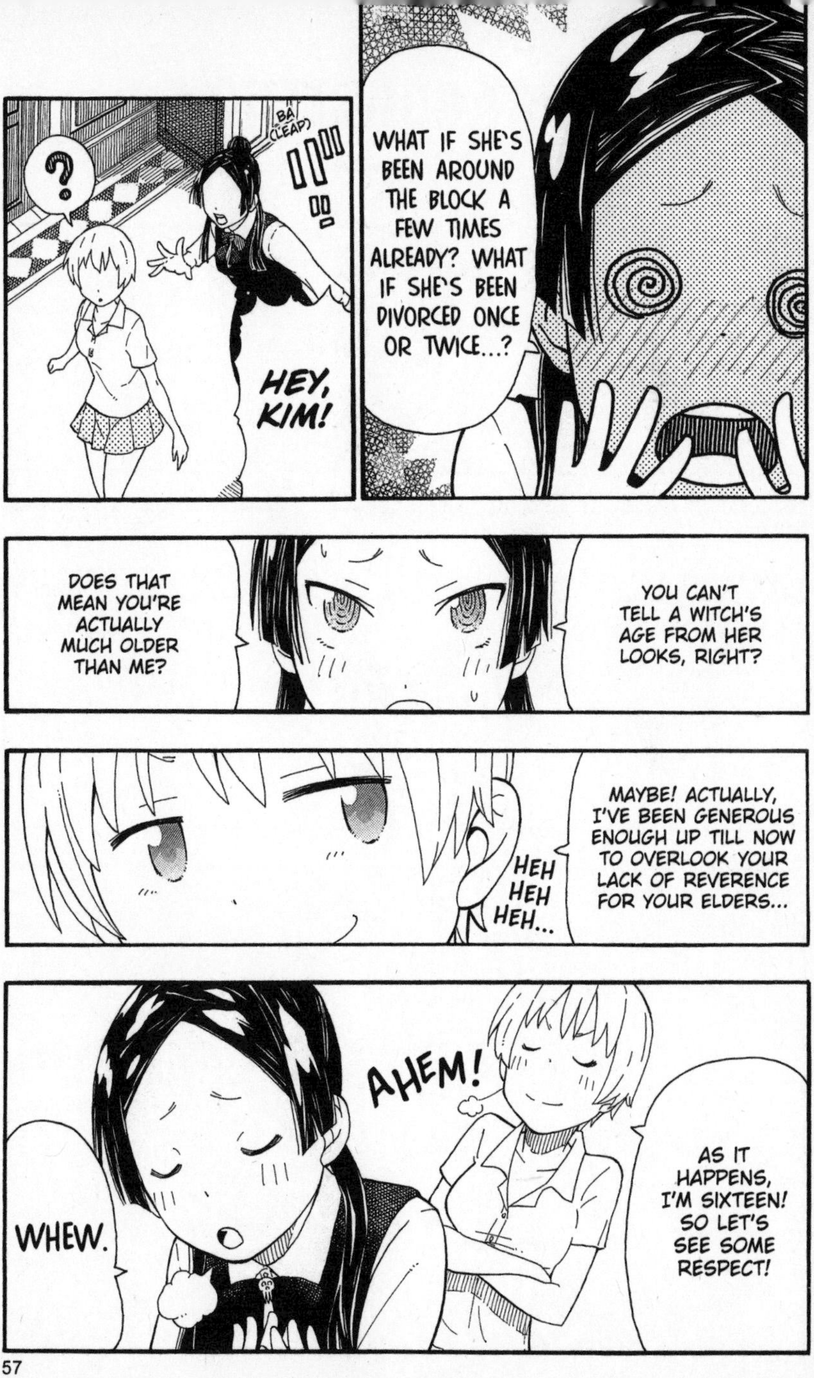
WHAT IF SHE'S BEEN AROUND THE BLOCK A FEW TIMES ALREADY? WHAT IF SHE'S BEEN DIVORCED ONCE OR TWICE...?
BA (LEAP)
?
HEY, KIM!
YOU CAN'T TELL A WITCH'S AGE FROM HER LOOKS, RIGHT?
DOES THAT MEAN YOU'RE ACTUALLY MUCH OLDER THAN ME?
MAYBE! ACTUALLY, I'VE BEEN GENEROUS ENOUGH UP TILL NOW TO OVERLOOK YOUR LACK OF REVERENCE FOR YOUR ELDERS...
HEH HEH HEH...
AS IT HAPPENS, I'M SIXTEEN! SO LET'S SEE SOME RESPECT!
AHEM!
WHEW.

A JOT SHORTER?

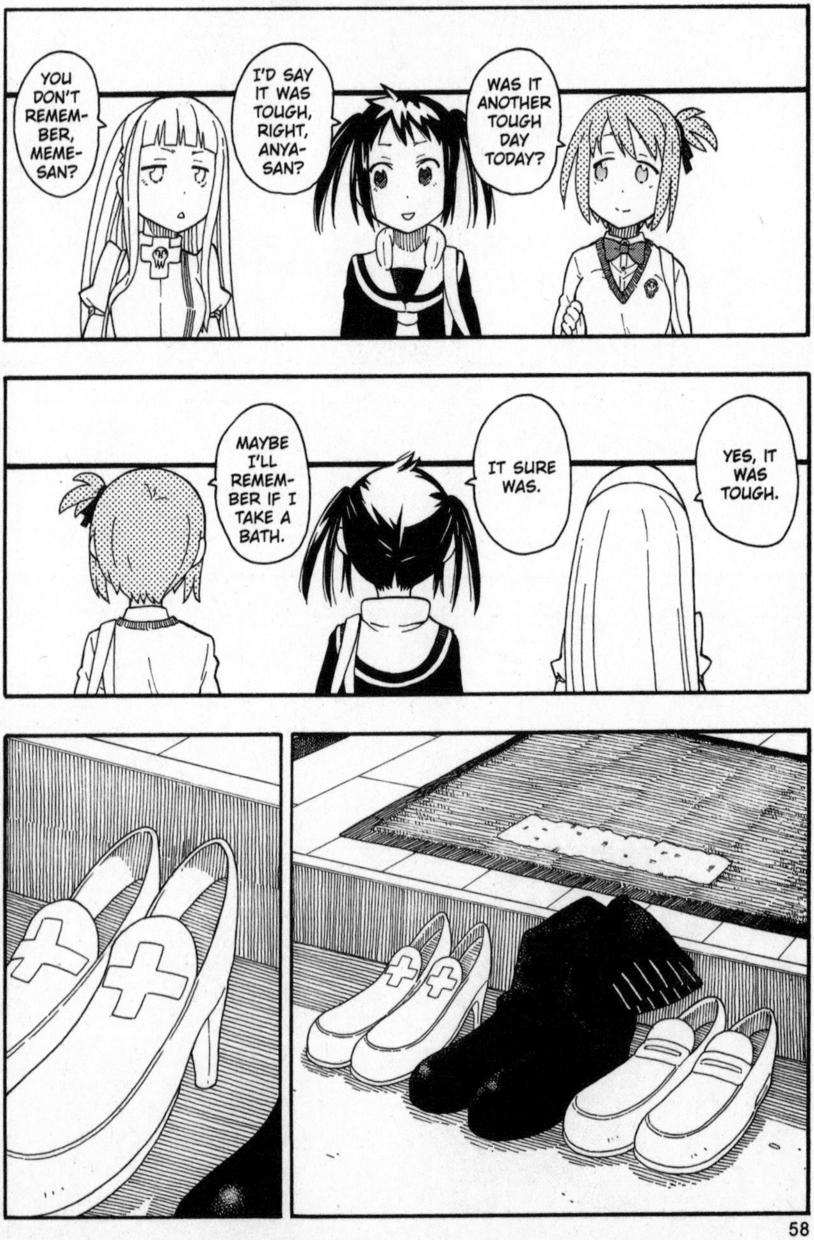
WAS IT ANOTHER TOUGH DAY TODAY?
I'D SAY IT WAS TOUGH, RIGHT, ANYA-SAN?
YOU DON'T REMEM-BER, MEME-SAN?
YES, IT WAS TOUGH.
IT SURE WAS.
MAYBE I'LL REMEM-BER IF I TAKE A BATH.

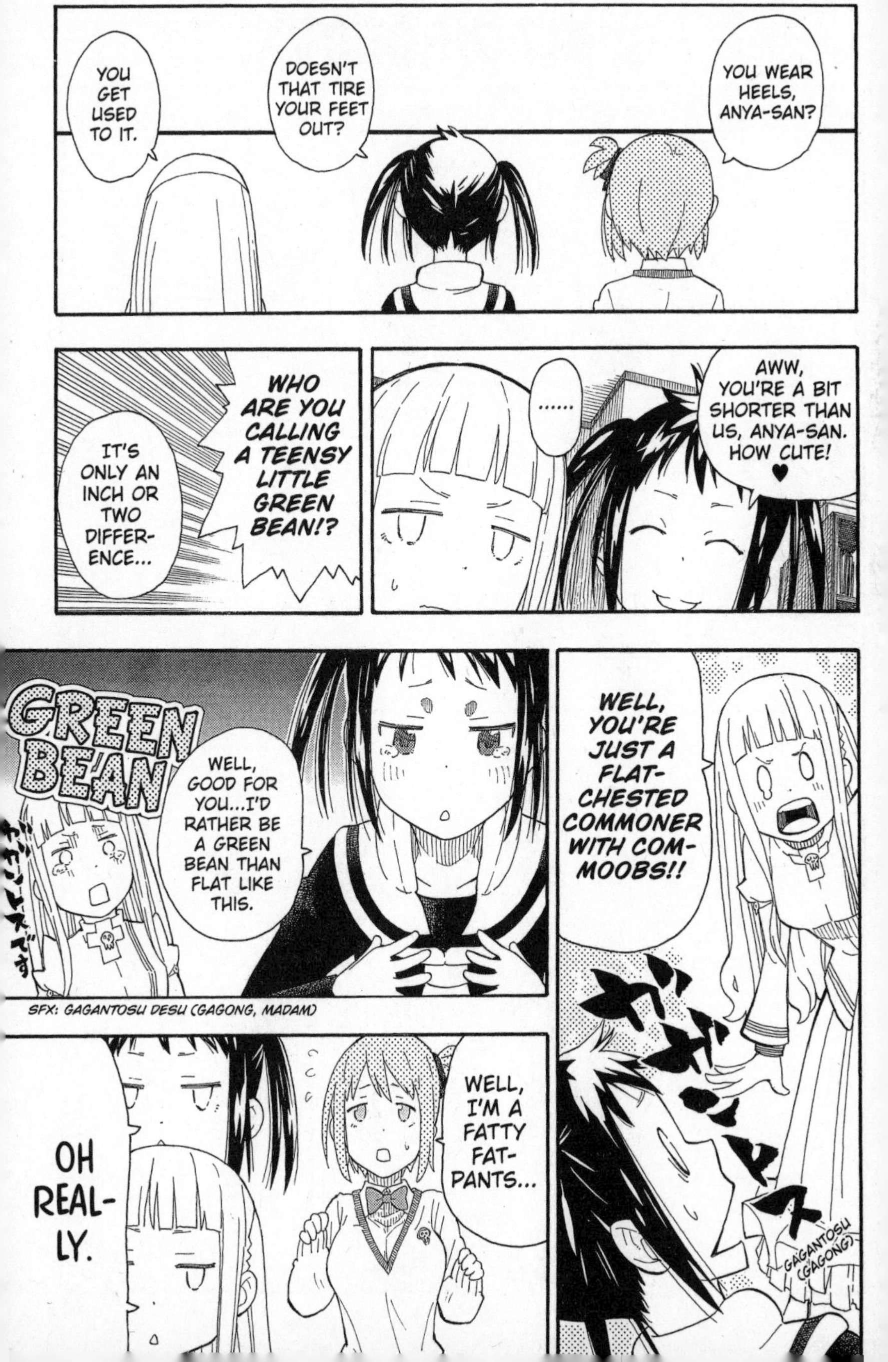
YOU WEAR HEELS, ANYA-SAN?
DOESN'T THAT TIRE YOUR FEET OUT?
YOU GET USED TO IT.
AWW, YOU'RE A BIT SHORTER THAN US, ANYA-SAN. HOW CUTE! ♥
......
WHO ARE YOU CALLING A TEENSY LITTLE GREEN BEAN!?
IT'S ONLY AN INCH OR TWO DIFFER-ENCE...
WELL, YOU'RE JUST A FLAT-CHESTED COMMONER WITH COM-MOOBS!!
GAGANTOSU (GAGONG)
GREEN BEAN
WELL, GOOD FOR YOU...I'D RATHER BE A GREEN BEAN THAN FLAT LIKE THIS.
SFX: GAGANTOSU DESU (GAGONG, MADAM)
WELL, I'M A FATTY FAT-PANTS...
OH REAL-LY.

A JOT WRONG?

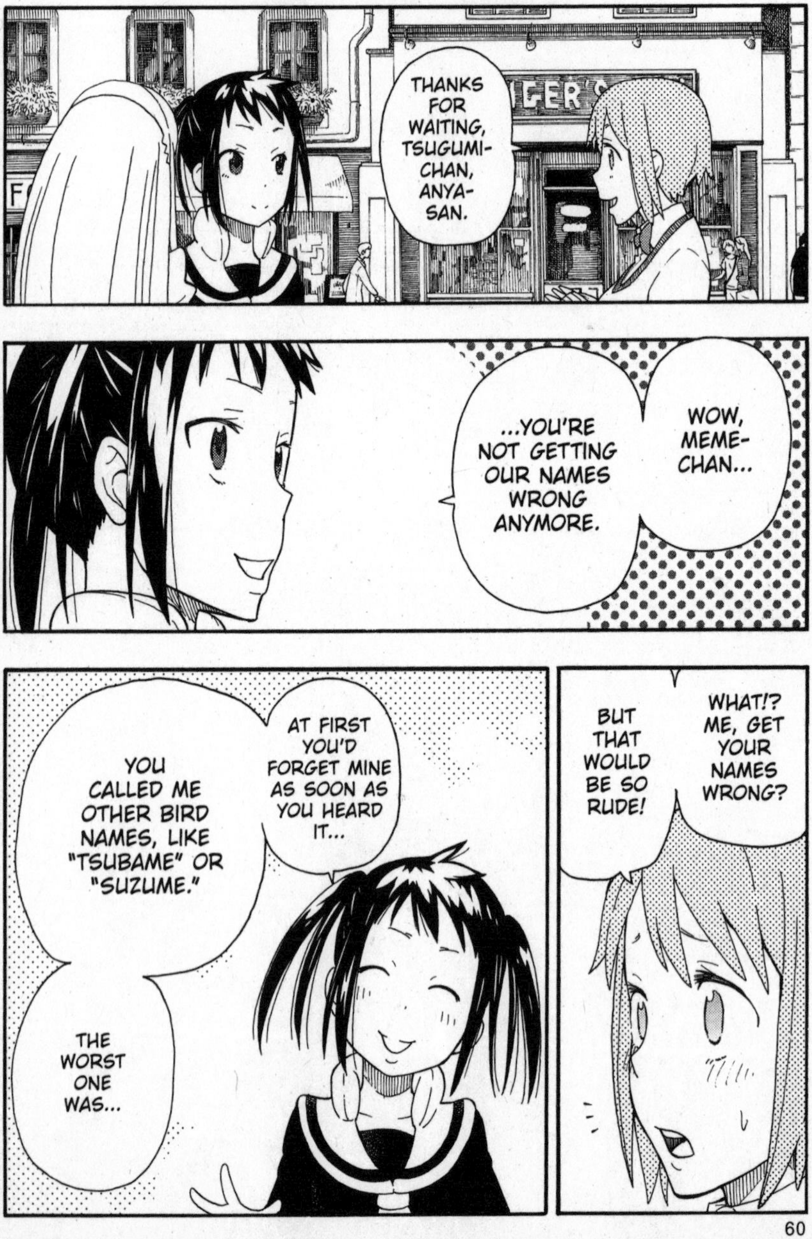
THANKS FOR WAITING, TSUGUMI-CHAN, ANYA-SAN.
WOW, MEME-CHAN...
...YOU'RE NOT GETTING OUR NAMES WRONG ANYMORE.
WHAT!? ME, GET YOUR NAMES WRONG?
BUT THAT WOULD BE SO RUDE!
AT FIRST YOU'D FORGET MINE AS SOON AS YOU HEARD IT...
YOU CALLED ME OTHER BIRD NAMES, LIKE "TSUBAME" OR "SUZUME."
THE WORST ONE WAS...

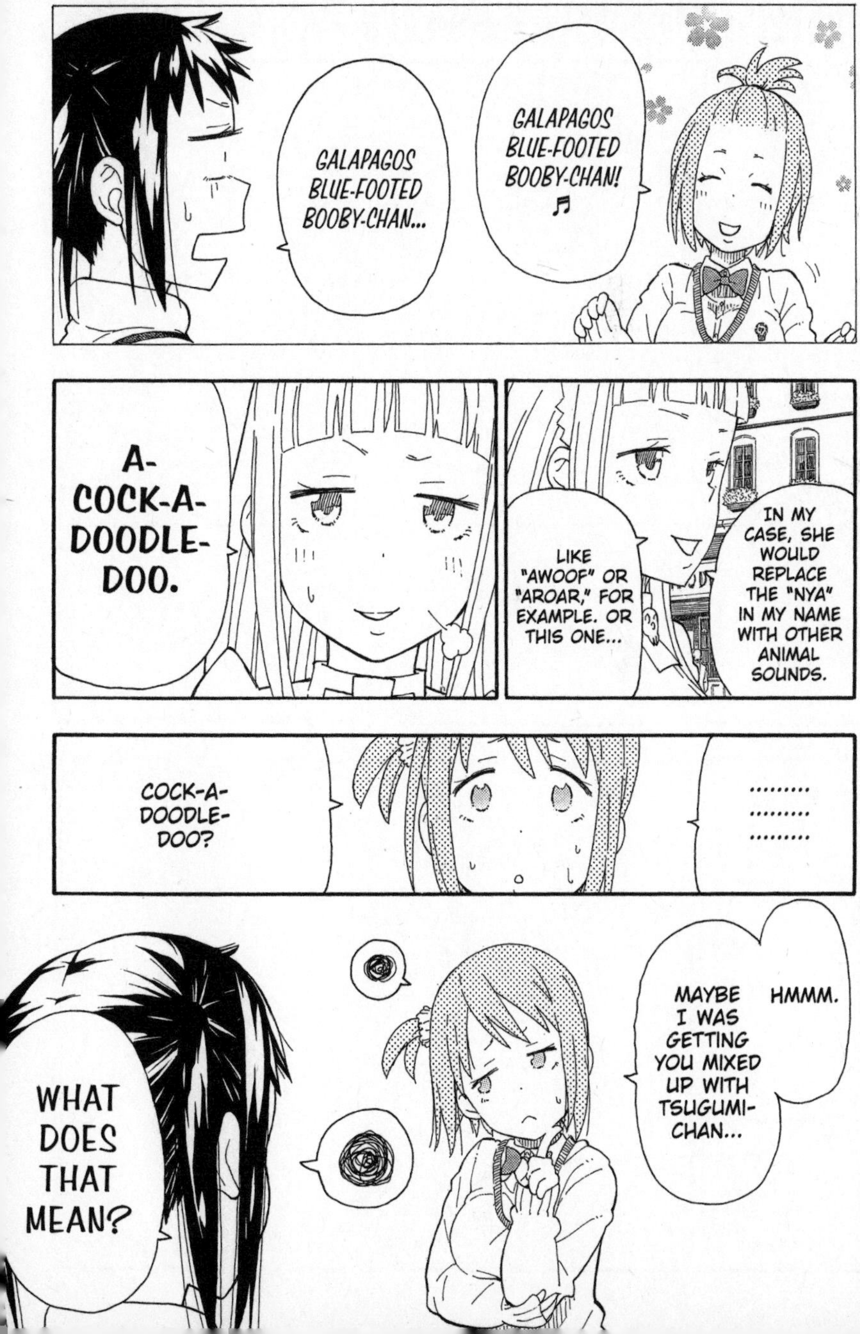
GALAPAGOS BLUE-FOOTED BOOBY-CHAN! ♪
GALAPAGOS BLUE-FOOTED BOOBY-CHAN...
IN MY CASE, SHE WOULD REPLACE THE "NYA" IN MY NAME WITH OTHER ANIMAL SOUNDS.
LIKE "AWOOF" OR "AROAR," FOR EXAMPLE. OR THIS ONE...
A-COCK-A-DOODLE-DOO.
....
....
....
COCK-A-DOODLE-DOO?
HMMM.
MAYBE I WAS GETTING YOU MIXED UP WITH TSUGUMI-CHAN...
WHAT DOES THAT MEAN?

THE MOST POWERFUL ANIMAL I CAN IMAGINE IS TOO CUTE

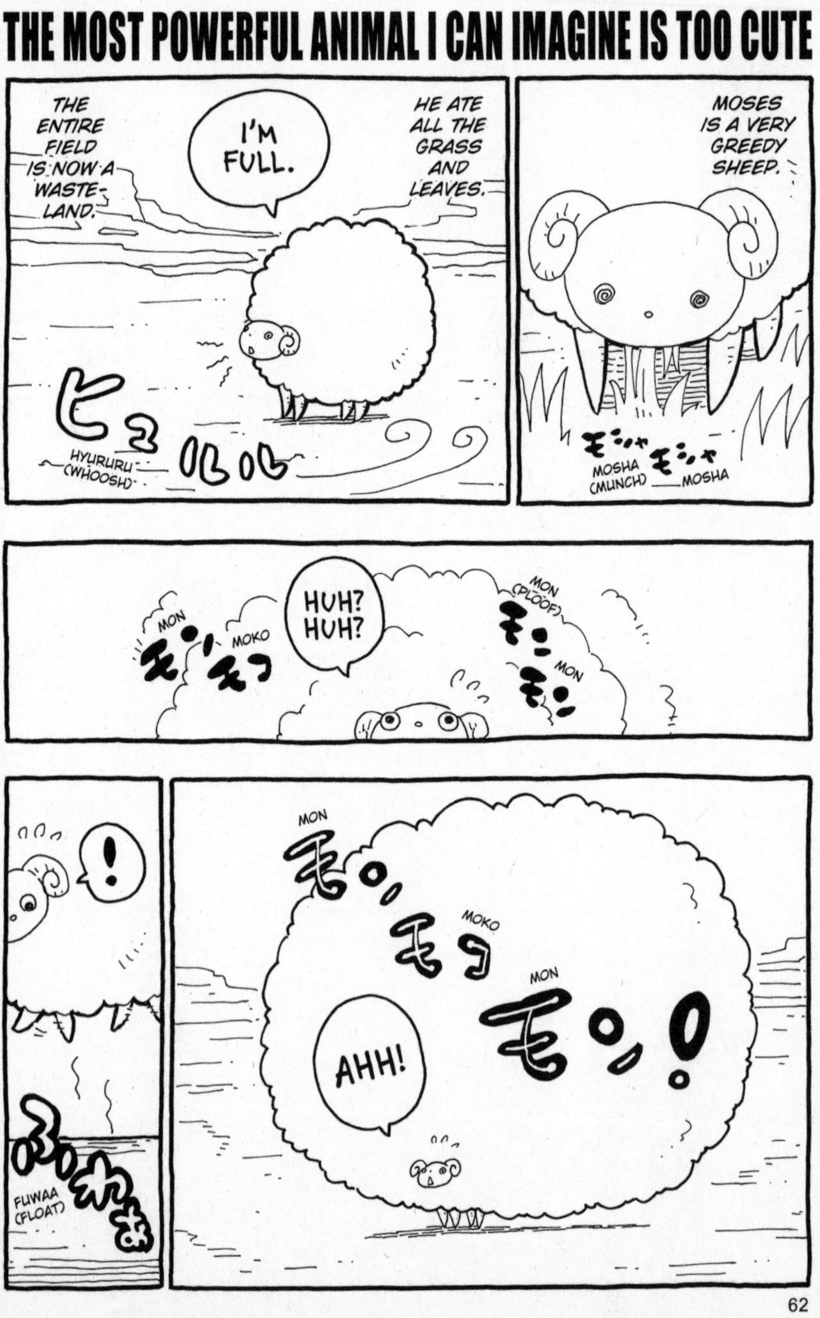

MOSES IS A VERY GREEDY SHEEP.
MOSHA (MUNCH) MOSHA
HE ATE ALL THE GRASS AND LEAVES.
I'M FULL.
THE ENTIRE FIELD IS NOW A WASTELAND.
HYURURU (WHOOSH)
MON (PLOOF)
MON
HUH? HUH?
MOKO
MON
MON
MOKO
MON
AHH!
!
FUWAA (FLOAT)

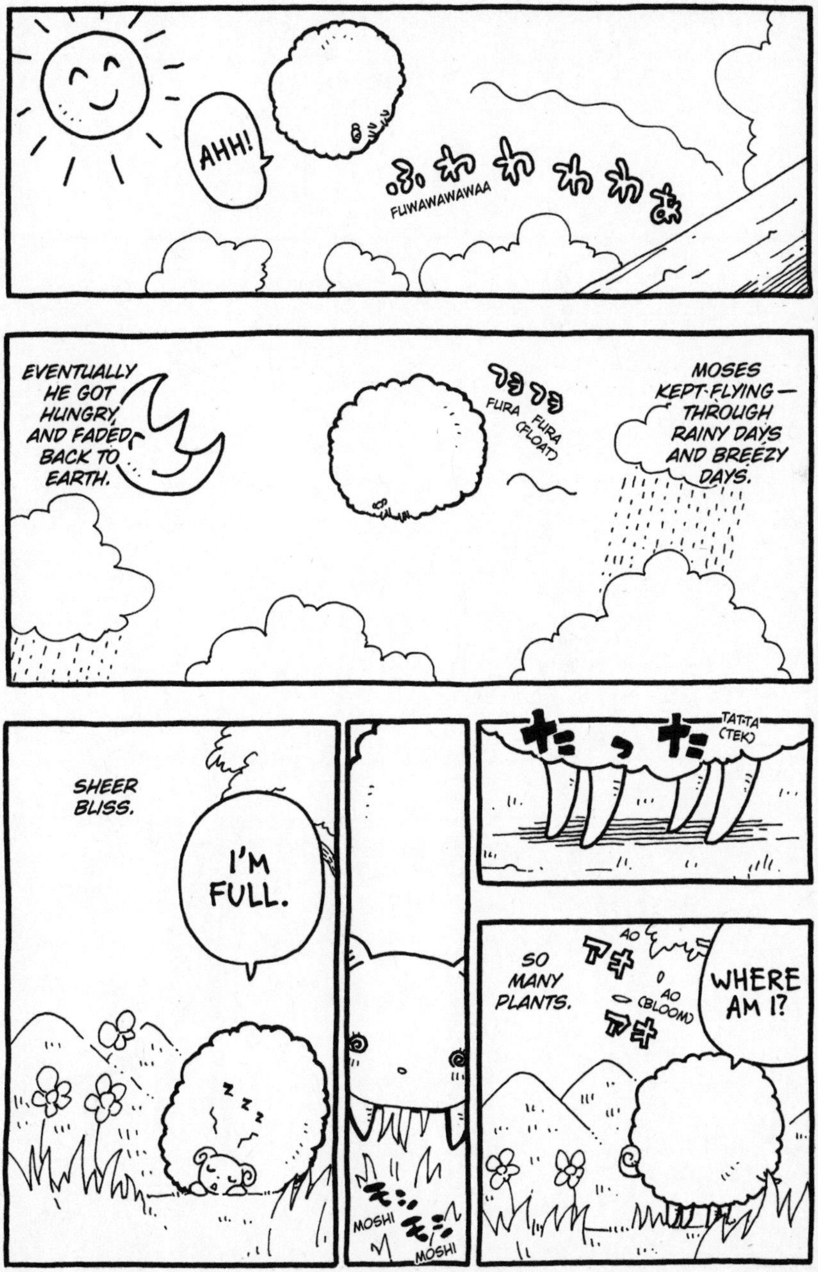
AHH!
ふわわわわぁ
FUWAWAWAWAA
MOSES KEPT FLYING— THROUGH RAINY DAYS AND BREEZY DAYS.
フラフラ
FURA FURA (FLOAT)
EVENTUALLY HE GOT HUNGRY, AND FADED BACK TO EARTH.
たっ た
TAT-TA (TEK)
WHERE AM I?
アオ
AO
アオ
AO (BLOOM)
SO MANY PLANTS.
モシ モシ
MOSHI MOSHI
I'M FULL.
SHEER BLISS.

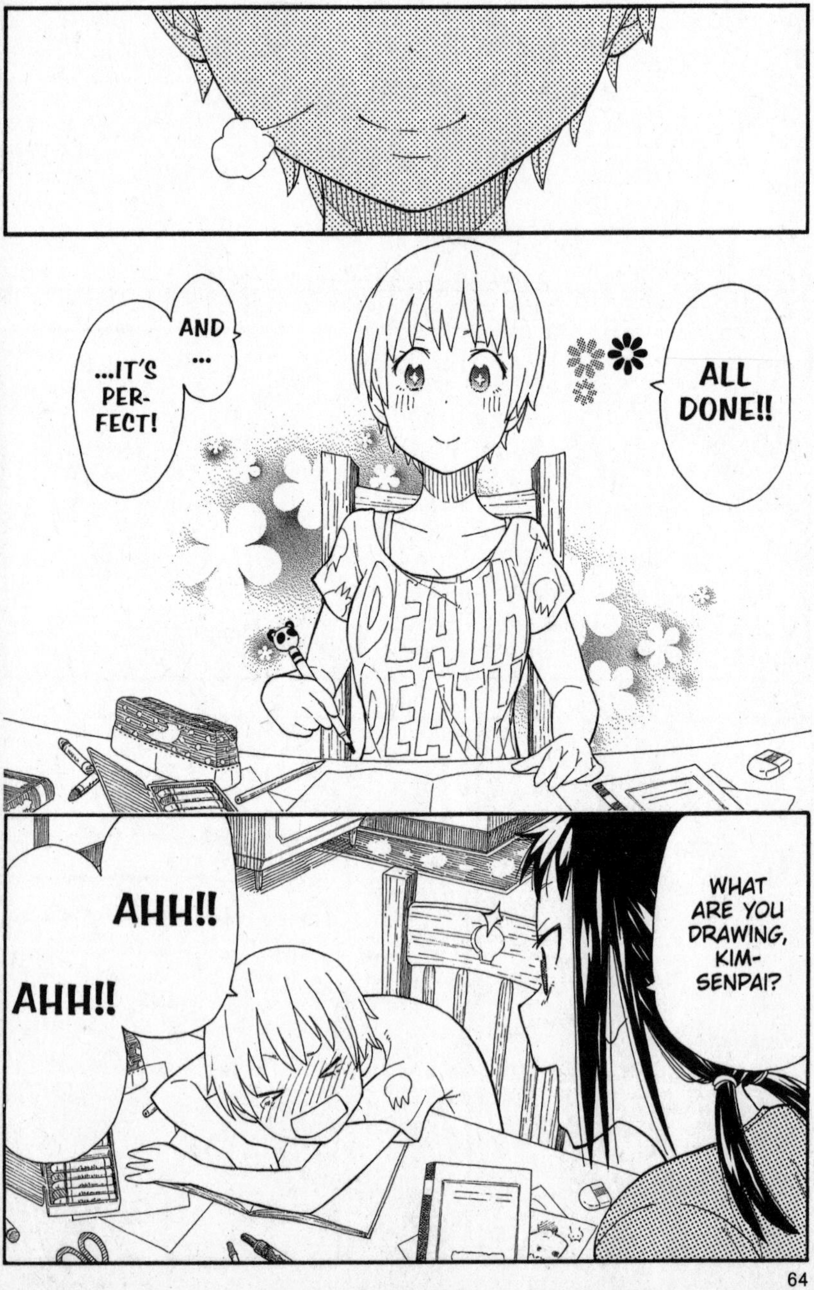
ALL DONE!!
AND ...
...IT'S PER-FECT!
WHAT ARE YOU DRAWING, KIM-SENPAI?
AHH!!
AHH!!

SOUL EATER NOT!

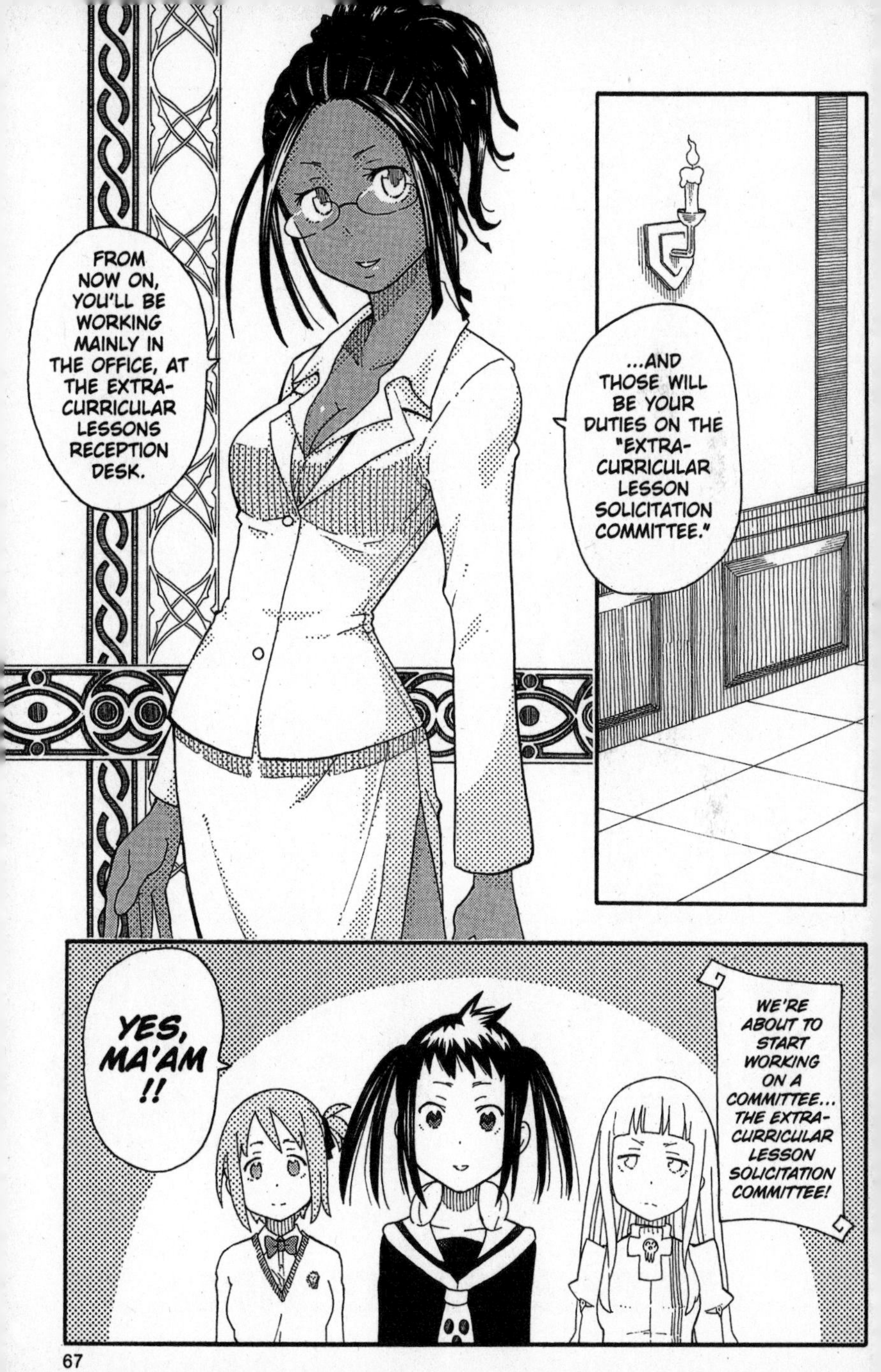
...AND THOSE WILL BE YOUR DUTIES ON THE "EXTRA-CURRICULAR LESSON SOLICITATION COMMITTEE."
FROM NOW ON, YOU'LL BE WORKING MAINLY IN THE OFFICE, AT THE EXTRA-CURRICULAR LESSONS RECEPTION DESK.
WE'RE ABOUT TO START WORKING ON A COMMITTEE... THE EXTRA-CURRICULAR LESSON SOLICITATION COMMITTEE!
YES, MA'AM!!

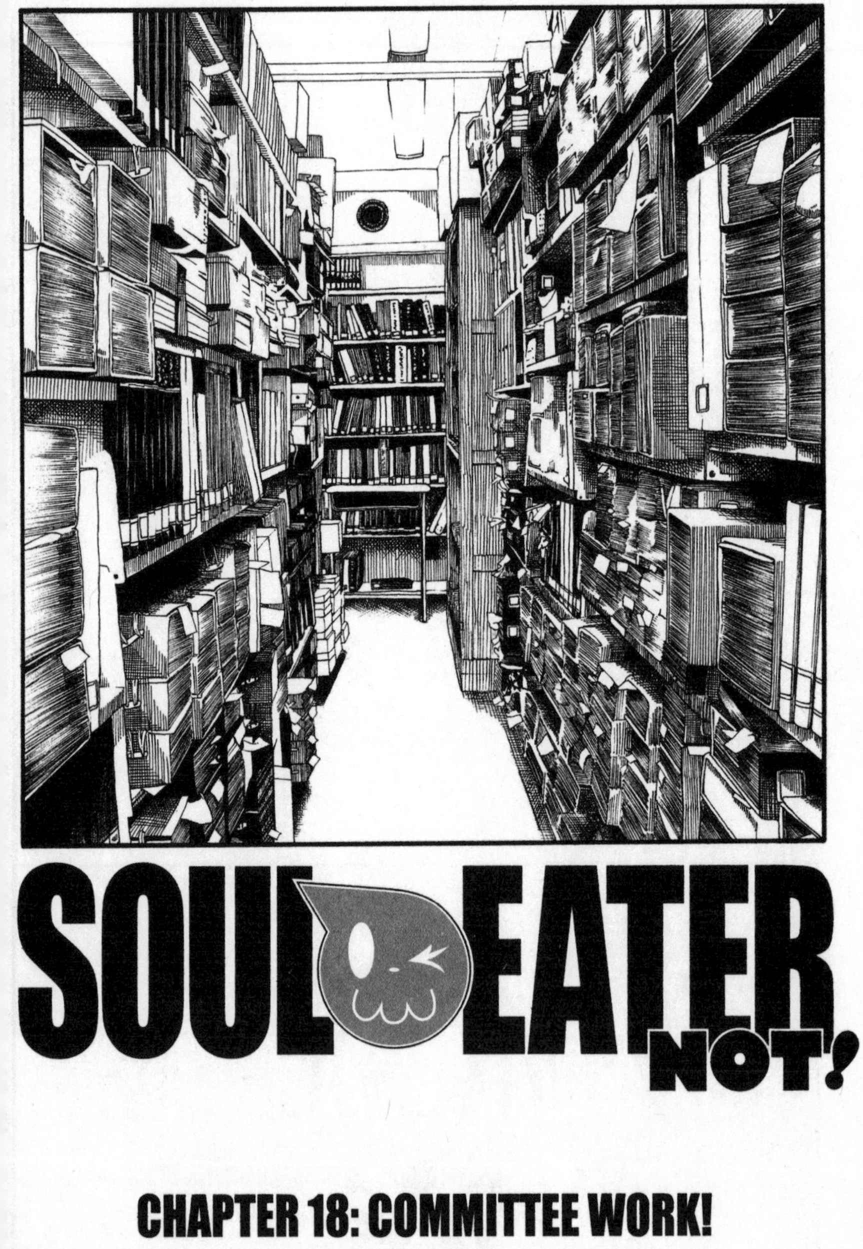

SOUL EATER NOT!

CHAPTER 18: COMMITTEE WORK!

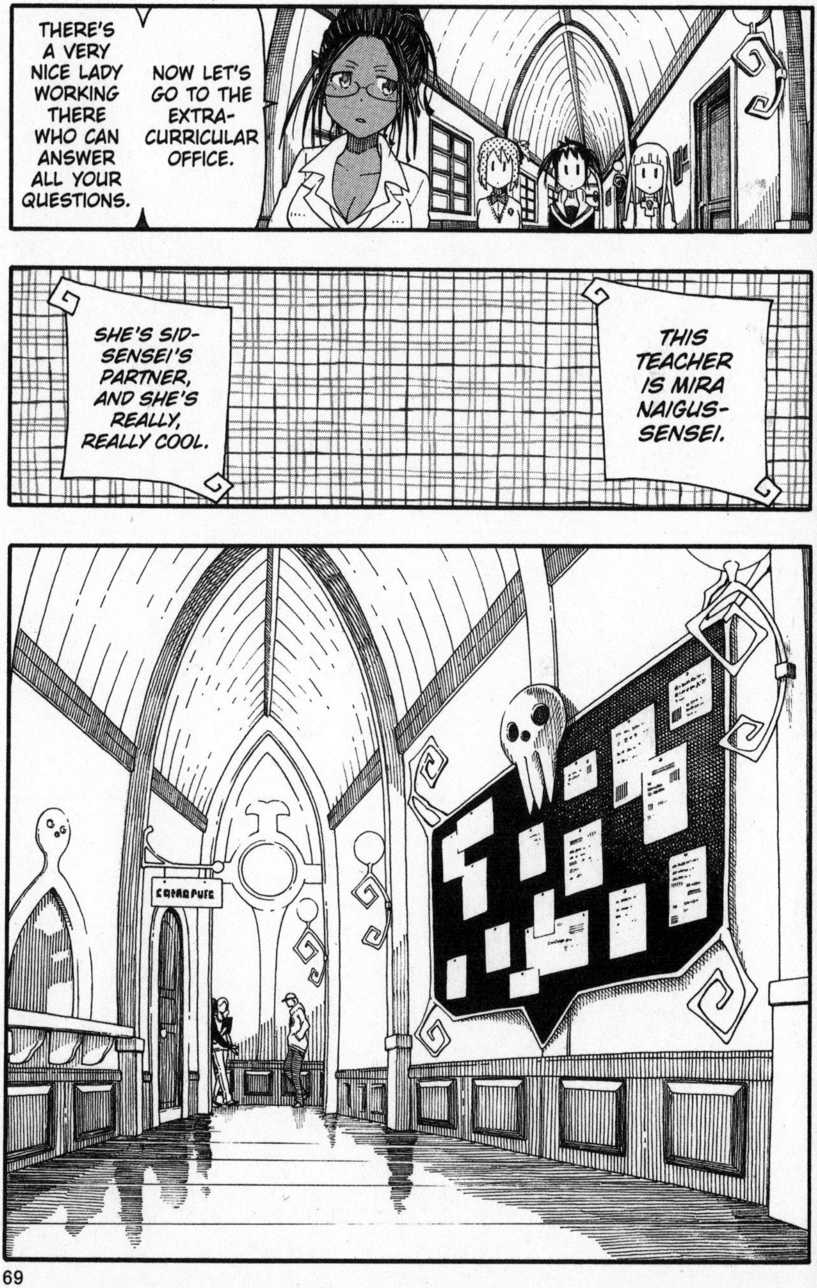
NOW LET'S GO TO THE EXTRA-CURRICULAR OFFICE.
THERE'S A VERY NICE LADY WORKING THERE WHO CAN ANSWER ALL YOUR QUESTIONS.
THIS TEACHER IS MIRA NAIGUS-SENSEI.
SHE'S SID-SENSEI'S PARTNER, AND SHE'S REALLY, REALLY COOL.

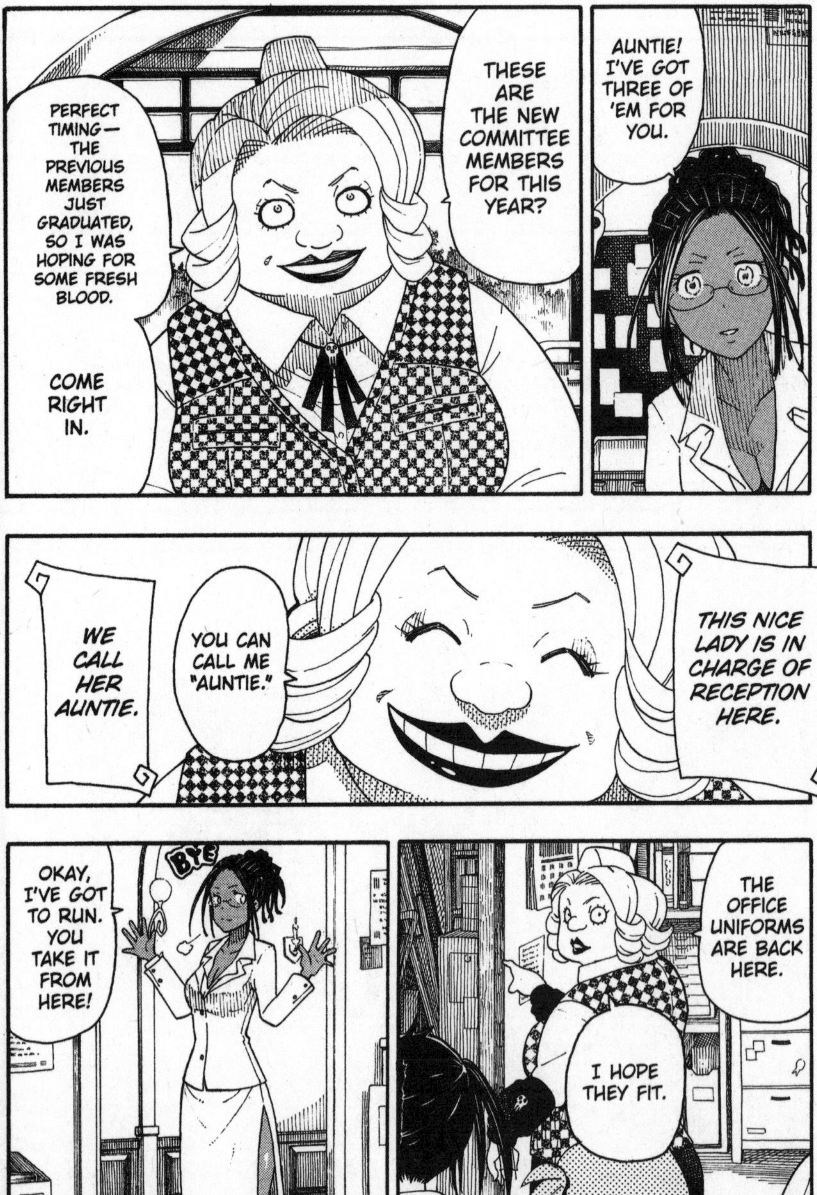
AUNTIE! I'VE GOT THREE OF 'EM FOR YOU.
THESE ARE THE NEW COMMITTEE MEMBERS FOR THIS YEAR?
PERFECT TIMING—THE PREVIOUS MEMBERS JUST GRADUATED, SO I WAS HOPING FOR SOME FRESH BLOOD.
COME RIGHT IN.
THIS NICE LADY IS IN CHARGE OF RECEPTION HERE.
YOU CAN CALL ME "AUNTIE."
WE CALL HER AUNTIE.
THE OFFICE UNIFORMS ARE BACK HERE.
I HOPE THEY FIT.
BYE
OKAY, I'VE GOT TO RUN. YOU TAKE IT FROM HERE!

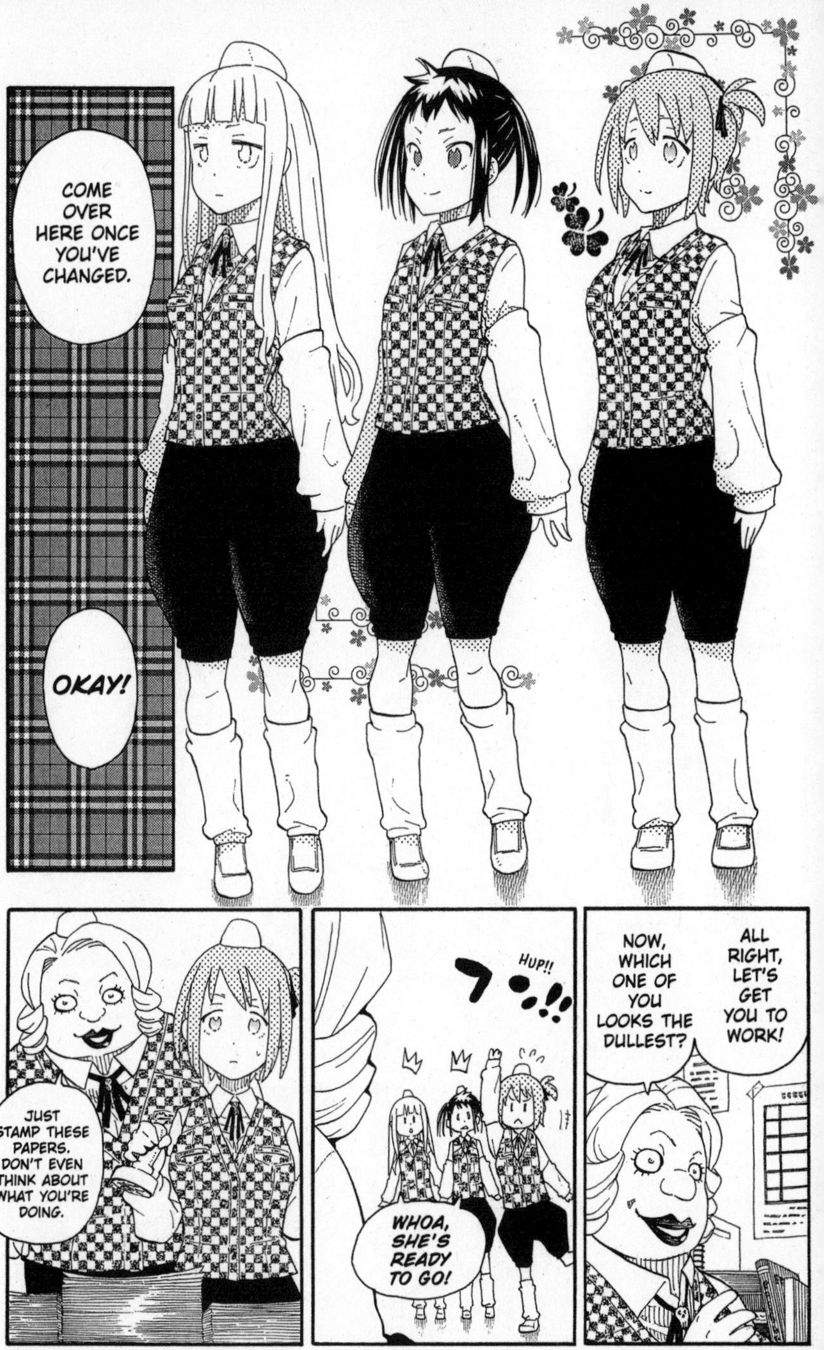
COME OVER HERE ONCE YOU'VE CHANGED.
OKAY!
ALL RIGHT, LET'S GET YOU TO WORK!
NOW, WHICH ONE OF YOU LOOKS THE DULLEST?
HUP!!
WHOA, SHE'S READY TO GO!
JUST STAMP THESE PAPERS. DON'T EVEN THINK ABOUT WHAT YOU'RE DOING.

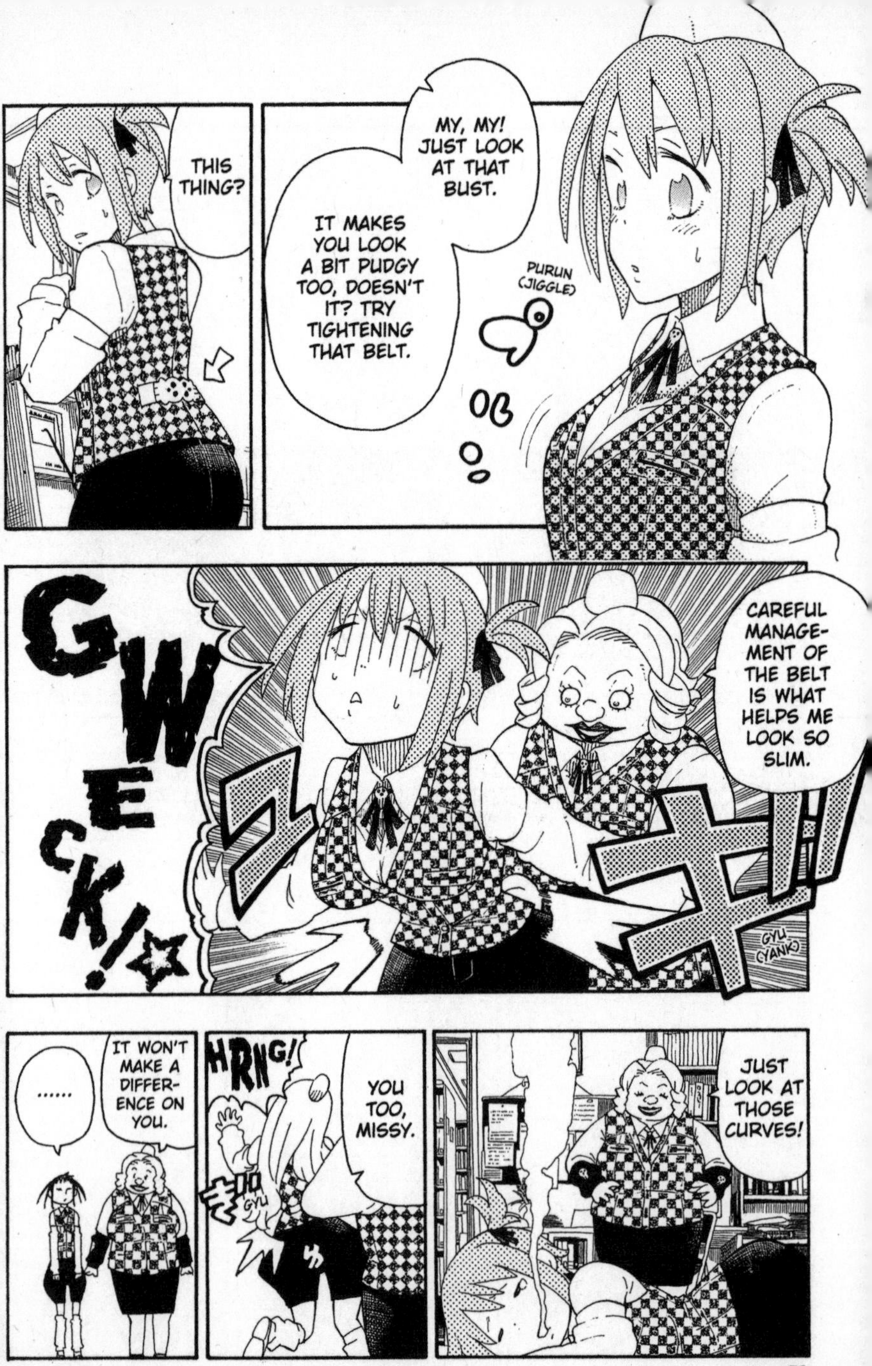

MY, MY! JUST LOOK AT THAT BUST.
IT MAKES YOU LOOK A BIT PUDGY TOO, DOESN'T IT? TRY TIGHTENING THAT BELT.
PURUN (JIGGLE)
THIS THING?
CAREFUL MANAGE-MENT OF THE BELT IS WHAT HELPS ME LOOK SO SLIM.
GYU (YANK)
GWECK!
JUST LOOK AT THOSE CURVES!
YOU TOO, MISSY.
HRNG!
GYU
IT WON'T MAKE A DIFFER-ENCE ON YOU.
......

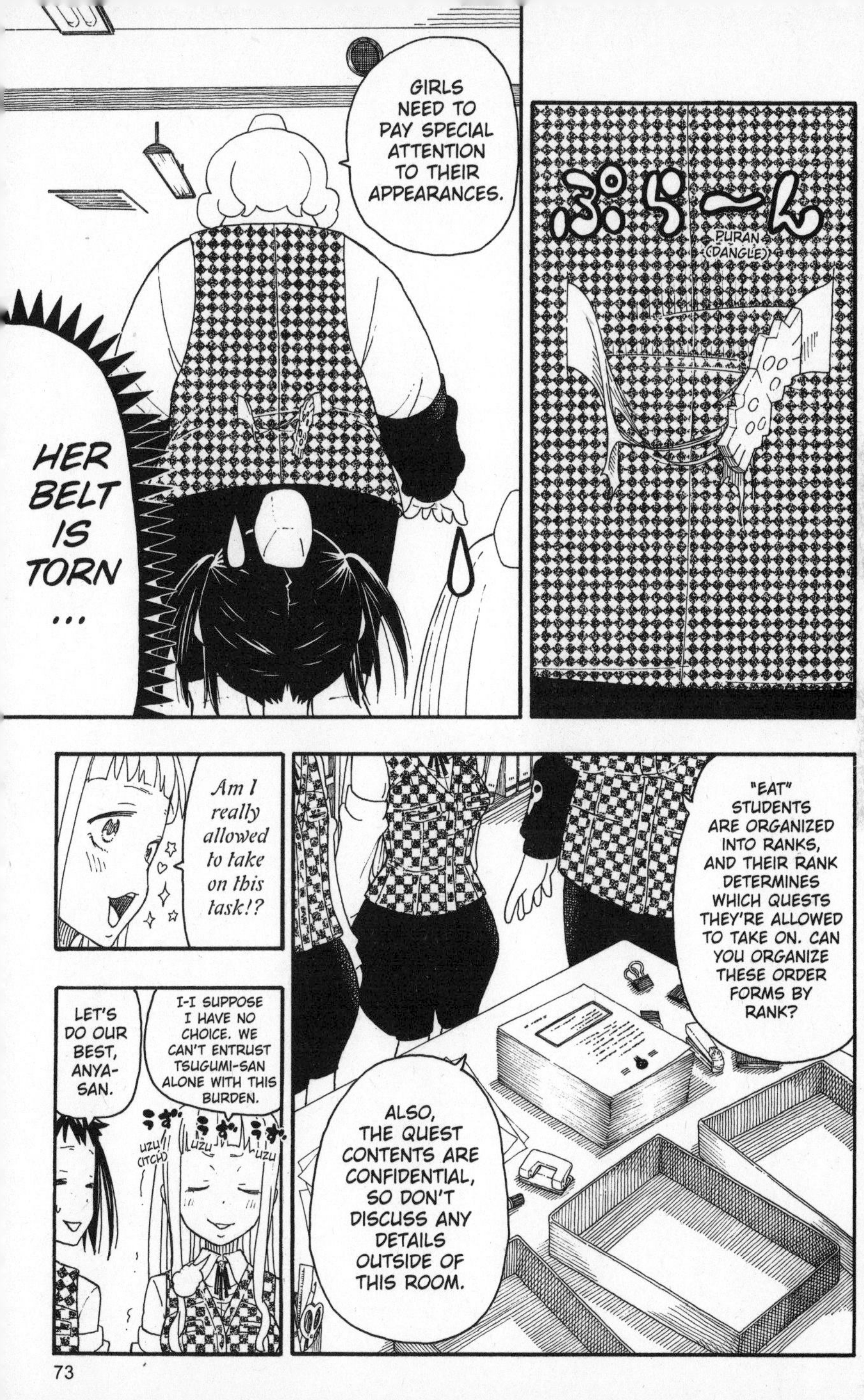
ぷら〜ん
PURAN (DANGLE)
GIRLS NEED TO PAY SPECIAL ATTENTION TO THEIR APPEARANCES.
HER BELT IS TORN ...
"EAT" STUDENTS ARE ORGANIZED INTO RANKS, AND THEIR RANK DETERMINES WHICH QUESTS THEY'RE ALLOWED TO TAKE ON. CAN YOU ORGANIZE THESE ORDER FORMS BY RANK?
ALSO, THE QUEST CONTENTS ARE CONFIDENTIAL, SO DON'T DISCUSS ANY DETAILS OUTSIDE OF THIS ROOM.
Am I really allowed to take on this task!?
I-I SUPPOSE I HAVE NO CHOICE. WE CAN'T ENTRUST TSUGUMI-SAN ALONE WITH THIS BURDEN.
LET'S DO OUR BEST, ANYA-SAN.
うず うず うず
UZU UZU UZU (ITCH)

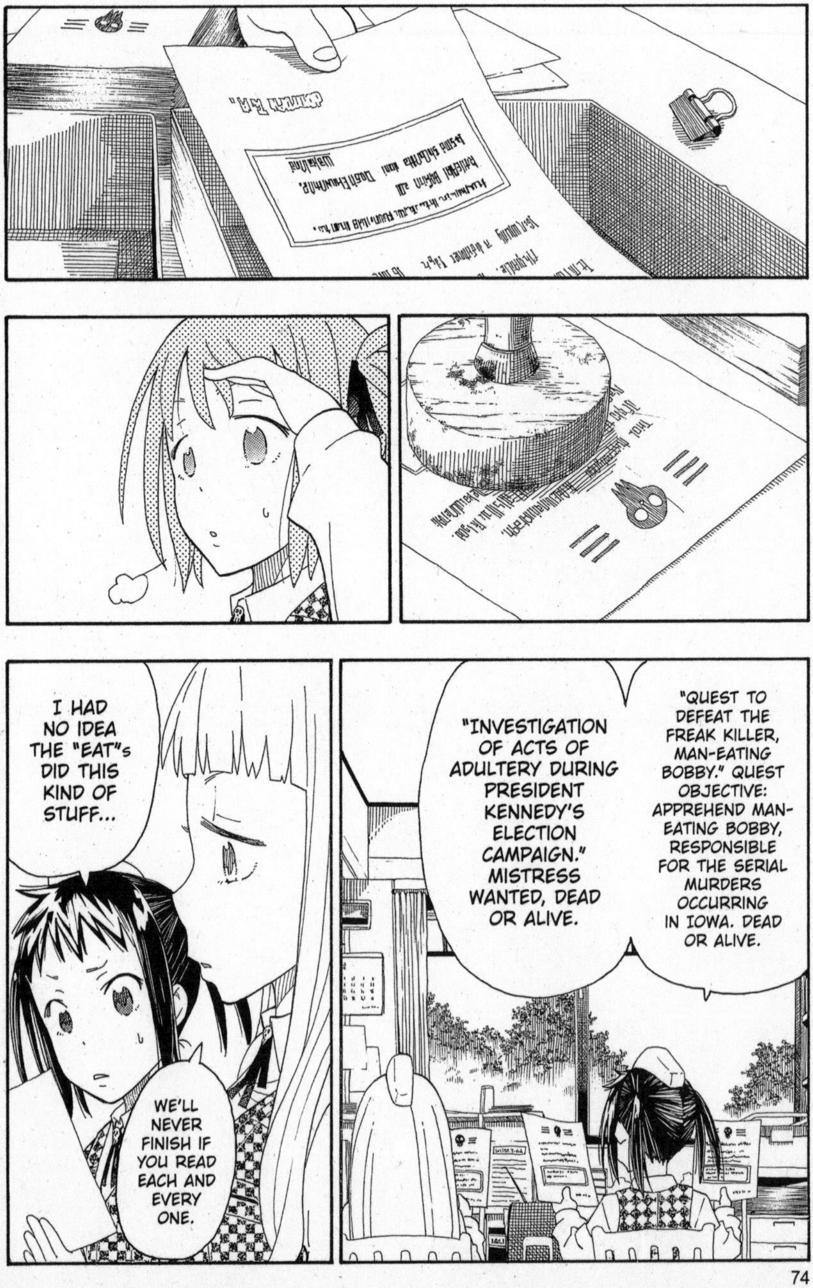
"QUEST TO DEFEAT THE FREAK KILLER, MAN-EATING BOBBY." QUEST OBJECTIVE: APPREHEND MAN-EATING BOBBY, RESPONSIBLE FOR THE SERIAL MURDERS OCCURRING IN IOWA. DEAD OR ALIVE.
"INVESTIGATION OF ACTS OF ADULTERY DURING PRESIDENT KENNEDY'S ELECTION CAMPAIGN." MISTRESS WANTED, DEAD OR ALIVE.
I HAD NO IDEA THE "EAT"s DID THIS KIND OF STUFF...
WE'LL NEVER FINISH IF YOU READ EACH AND EVERY ONE.

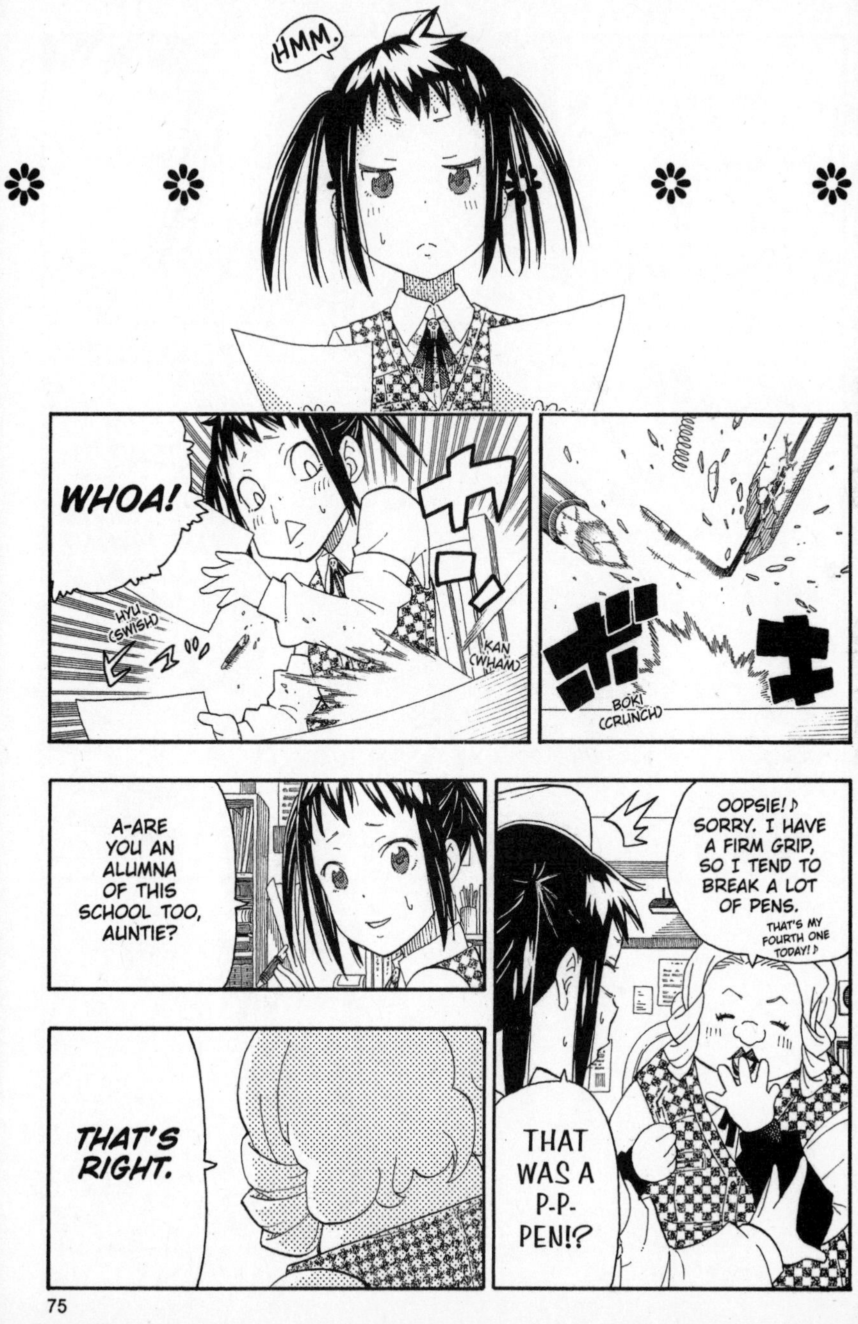
HMM.
BOKI (CRUNCH)
WHOA!
HYU (SWISH)
KAN (WHAM)
OOPSIE!♪ SORRY. I HAVE A FIRM GRIP, SO I TEND TO BREAK A LOT OF PENS.
THAT'S MY FOURTH ONE TODAY!♪
A-ARE YOU AN ALUMNA OF THIS SCHOOL TOO, AUNTIE?
THAT WAS A P-P-PEN!?
THAT'S RIGHT.

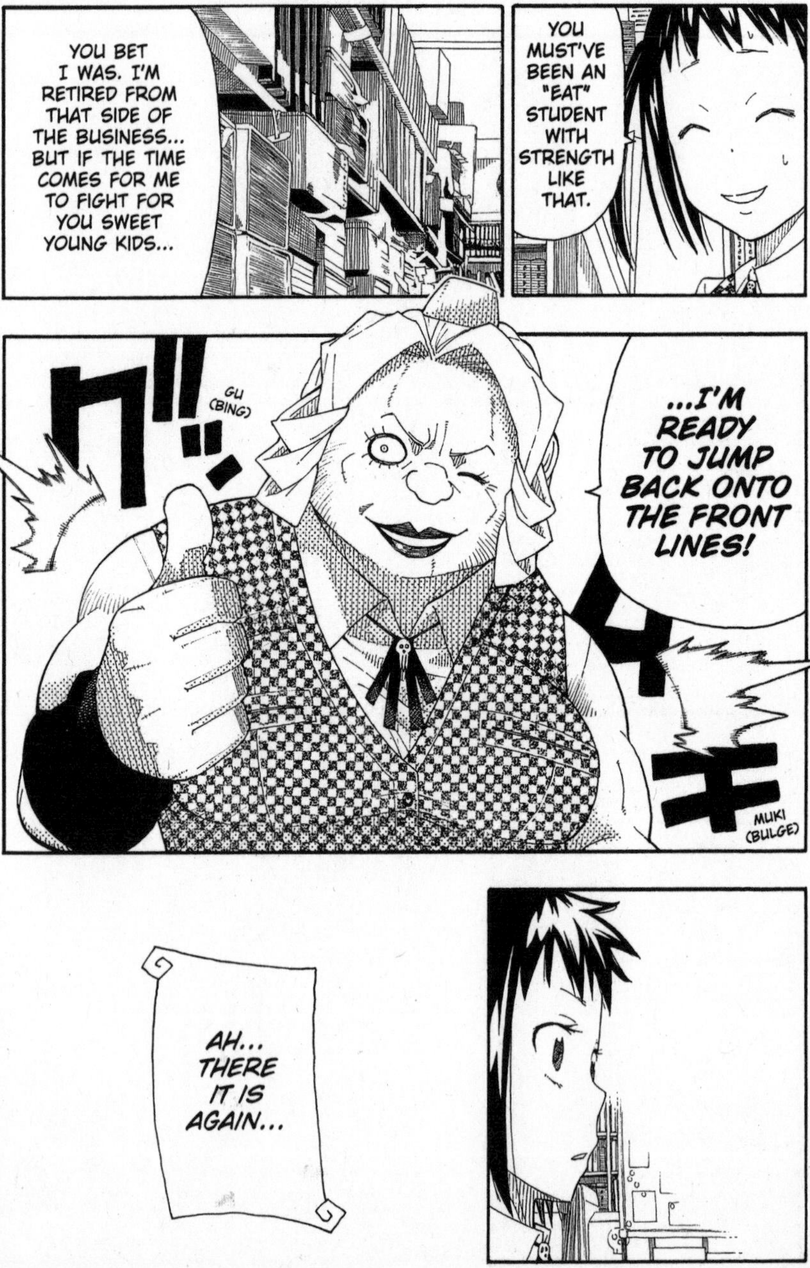

YOU MUST'VE BEEN AN "EAT" STUDENT WITH STRENGTH LIKE THAT.
YOU BET I WAS. I'M RETIRED FROM THAT SIDE OF THE BUSINESS... BUT IF THE TIME COMES FOR ME TO FIGHT FOR YOU SWEET YOUNG KIDS...
...I'M READY TO JUMP BACK ONTO THE FRONT LINES!
GU (BING)
MUKI (BULGE)
AH... THERE IT IS AGAIN...

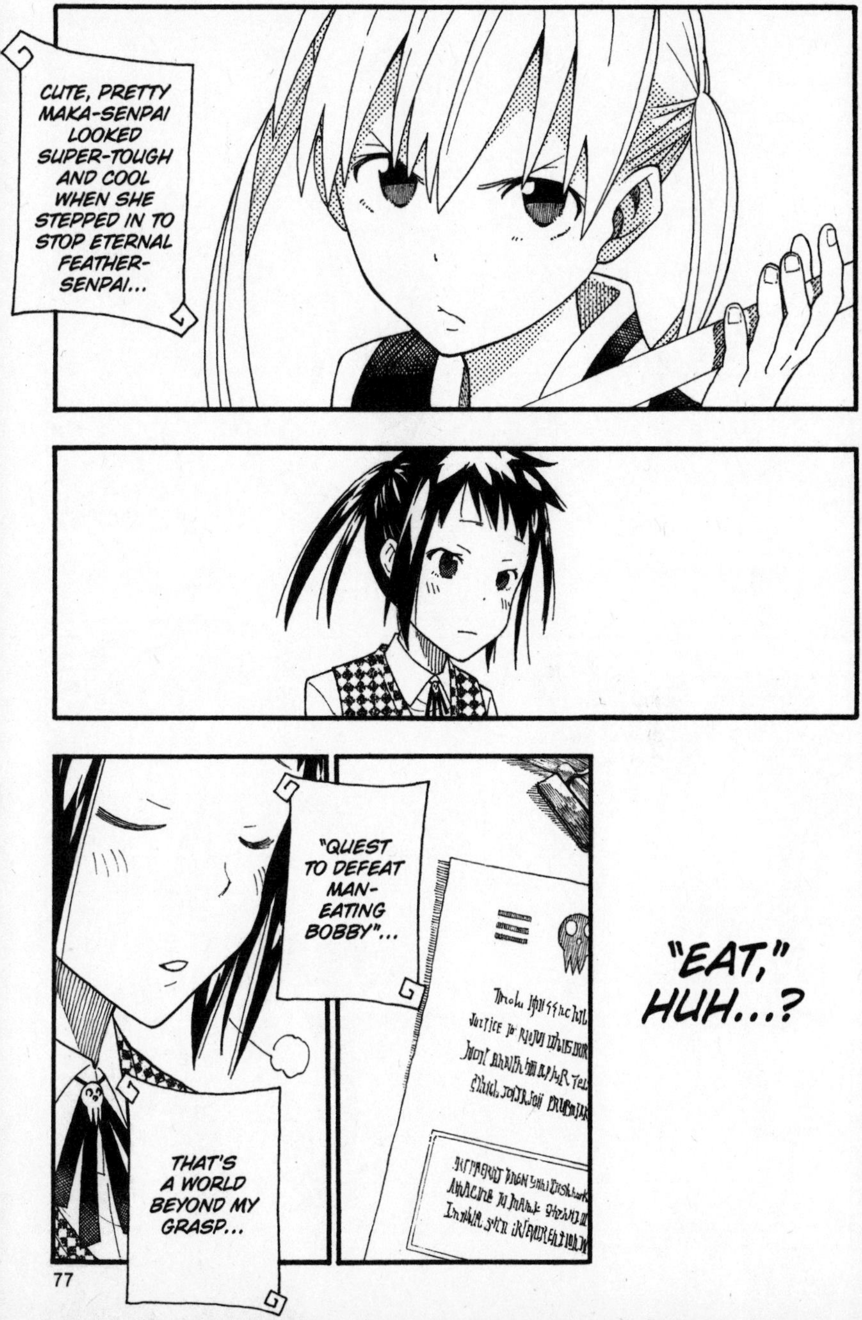
CUTE, PRETTY MAKA-SENPAI LOOKED SUPER-TOUGH AND COOL WHEN SHE STEPPED IN TO STOP ETERNAL FEATHER-SENPAI...
"QUEST TO DEFEAT MAN-EATING BOBBY"...
"EAT," HUH...?
THAT'S A WORLD BEYOND MY GRASP...

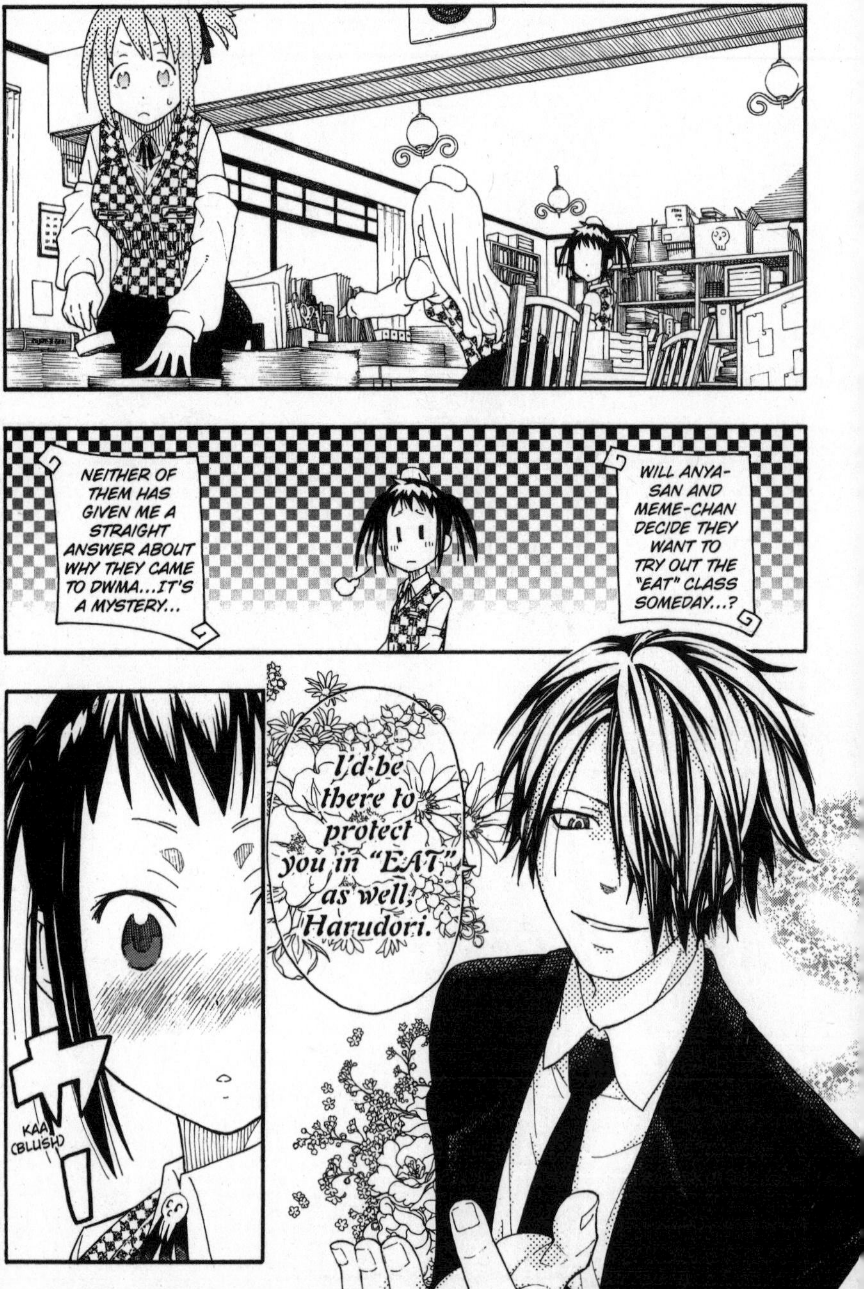
WILL ANYA-SAN AND MEME-CHAN DECIDE THEY WANT TO TRY OUT THE "EAT" CLASS SOMEDAY...?
NEITHER OF THEM HAS GIVEN ME A STRAIGHT ANSWER ABOUT WHY THEY CAME TO DWMA...IT'S A MYSTERY...
I'd be there to protect you in "EAT" as well, Harudori.
KAA (BLUSH)

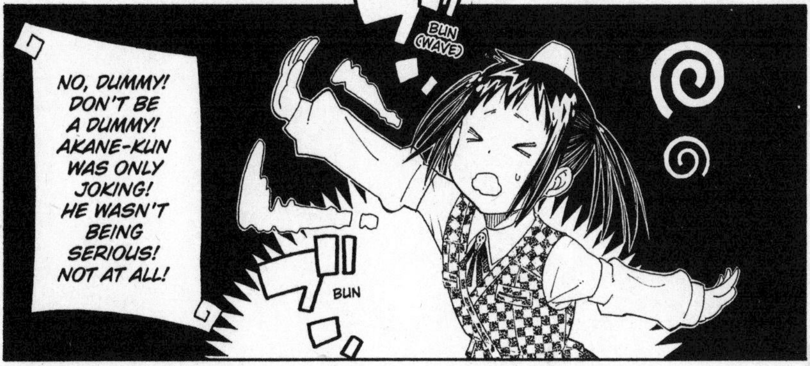
BUN (WAVE)
NO, DUMMY! DON'T BE A DUMMY! AKANE-KUN WAS ONLY JOKING! HE WASN'T BEING SERIOUS! NOT AT ALL!
BUN

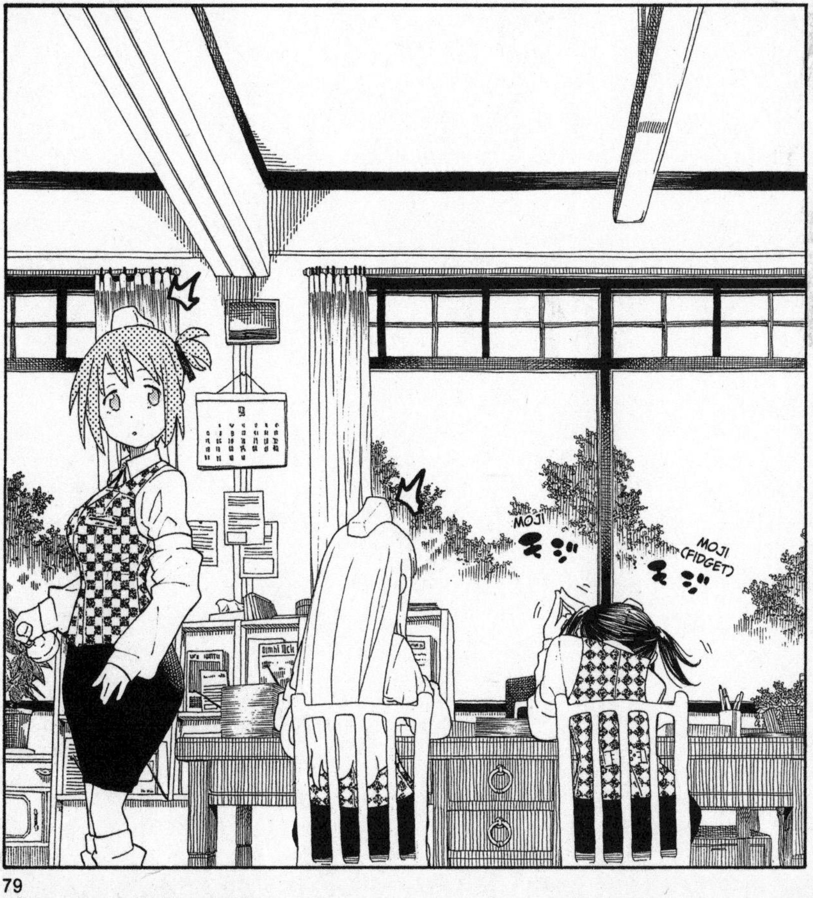
MOJI (FIDGET)
MOJI

SOUL EATER NOT!

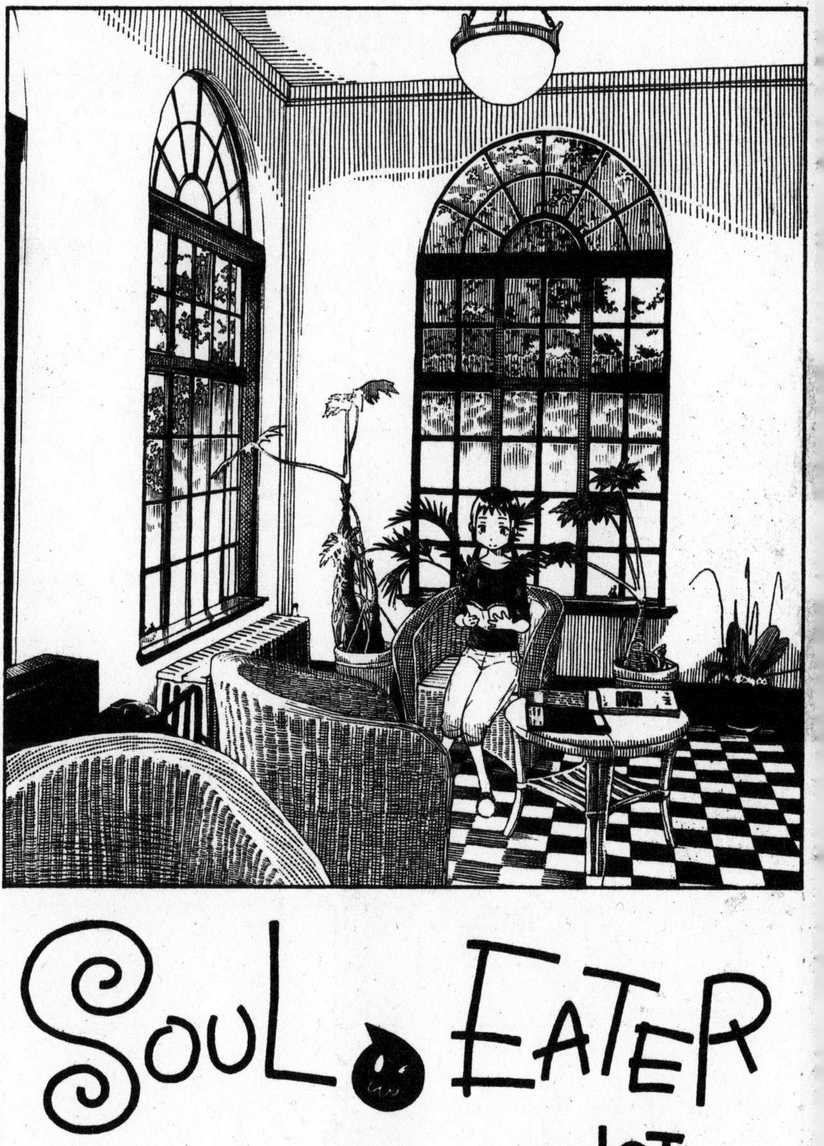

SOUL EATER

JOT

PART 3

QUAGMIRED

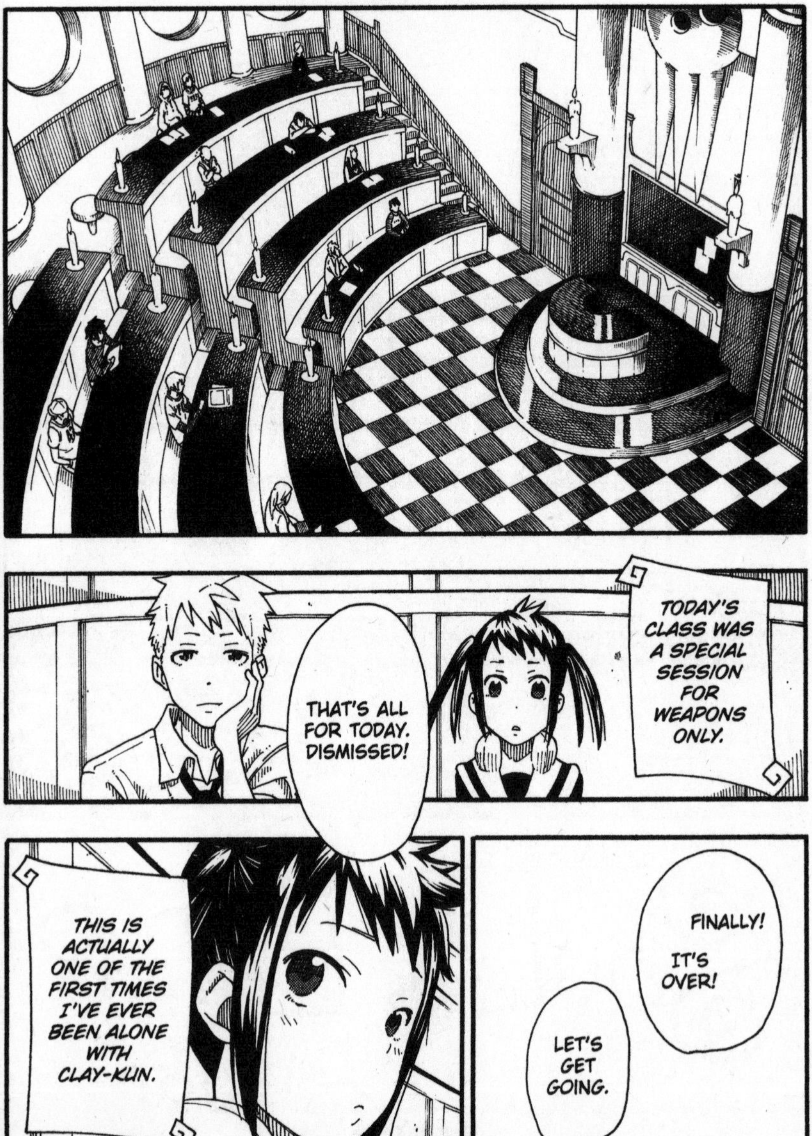
TODAY'S CLASS WAS A SPECIAL SESSION FOR WEAPONS ONLY.
THAT'S ALL FOR TODAY. DISMISSED!
FINALLY! IT'S OVER!
LET'S GET GOING.
THIS IS ACTUALLY ONE OF THE FIRST TIMES I'VE EVER BEEN ALONE WITH CLAY-KUN.

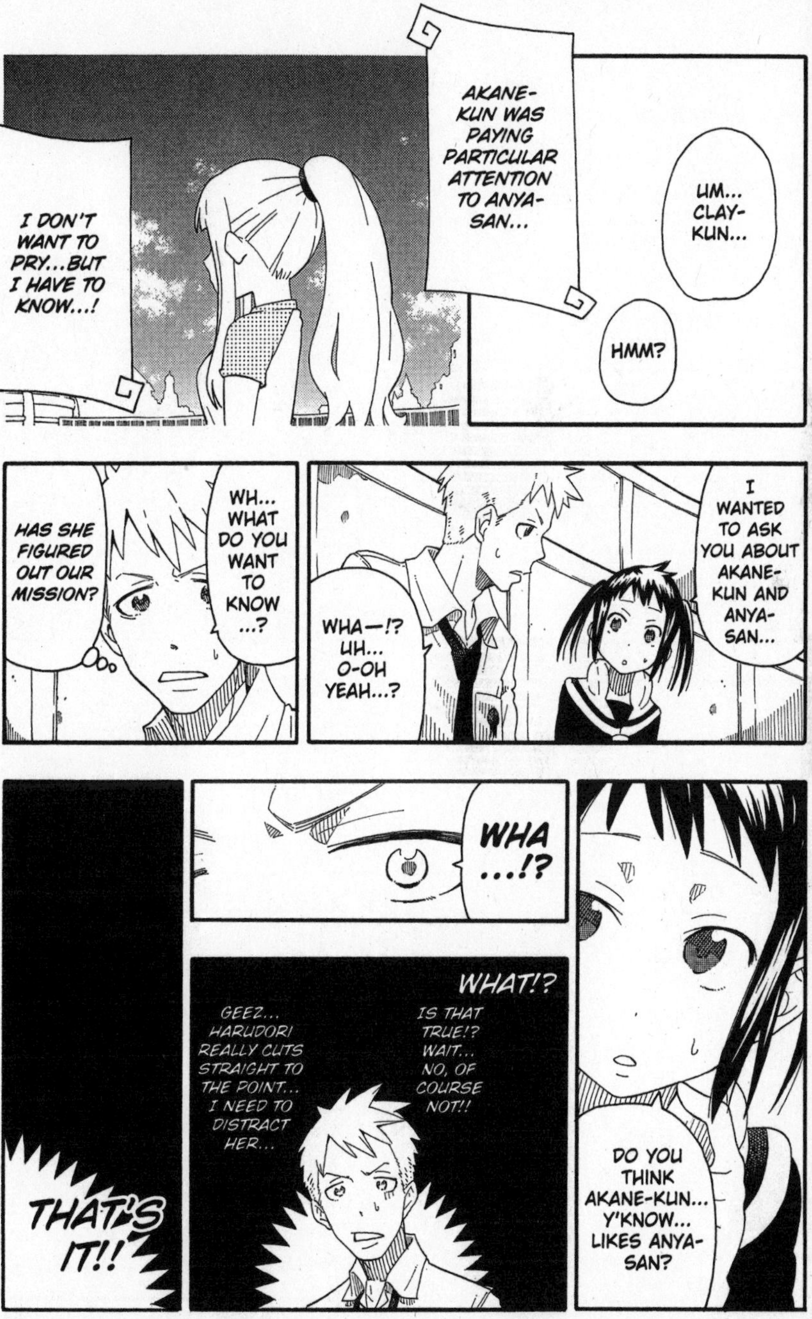
UM... CLAY-KUN...
HMM?
AKANE-KUN WAS PAYING PARTICULAR ATTENTION TO ANYA-SAN...
I DON'T WANT TO PRY...BUT I HAVE TO KNOW...!
I WANTED TO ASK YOU ABOUT AKANE-KUN AND ANYA-SAN...
WHA—!? UH... O-OH YEAH...?
WH... WHAT DO YOU WANT TO KNOW ...?
HAS SHE FIGURED OUT OUR MISSION?
DO YOU THINK AKANE-KUN... Y'KNOW... LIKES ANYA-SAN?
WHA ...!?
WHAT!?
IS THAT TRUE!? WAIT... NO, OF COURSE NOT!!
GEEZ... HARUDORI REALLY CUTS STRAIGHT TO THE POINT... I NEED TO DISTRACT HER...
THAT'S IT!!

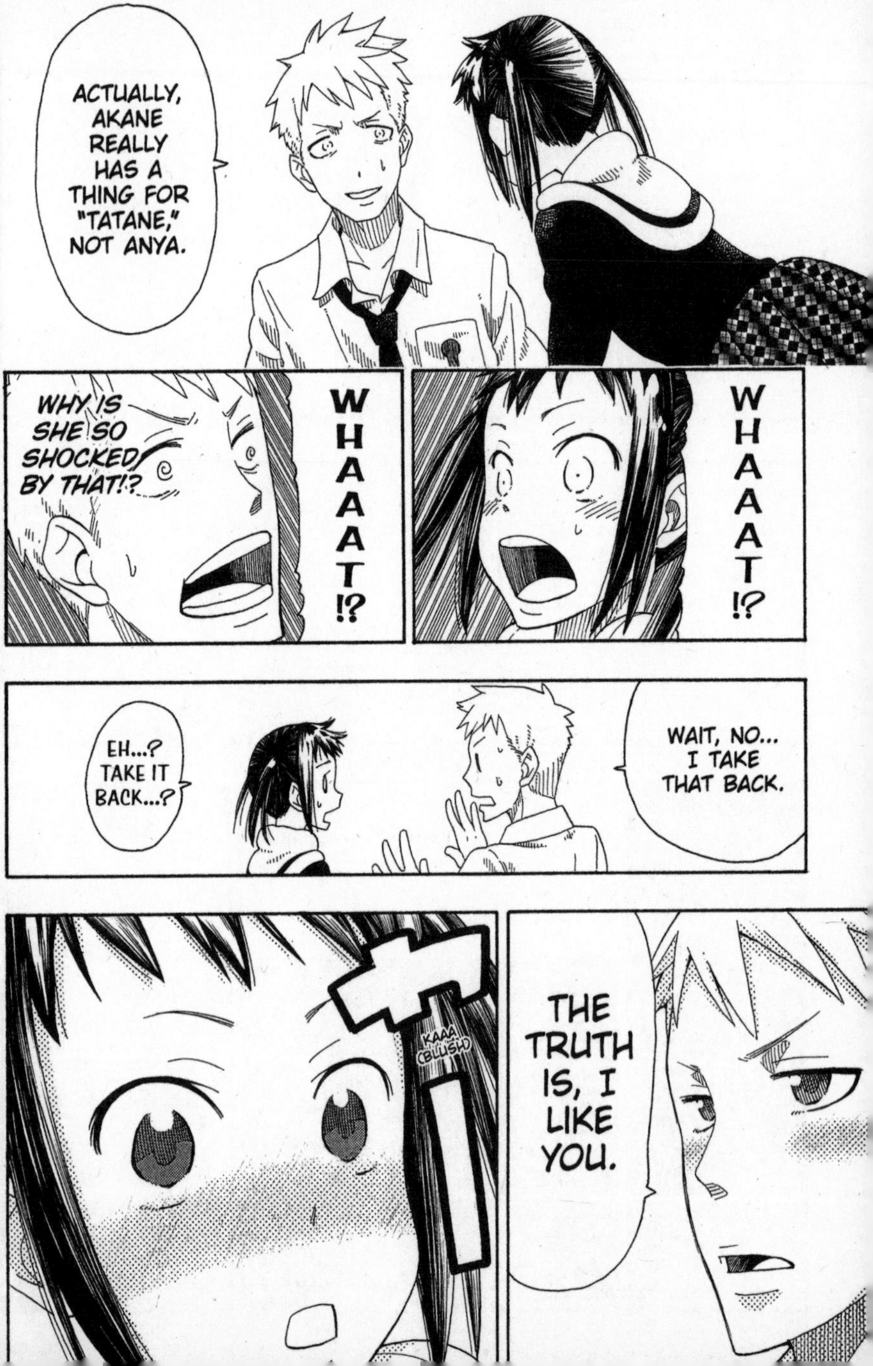
ACTUALLY, AKANE REALLY HAS A THING FOR "TATANE," NOT ANYA.
WHAAAT!?
WHAAAT!?
WHY IS SHE SO SHOCKED BY THAT!?
WAIT, NO... I TAKE THAT BACK.
EH...? TAKE IT BACK...?
THE TRUTH IS, I LIKE YOU.
KAAA (BLUSH)

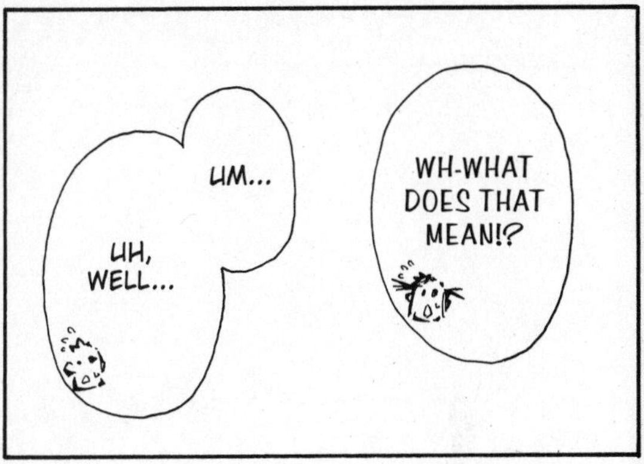
WH-WHAT DOES THAT MEAN!?
UM...
UH, WELL...

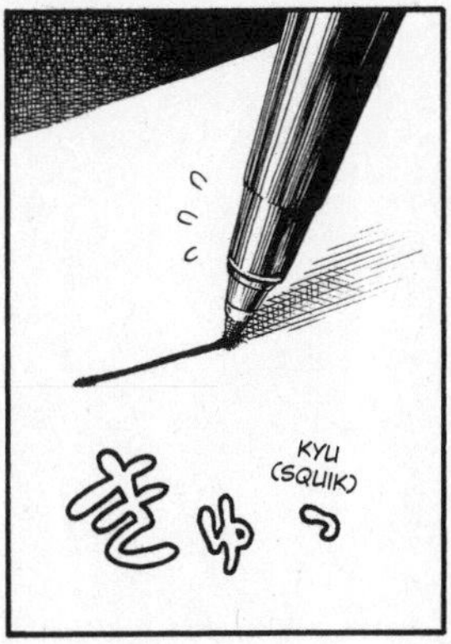
きゅっ
KYU (SQUIK)

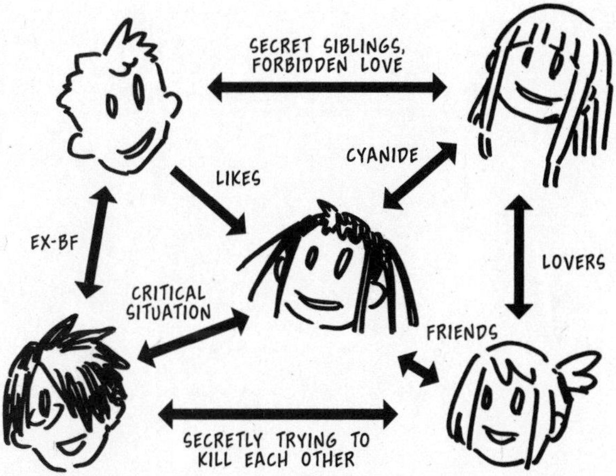
SECRET SIBLINGS, FORBIDDEN LOVE
CYANIDE
LIKES
EX-BF
LOVERS
CRITICAL SITUATION
FRIENDS
SECRETLY TRYING TO KILL EACH OTHER

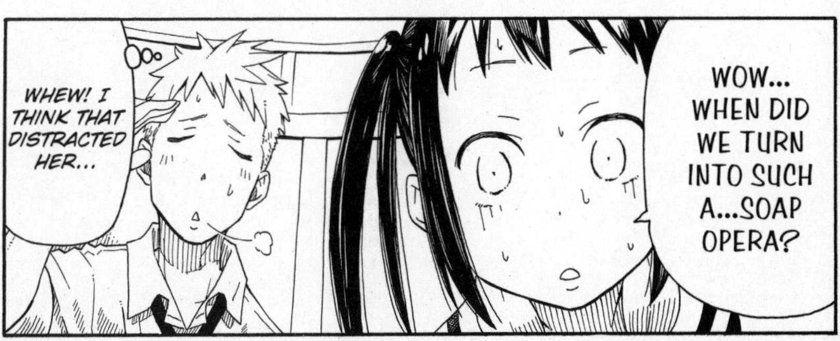
WOW... WHEN DID WE TURN INTO SUCH A...SOAP OPERA?
WHEW! I THINK THAT DISTRACTED HER...

HELP ME, AKANE-SAN

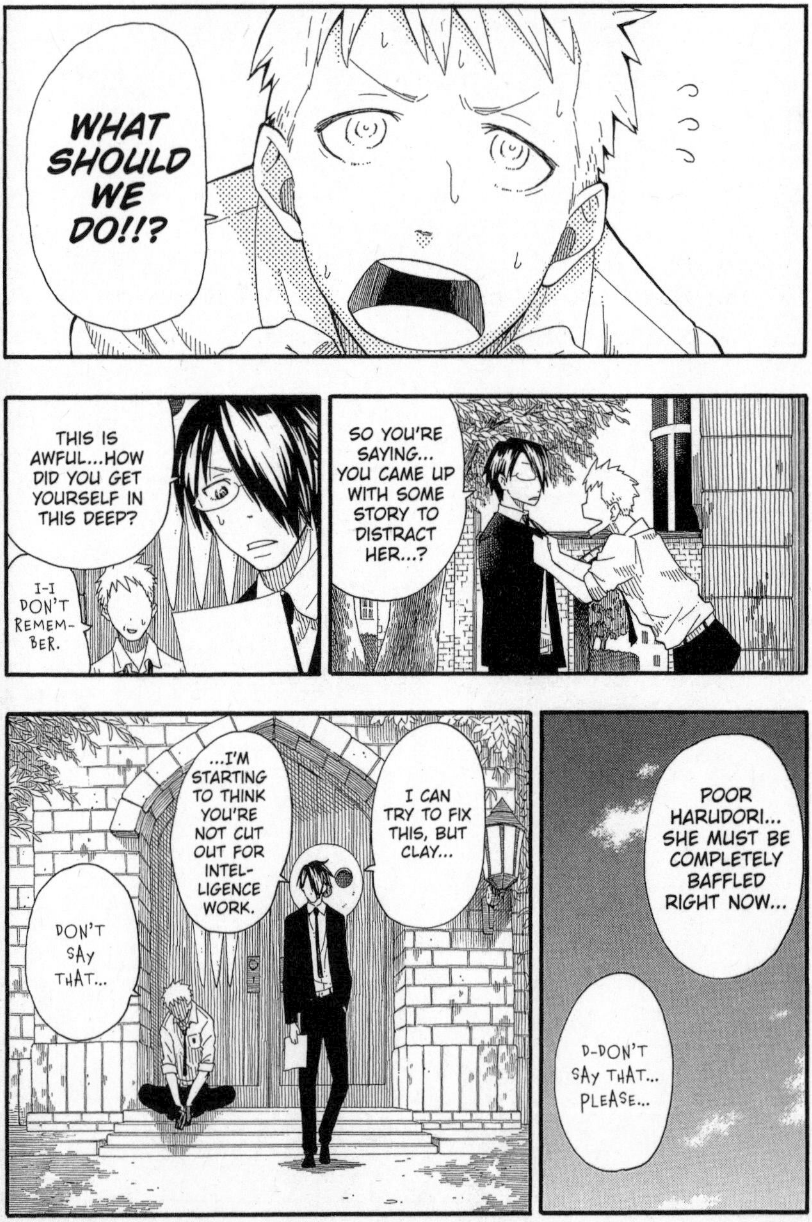
WHAT SHOULD WE DO!!?
SO YOU'RE SAYING... YOU CAME UP WITH SOME STORY TO DISTRACT HER...?
THIS IS AWFUL...HOW DID YOU GET YOURSELF IN THIS DEEP?
I-I DON'T REMEM-BER.
POOR HARUDORI... SHE MUST BE COMPLETELY BAFFLED RIGHT NOW...
D-DON'T SAY THAT... PLEASE...
I CAN TRY TO FIX THIS, BUT CLAY...
...I'M STARTING TO THINK YOU'RE NOT CUT OUT FOR INTEL-LIGENCE WORK.
DON'T SAY THAT...

DEATH CHILD

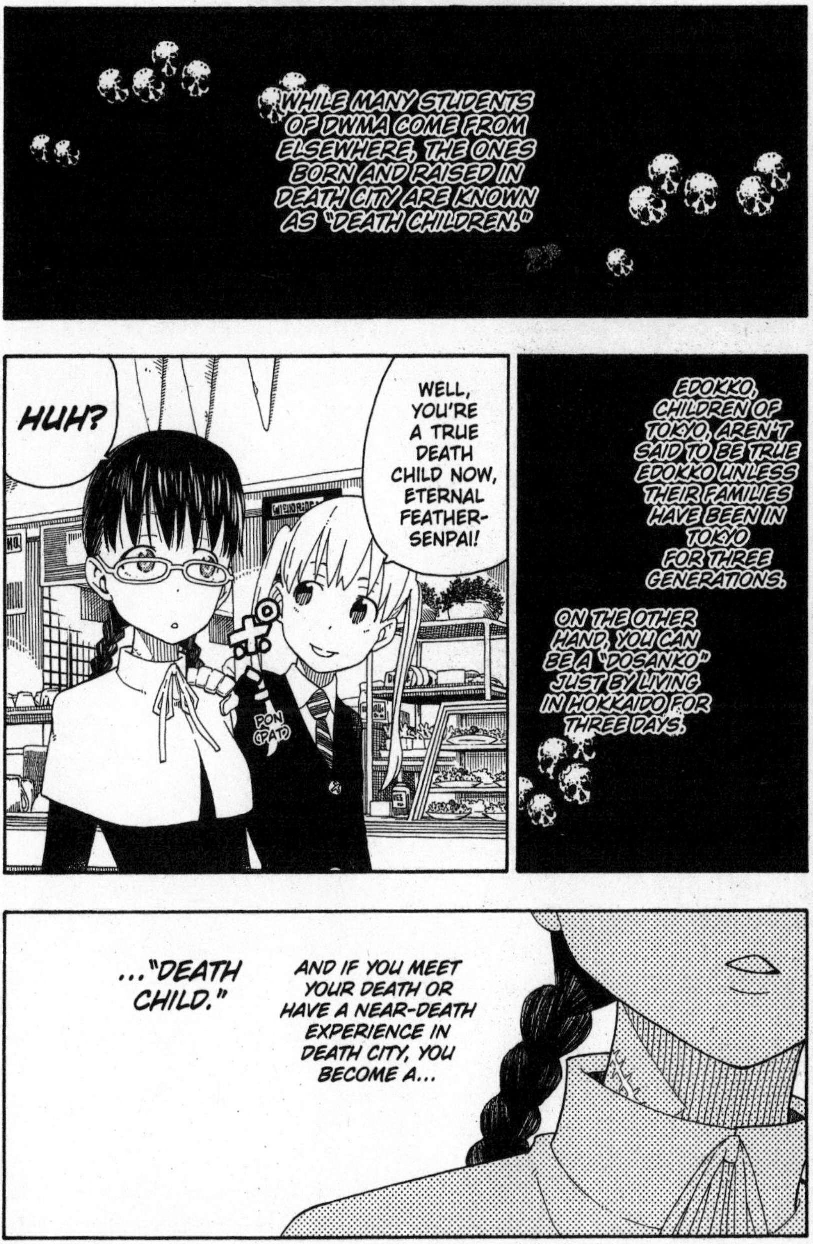
WHILE MANY STUDENTS OF DWMA COME FROM ELSEWHERE, THE ONES BORN AND RAISED IN DEATH CITY ARE KNOWN AS "DEATH CHILDREN."
EDOKKO, CHILDREN OF TOKYO, AREN'T SAID TO BE TRUE EDOKKO UNLESS THEIR FAMILIES HAVE BEEN IN TOKYO FOR THREE GENERATIONS.
ON THE OTHER HAND, YOU CAN BE A "DOSANKO" JUST BY LIVING IN HOKKAIDO FOR THREE DAYS.
WELL, YOU'RE A TRUE DEATH CHILD NOW, ETERNAL FEATHER-SENPAI!
HUH?
PON (PAT)
AND IF YOU MEET YOUR DEATH OR HAVE A NEAR-DEATH EXPERIENCE IN DEATH CITY, YOU BECOME A...
..."DEATH CHILD."

TELL ME, FEATHER-SAN

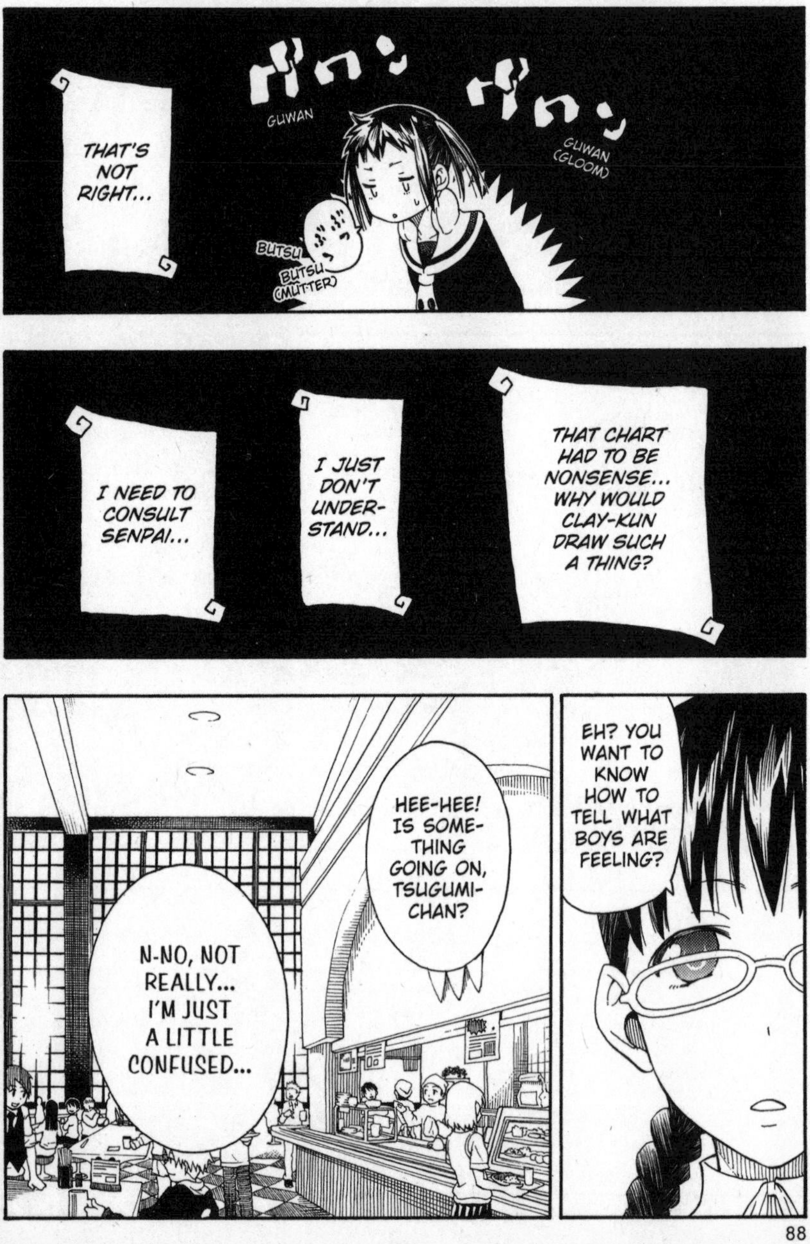
GUWAN (GLOOM)
GUWAN
THAT'S NOT RIGHT...
BUTSU BUTSU (MUTTER)
THAT CHART HAD TO BE NONSENSE... WHY WOULD CLAY-KUN DRAW SUCH A THING?
I JUST DON'T UNDER-STAND...
I NEED TO CONSULT SENPAI...
EH? YOU WANT TO KNOW HOW TO TELL WHAT BOYS ARE FEELING?
HEE-HEE! IS SOME-THING GOING ON, TSUGUMI-CHAN?
N-NO, NOT REALLY... I'M JUST A LITTLE CONFUSED...

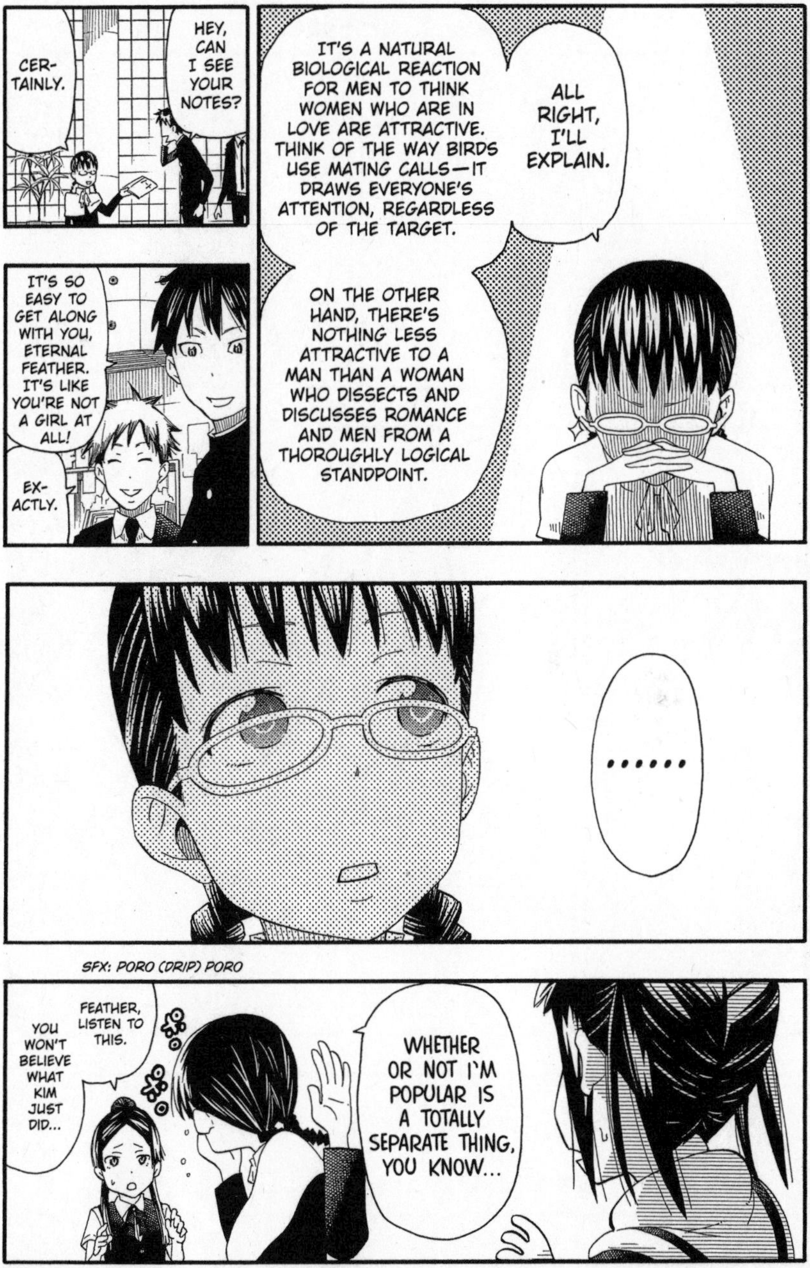
ALL RIGHT, I'LL EXPLAIN.
IT'S A NATURAL BIOLOGICAL REACTION FOR MEN TO THINK WOMEN WHO ARE IN LOVE ARE ATTRACTIVE. THINK OF THE WAY BIRDS USE MATING CALLS—IT DRAWS EVERYONE'S ATTENTION, REGARDLESS OF THE TARGET.
ON THE OTHER HAND, THERE'S NOTHING LESS ATTRACTIVE TO A MAN THAN A WOMAN WHO DISSECTS AND DISCUSSES ROMANCE AND MEN FROM A THOROUGHLY LOGICAL STANDPOINT.
HEY, CAN I SEE YOUR NOTES?
CER-TAINLY.
IT'S SO EASY TO GET ALONG WITH YOU, ETERNAL FEATHER. IT'S LIKE YOU'RE NOT A GIRL AT ALL!
EX-ACTLY.
......
SFX: PORO (DRIP) PORO
WHETHER OR NOT I'M POPULAR IS A TOTALLY SEPARATE THING, YOU KNOW...
FEATHER, LISTEN TO THIS.
YOU WON'T BELIEVE WHAT KIM JUST DID...

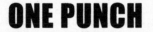

ONE PUNCH

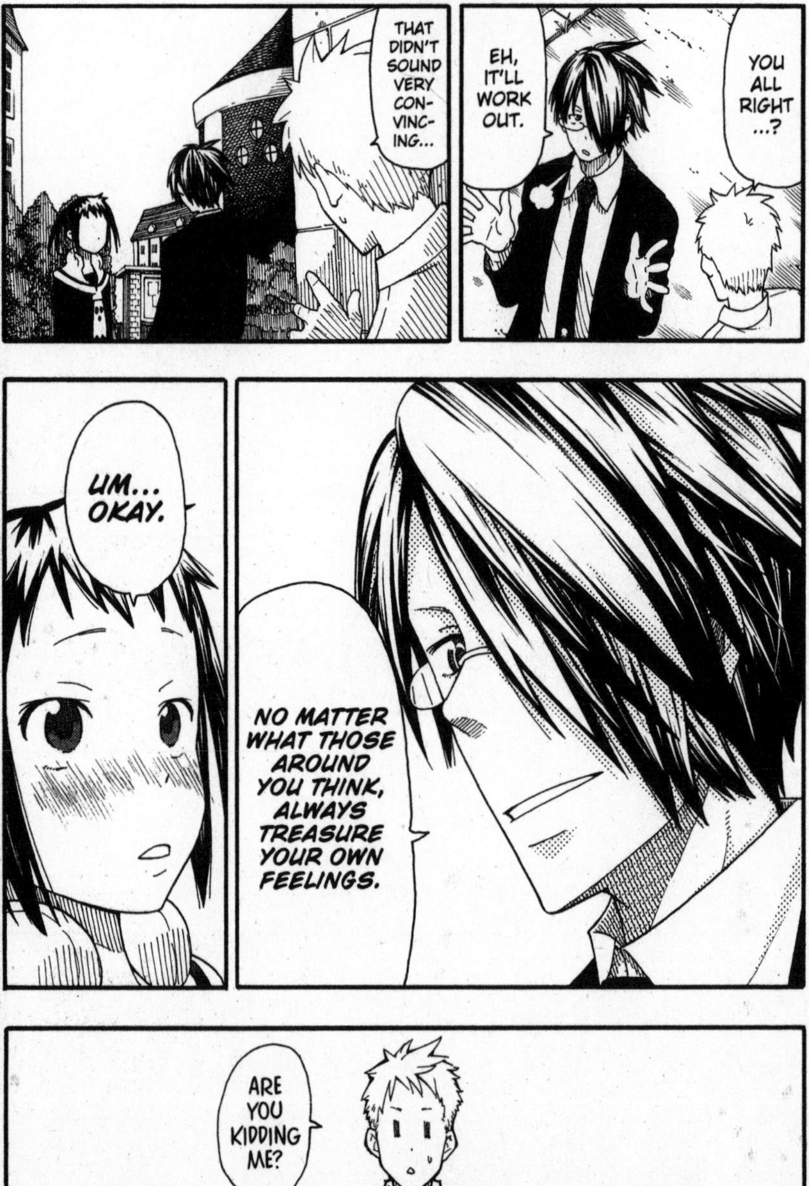

YOU ALL RIGHT ...?
EH, IT'LL WORK OUT.
THAT DIDN'T SOUND VERY CON-VINC-ING...
NO MATTER WHAT THOSE AROUND YOU THINK, ALWAYS TREASURE YOUR OWN FEELINGS.
UM... OKAY.
ARE YOU KIDDING ME?

SOUL EATER NOT!

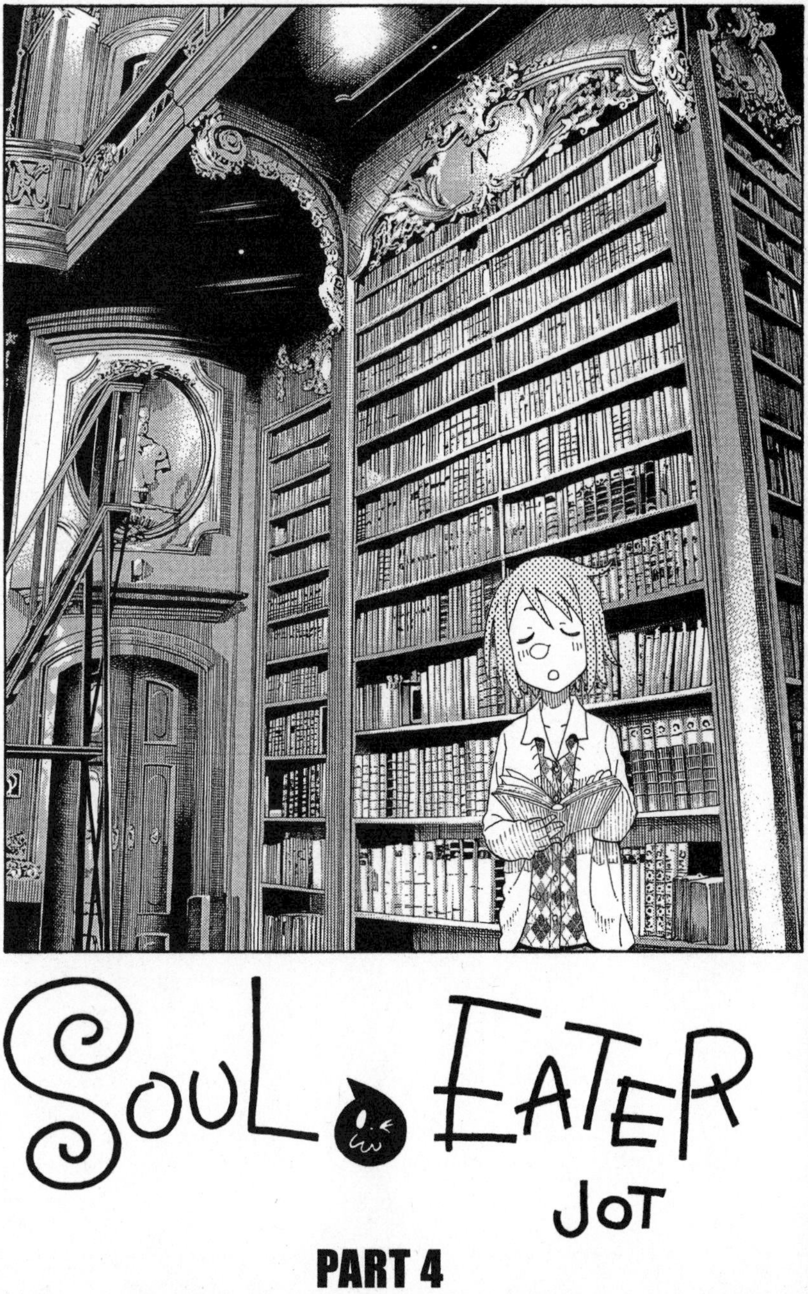

SOUL EATER

JOT

PART 4

TEXAS HOLSTEIN

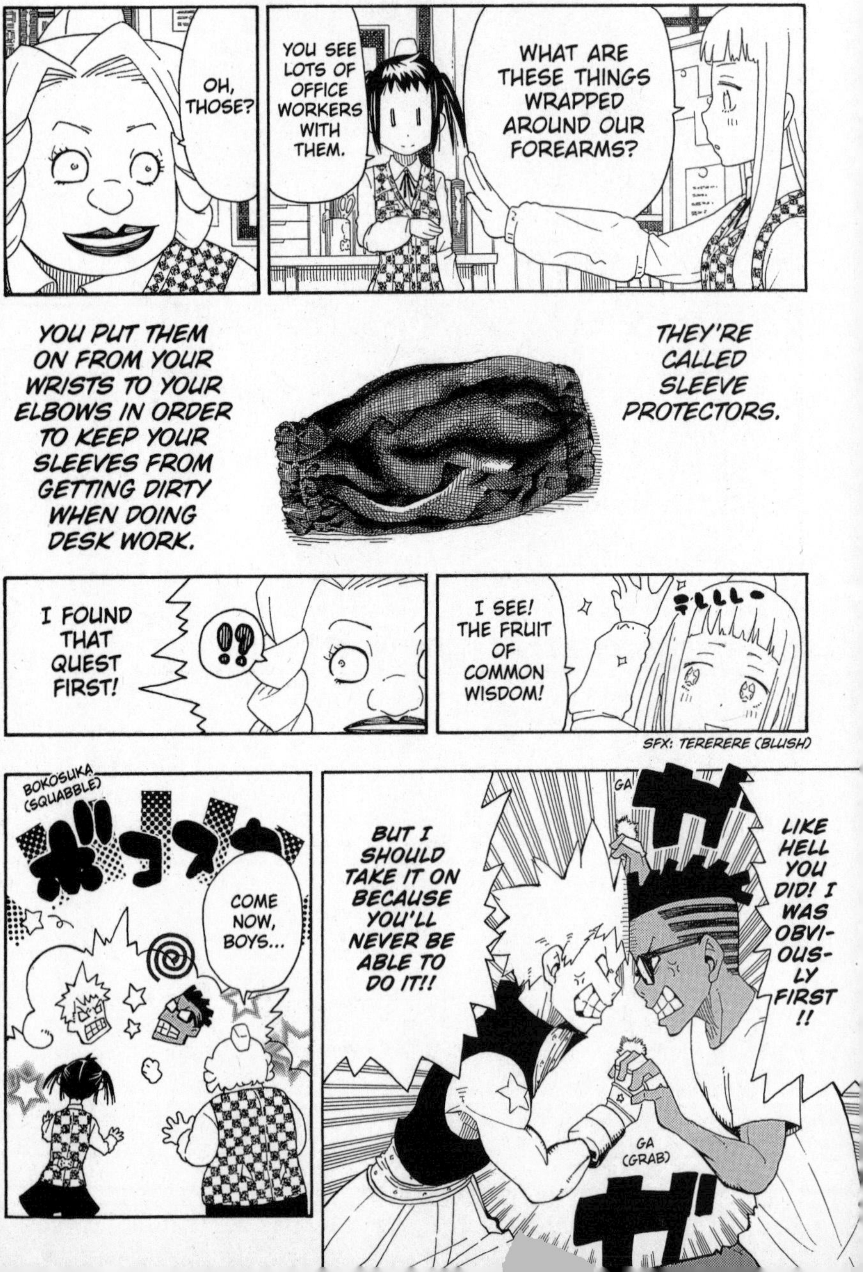
WHAT ARE THESE THINGS WRAPPED AROUND OUR FOREARMS?
YOU SEE LOTS OF OFFICE WORKERS WITH THEM.
OH, THOSE?
THEY'RE CALLED SLEEVE PROTECTORS.
YOU PUT THEM ON FROM YOUR WRISTS TO YOUR ELBOWS IN ORDER TO KEEP YOUR SLEEVES FROM GETTING DIRTY WHEN DOING DESK WORK.
I SEE! THE FRUIT OF COMMON WISDOM!
SFX: TERERERE (BLUSH)
I FOUND THAT QUEST FIRST!
GA
LIKE HELL YOU DID! I WAS OBVIOUSLY FIRST!!
BUT I SHOULD TAKE IT ON BECAUSE YOU'LL NEVER BE ABLE TO DO IT!!
GA (GRAB)
BOKOSUKA (SQUABBLE)
COME NOW, BOYS...

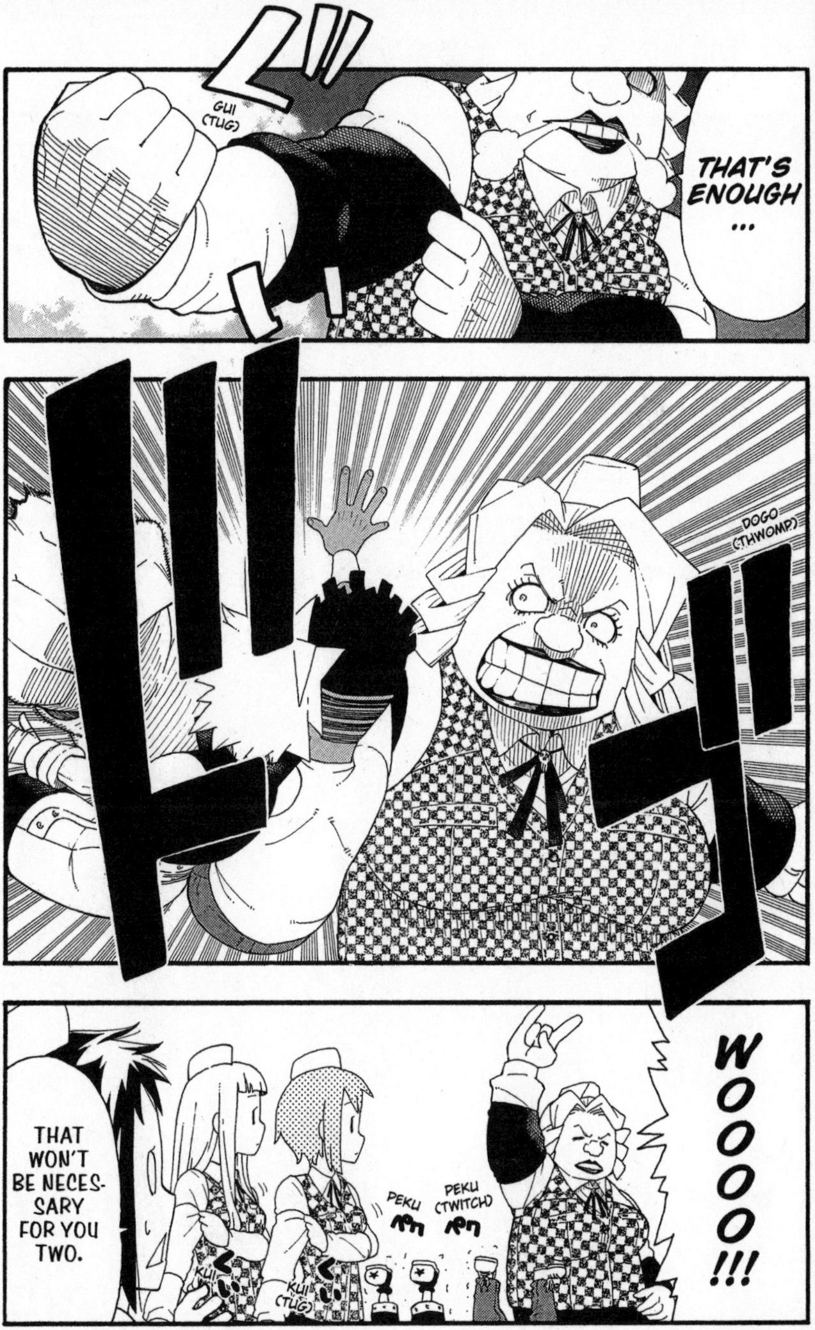
THAT'S ENOUGH ...
GUI (TUG)
DOGO (THWOMP)
WOOOOO!!!
PEKU (TWITCH)
PEKU
KUI (TUG)
KUI
THAT WON'T BE NECES-SARY FOR YOU TWO.

FAKE

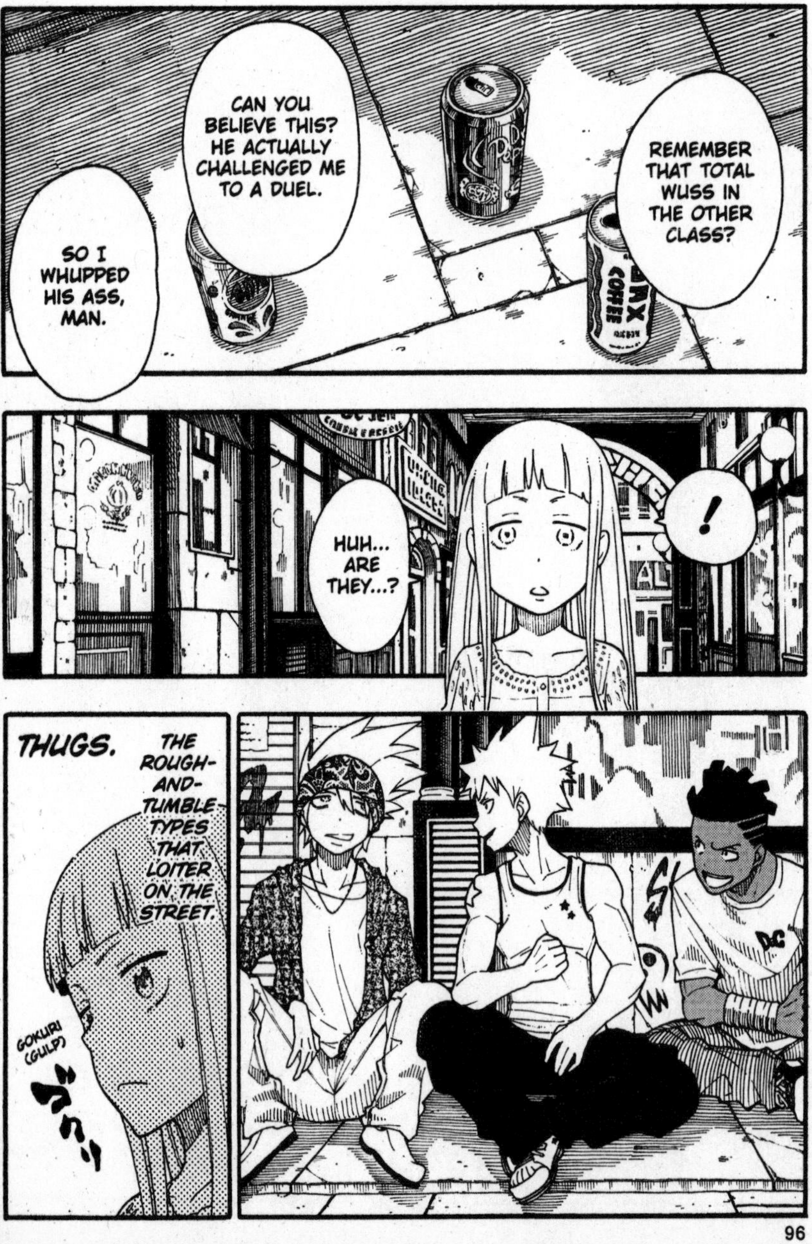
REMEMBER THAT TOTAL WUSS IN THE OTHER CLASS?
CAN YOU BELIEVE THIS? HE ACTUALLY CHALLENGED ME TO A DUEL.
SO I WHUPPED HIS ASS, MAN.
!
HUH... ARE THEY...?
THE ROUGH-AND-TUMBLE TYPES THAT LOITER ON THE STREET.
THUGS.
GOKURI (GULP)

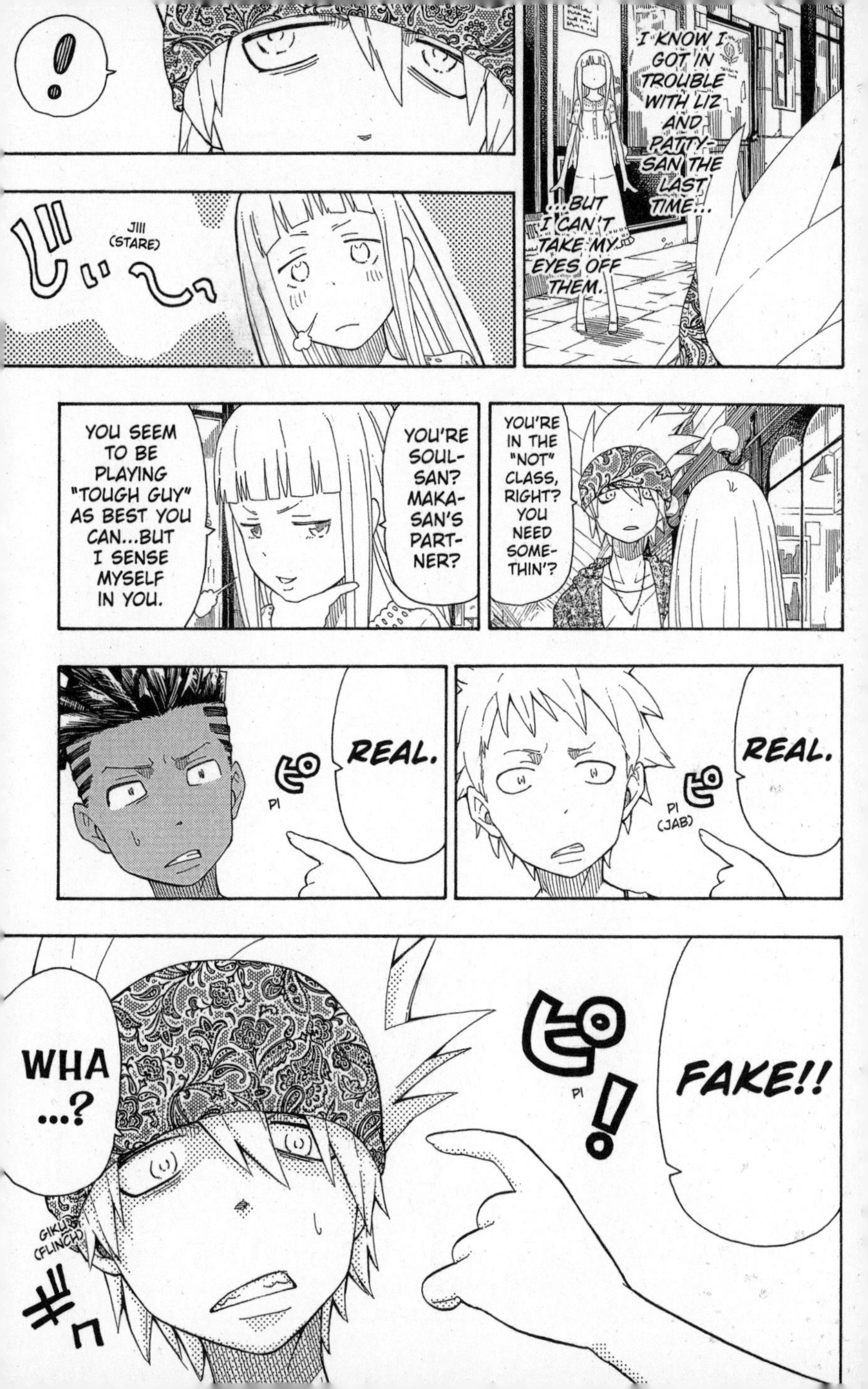
I KNOW I GOT IN TROUBLE WITH LIZ AND PATTY-SAN THE LAST TIME...
...BUT I CAN'T TAKE MY EYES OFF THEM.
!
JIII (STARE)
YOU'RE IN THE "NOT" CLASS, RIGHT? YOU NEED SOMETHIN'?
YOU'RE SOUL-SAN? MAKA-SAN'S PARTNER?
YOU SEEM TO BE PLAYING "TOUGH GUY" AS BEST YOU CAN...BUT I SENSE MYSELF IN YOU.
REAL.
PI (JAB)
REAL.
PI
FAKE!!
PI
WHA...?
GIKU (FLINCH)

BAD AT THIS

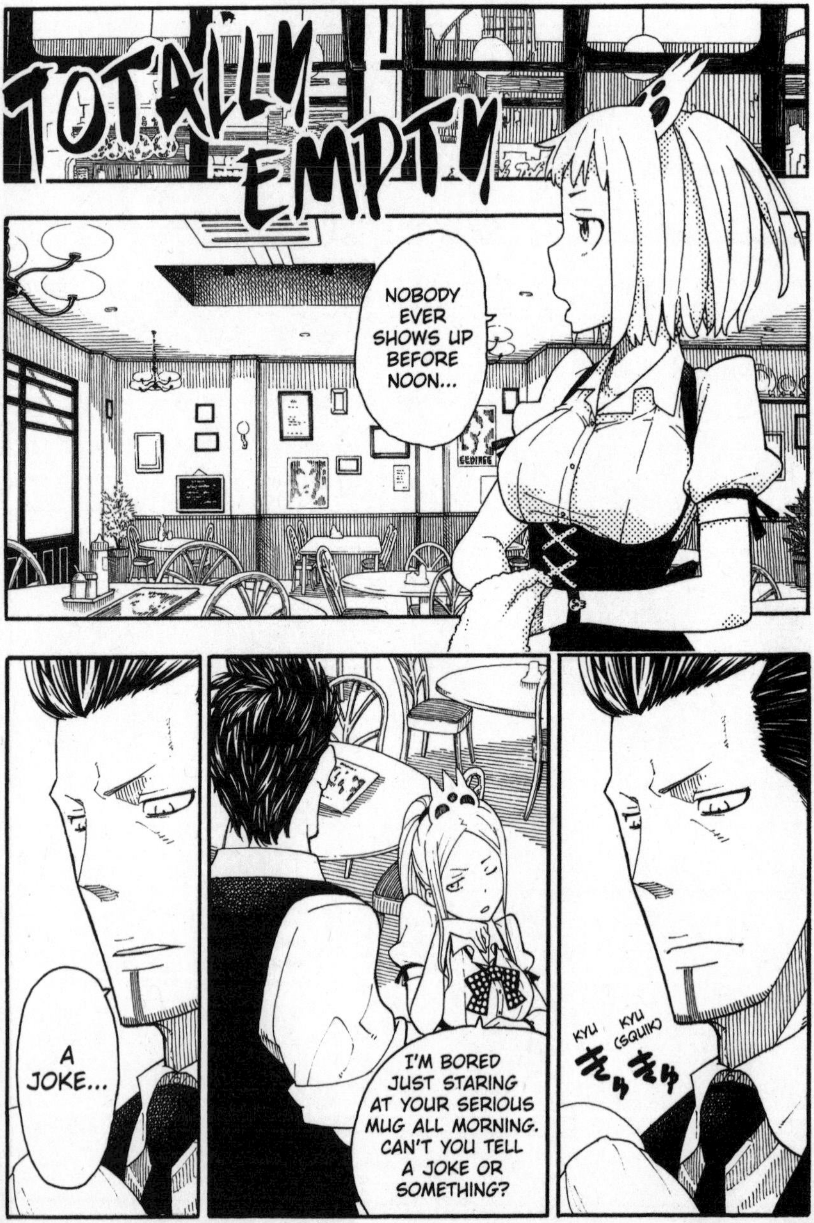
TOTALLY EMPTY
NOBODY EVER SHOWS UP BEFORE NOON...
KYU KYU (SQUIK)
I'M BORED JUST STARING AT YOUR SERIOUS MUG ALL MORNING. CAN'T YOU TELL A JOKE OR SOMETHING?
A JOKE...

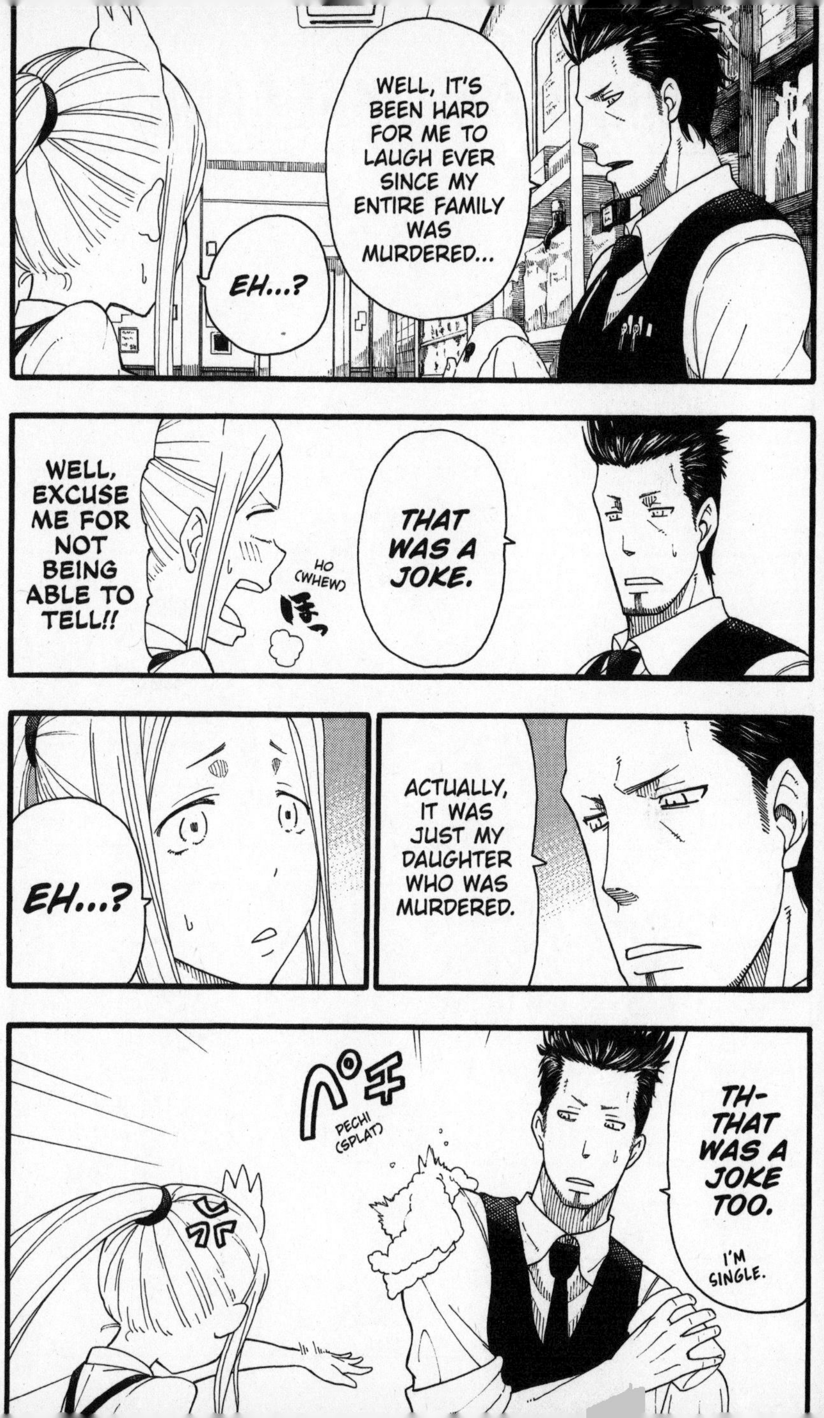
WELL, IT'S BEEN HARD FOR ME TO LAUGH EVER SINCE MY ENTIRE FAMILY WAS MURDERED...
EH...?
THAT WAS A JOKE.
ほっ
HO (WHEW)
WELL, EXCUSE ME FOR NOT BEING ABLE TO TELL!!
ACTUALLY, IT WAS JUST MY DAUGHTER WHO WAS MURDERED.
EH...?
TH-THAT WAS A JOKE TOO.
I'M SINGLE.
ペチ
PECHI (SPLAT)

KANA'S ORIGINAL CARDS

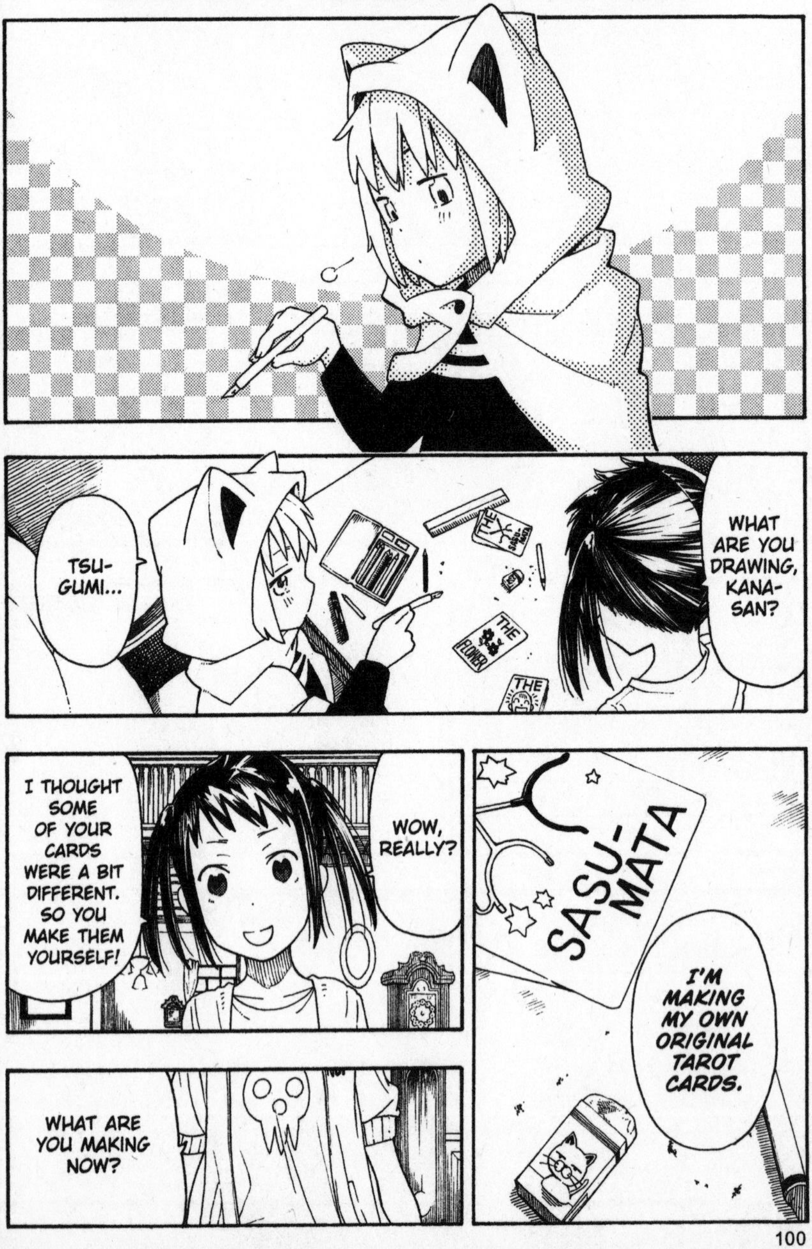
WHAT ARE YOU DRAWING, KANA-SAN?
THE SASU-MATA
THE FLOWER
THE
TSU-GUMI...
SASU-MATA
I'M MAKING MY OWN ORIGINAL TAROT CARDS.
WOW, REALLY?
I THOUGHT SOME OF YOUR CARDS WERE A BIT DIFFERENT. SO YOU MAKE THEM YOURSELF!
WHAT ARE YOU MAKING NOW?

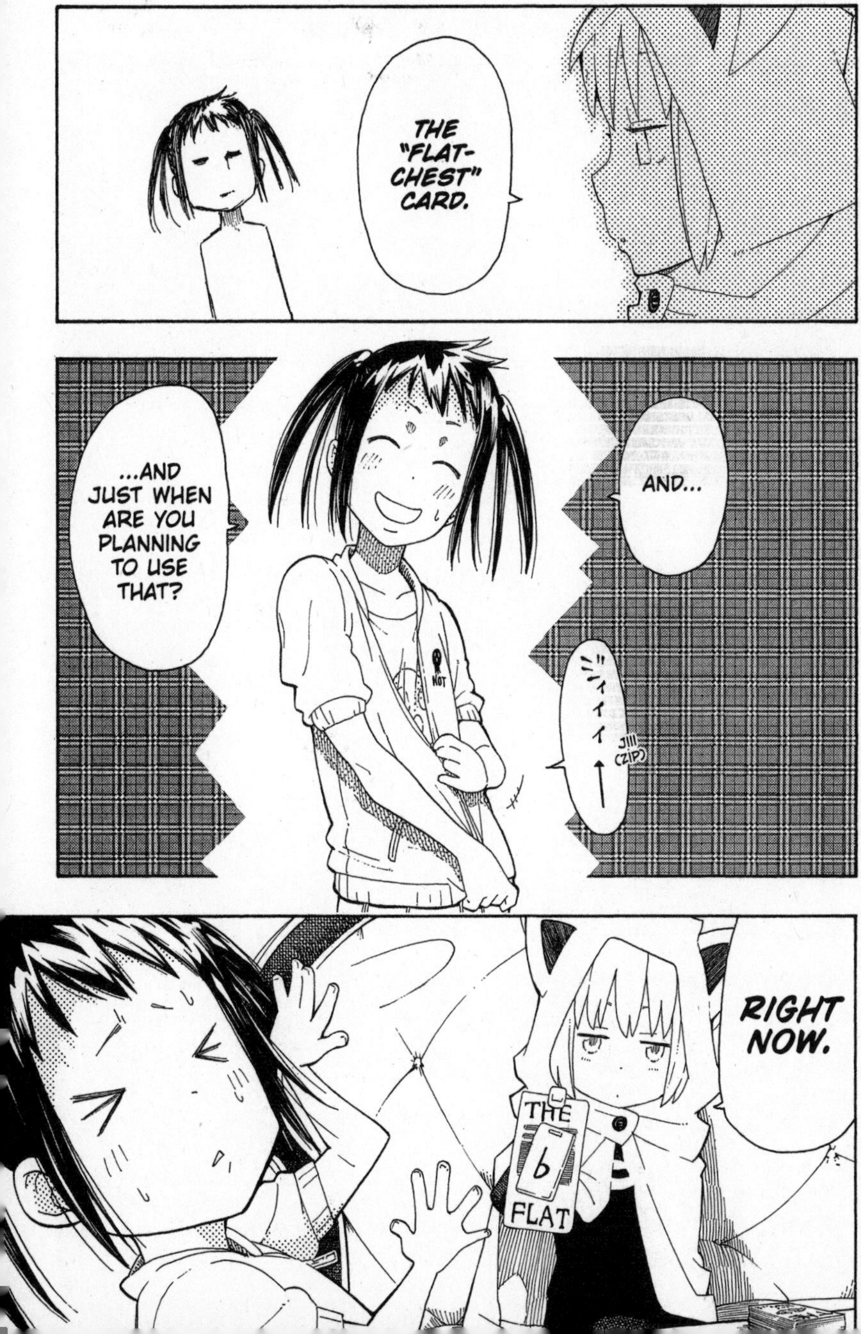
THE "FLAT-CHEST" CARD.
AND...
ジィイイ↑ JIII (ZIP)
...AND JUST WHEN ARE YOU PLANNING TO USE THAT?
RIGHT NOW.
THE ♭ FLAT
NOT

DEATH CHILD

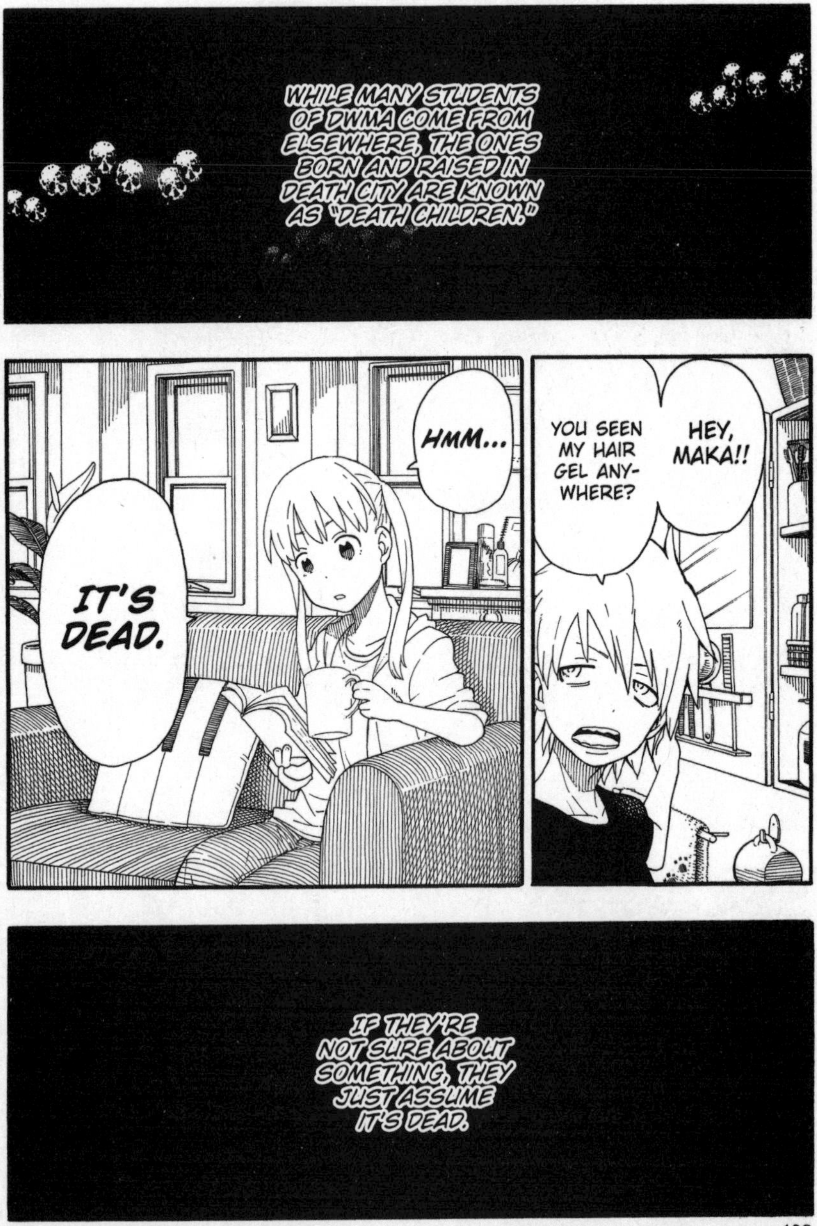
WHILE MANY STUDENTS OF DWMA COME FROM ELSEWHERE, THE ONES BORN AND RAISED IN DEATH CITY ARE KNOWN AS "DEATH CHILDREN."
HEY, MAKA!!
YOU SEEN MY HAIR GEL ANY-WHERE?
HMM...
IT'S DEAD.
IF THEY'RE NOT SURE ABOUT SOMETHING, THEY JUST ASSUME IT'S DEAD.

SOUL EATER NOT!

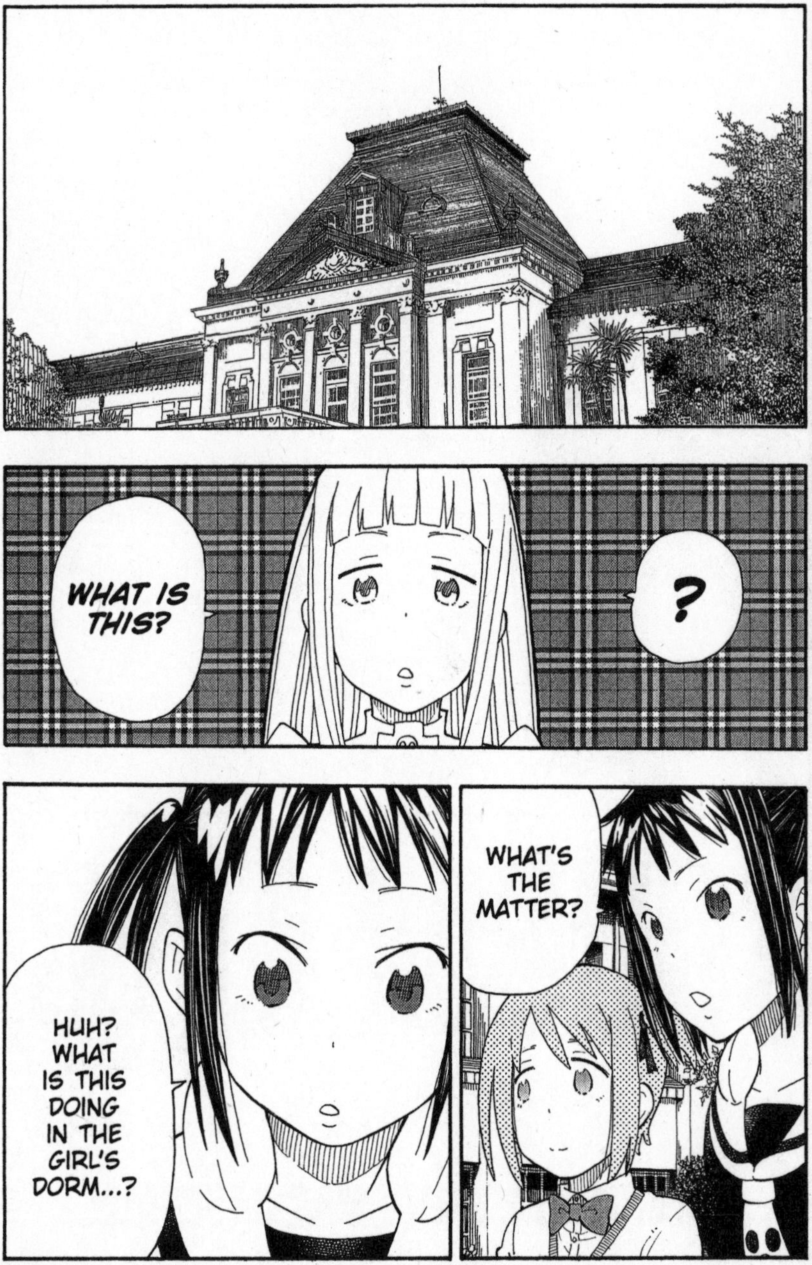
?
WHAT IS THIS?
WHAT'S THE MATTER?
HUH? WHAT IS THIS DOING IN THE GIRL'S DORM...?

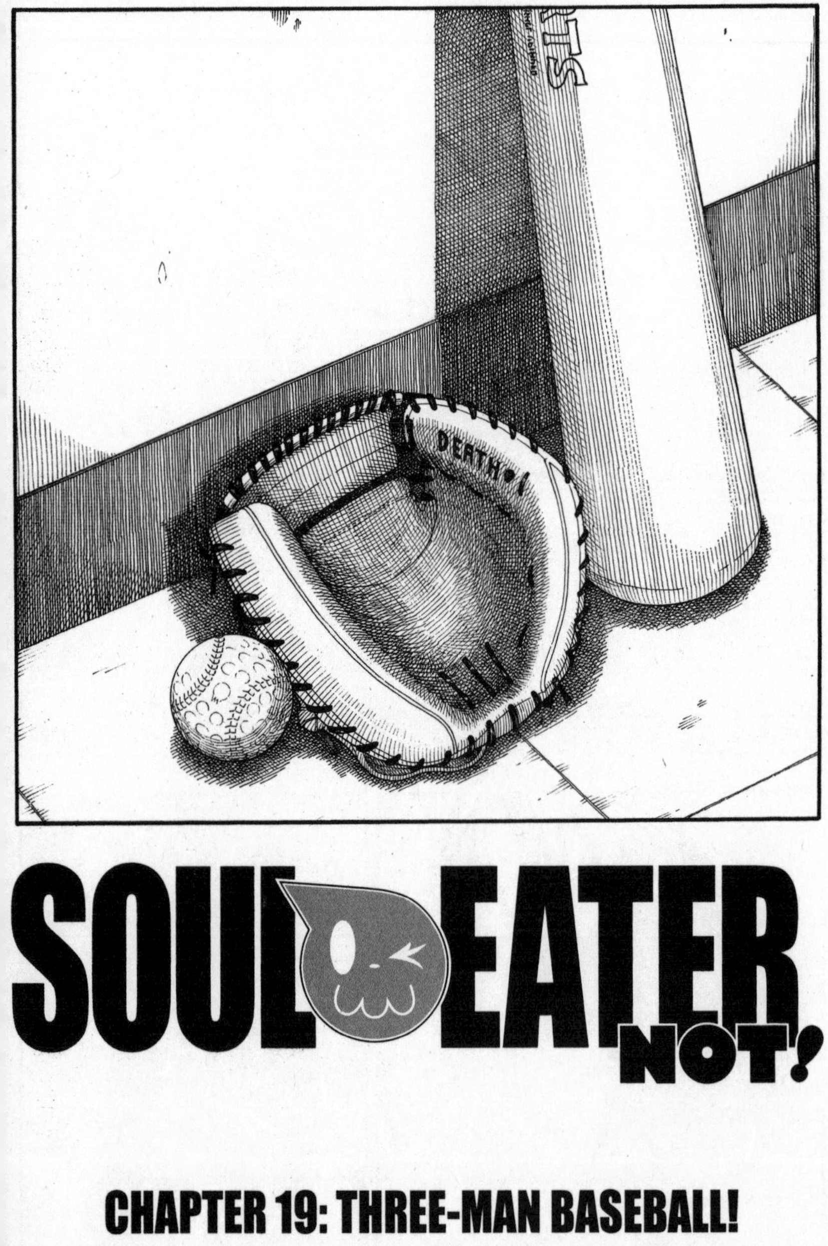

SOUL EATER NOT!

CHAPTER 19: THREE-MAN BASEBALL!

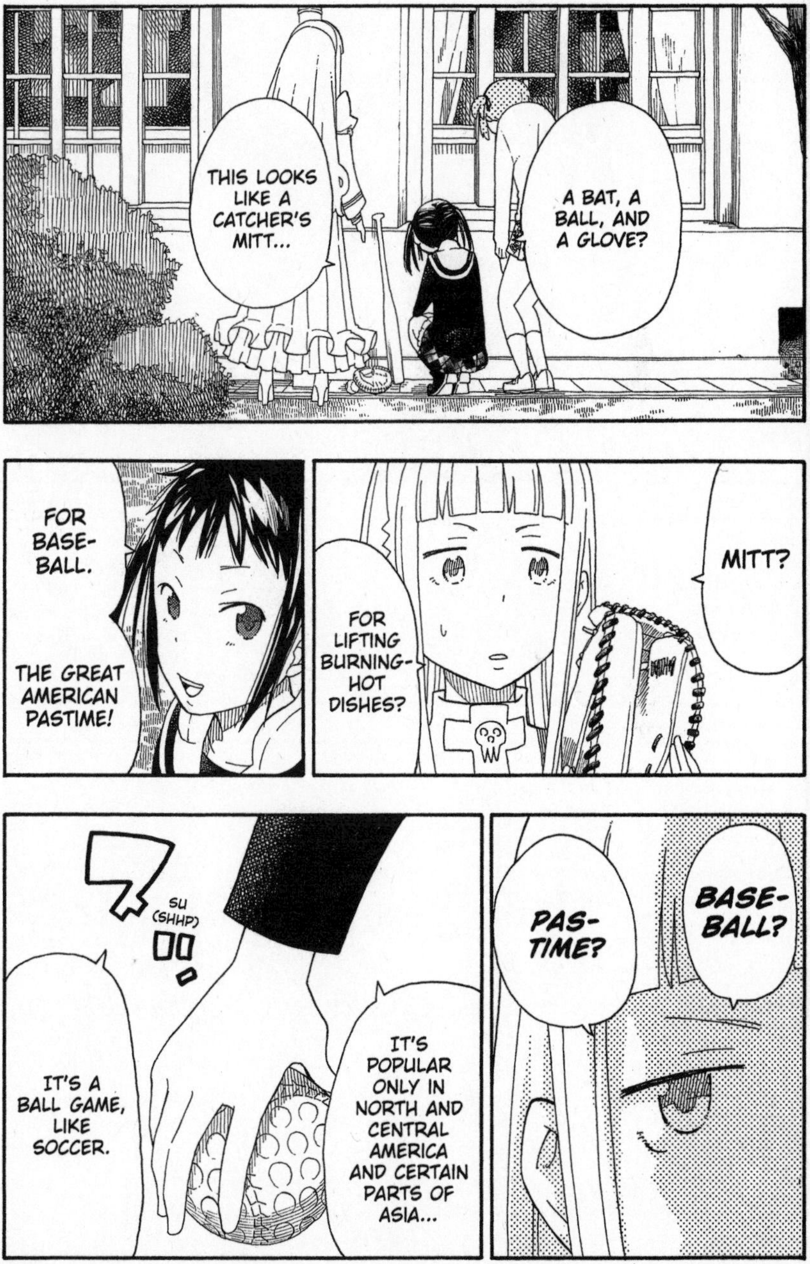
A BAT, A BALL, AND A GLOVE?
THIS LOOKS LIKE A CATCHER'S MITT...
MITT?
FOR LIFTING BURNING-HOT DISHES?
FOR BASEBALL.
THE GREAT AMERICAN PASTIME!
BASEBALL?
PASTIME?
SU (SHHP)
IT'S POPULAR ONLY IN NORTH AND CENTRAL AMERICA AND CERTAIN PARTS OF ASIA...
IT'S A BALL GAME, LIKE SOCCER.

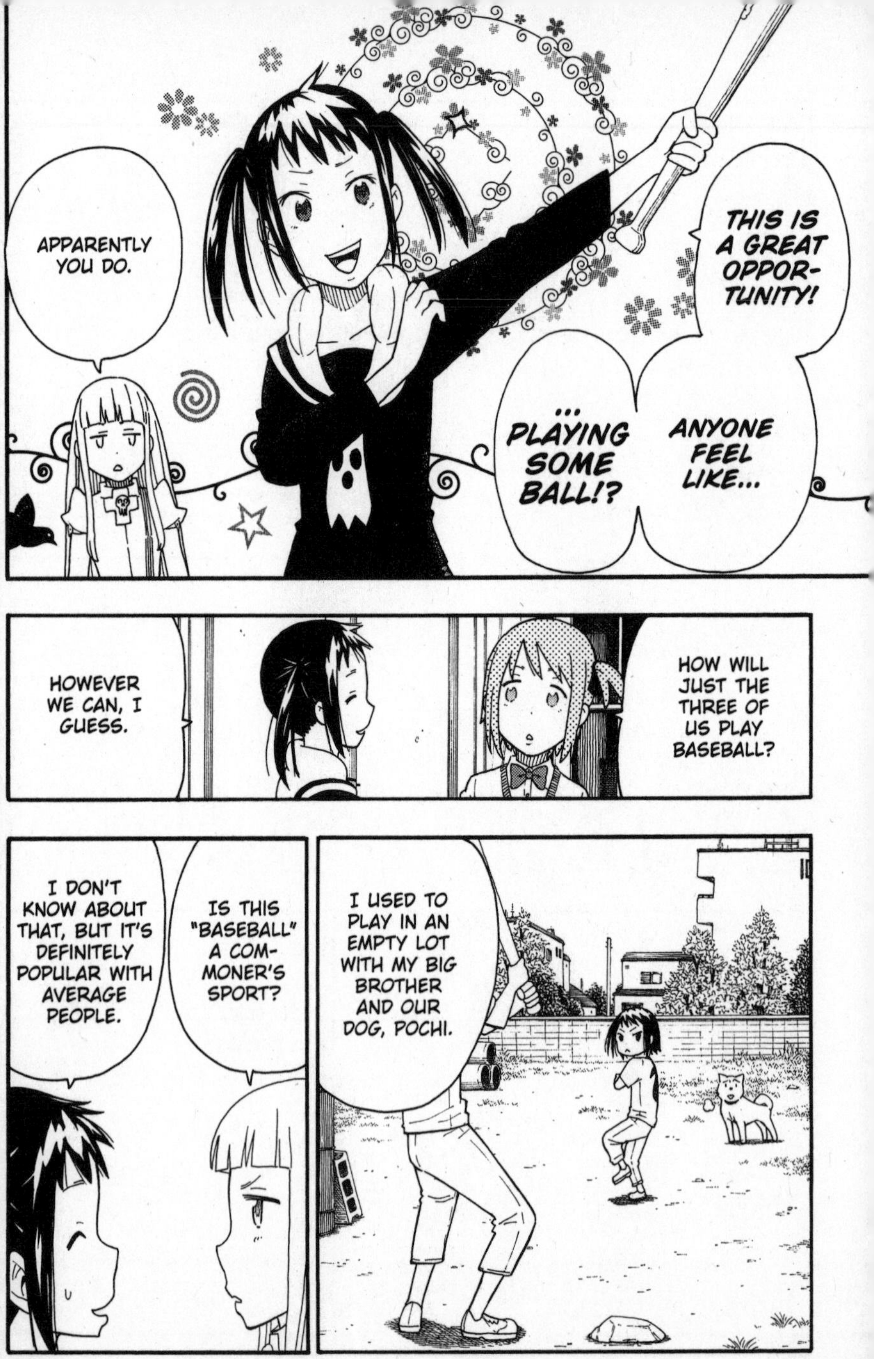
THIS IS A GREAT OPPORTUNITY!
ANYONE FEEL LIKE...
...PLAYING SOME BALL!?
APPARENTLY YOU DO.
HOW WILL JUST THE THREE OF US PLAY BASEBALL?
HOWEVER WE CAN, I GUESS.
I USED TO PLAY IN AN EMPTY LOT WITH MY BIG BROTHER AND OUR DOG, POCHI.
IS THIS "BASEBALL" A COMMONER'S SPORT?
I DON'T KNOW ABOUT THAT, BUT IT'S DEFINITELY POPULAR WITH AVERAGE PEOPLE.

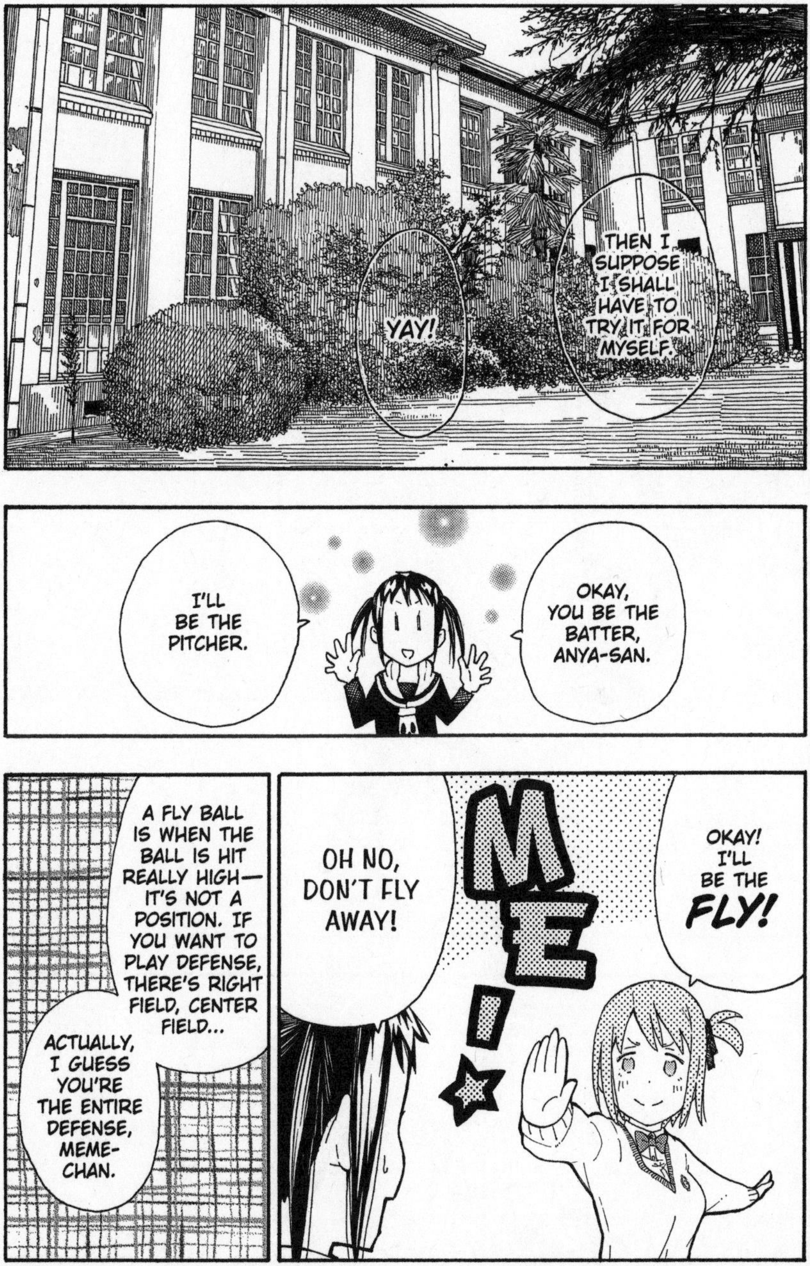
THEN I SUPPOSE I SHALL HAVE TO TRY IT FOR MYSELF.
YAY!
OKAY, YOU BE THE BATTER, ANYA-SAN.
I'LL BE THE PITCHER.
OKAY! I'LL BE THE *FLY!*
ME!
OH NO, DON'T FLY AWAY!
A FLY BALL IS WHEN THE BALL IS HIT REALLY HIGH—IT'S NOT A POSITION. IF YOU WANT TO PLAY DEFENSE, THERE'S RIGHT FIELD, CENTER FIELD...
ACTUALLY, I GUESS YOU'RE THE ENTIRE DEFENSE, MEME-CHAN.

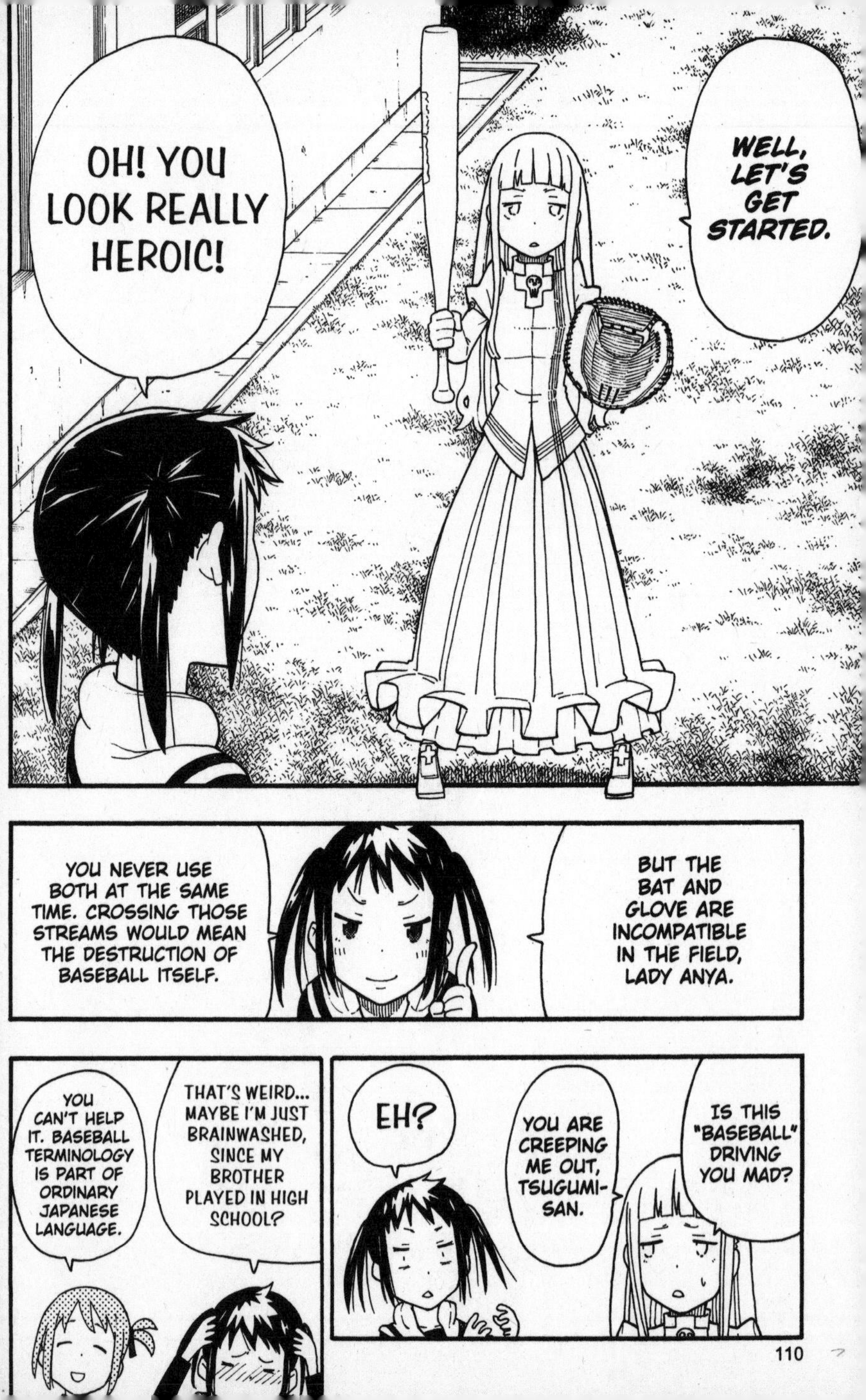
WELL, LET'S GET STARTED.
OH! YOU LOOK REALLY HEROIC!
BUT THE BAT AND GLOVE ARE INCOMPATIBLE IN THE FIELD, LADY ANYA.
YOU NEVER USE BOTH AT THE SAME TIME. CROSSING THOSE STREAMS WOULD MEAN THE DESTRUCTION OF BASEBALL ITSELF.
IS THIS "BASEBALL" DRIVING YOU MAD?
YOU ARE CREEPING ME OUT, TSUGUMI-SAN.
EH?
THAT'S WEIRD... MAYBE I'M JUST BRAINWASHED, SINCE MY BROTHER PLAYED IN HIGH SCHOOL?
YOU CAN'T HELP IT. BASEBALL TERMINOLOGY IS PART OF ORDINARY JAPANESE LANGUAGE.

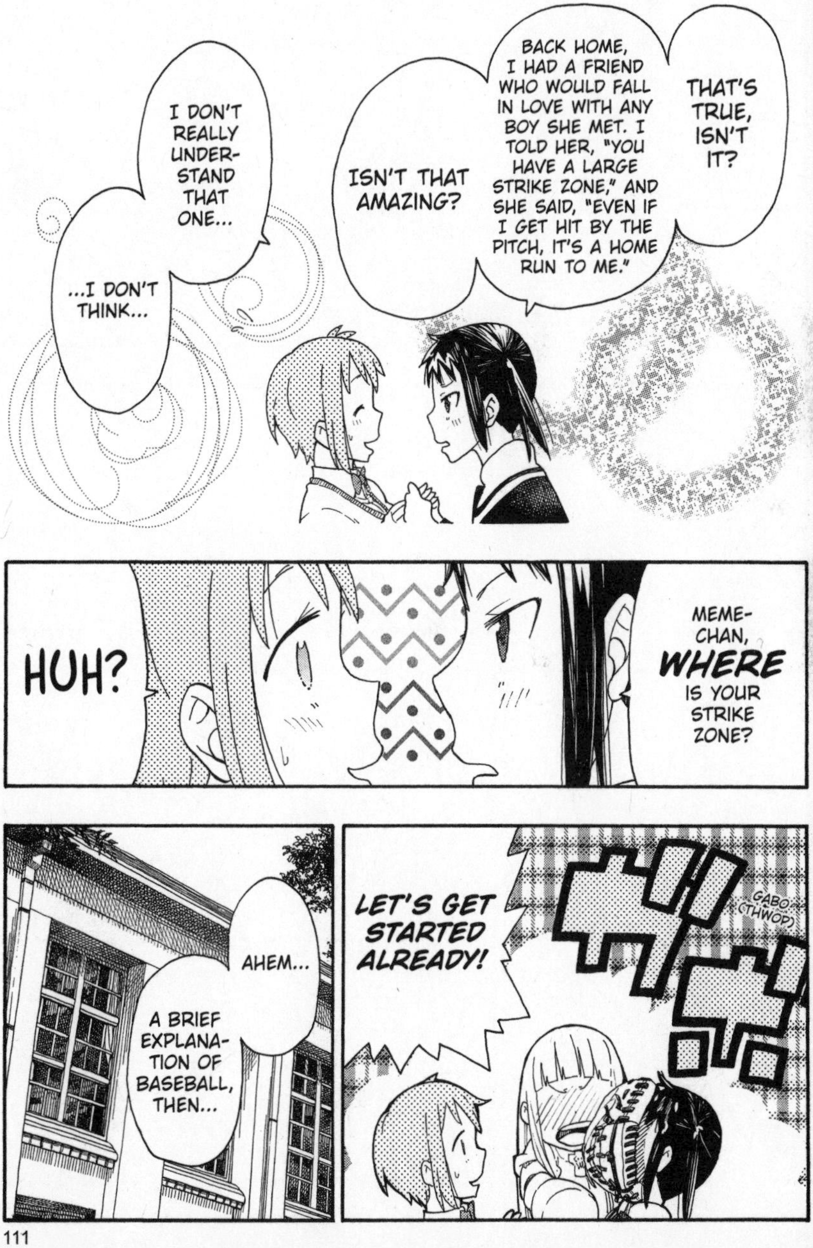
THAT'S TRUE, ISN'T IT?
BACK HOME, I HAD A FRIEND WHO WOULD FALL IN LOVE WITH ANY BOY SHE MET. I TOLD HER, "YOU HAVE A LARGE STRIKE ZONE," AND SHE SAID, "EVEN IF I GET HIT BY THE PITCH, IT'S A HOME RUN TO ME."
ISN'T THAT AMAZING?
I DON'T REALLY UNDER-STAND THAT ONE...
...I DON'T THINK...
MEME-CHAN, WHERE IS YOUR STRIKE ZONE?
HUH?
GABO (THWOP)
LET'S GET STARTED ALREADY!
AHEM...
A BRIEF EXPLANA-TION OF BASEBALL, THEN...

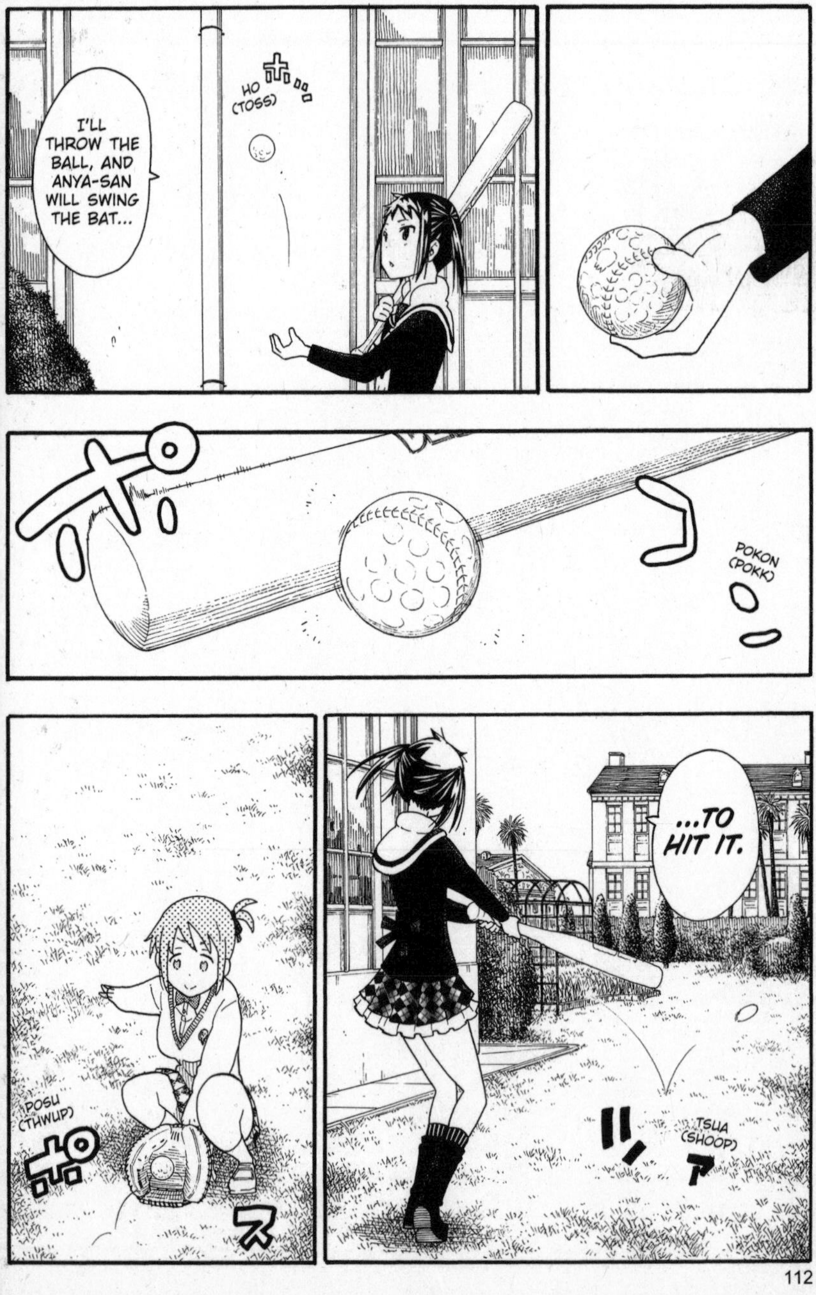
HO (TOSS)
I'LL THROW THE BALL, AND ANYA-SAN WILL SWING THE BAT...
POKON (POKK)
...TO HIT IT.
TSUA (SHOOP)
POSU (THWUP)

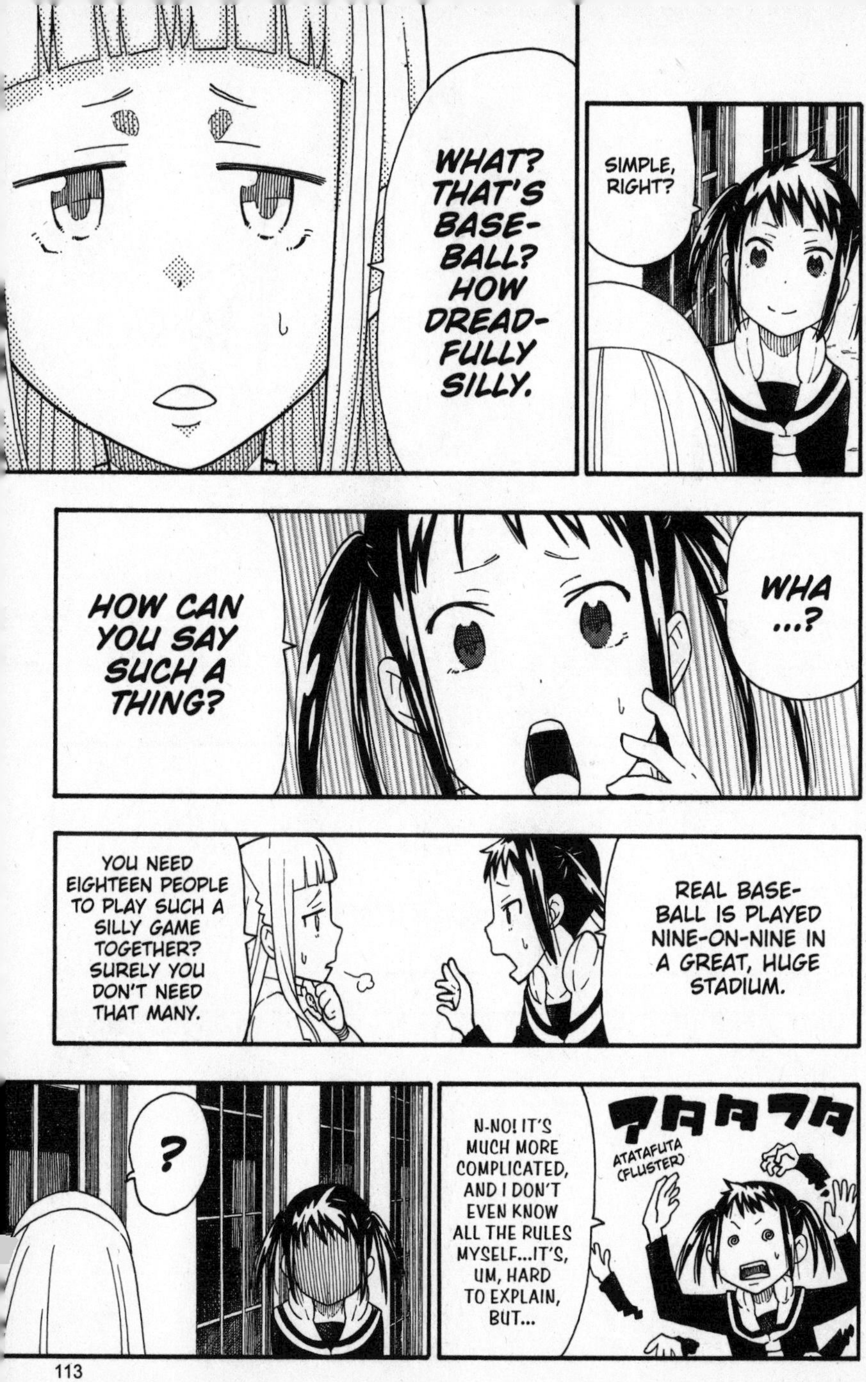
SIMPLE, RIGHT?
WHAT? THAT'S BASE-BALL? HOW DREAD-FULLY SILLY.
WHA...?
HOW CAN YOU SAY SUCH A THING?
REAL BASE-BALL IS PLAYED NINE-ON-NINE IN A GREAT, HUGE STADIUM.
YOU NEED EIGHTEEN PEOPLE TO PLAY SUCH A SILLY GAME TOGETHER? SURELY YOU DON'T NEED THAT MANY.
アタタフタ
ATATAFUTA (FLUSTER)
N-NO! IT'S MUCH MORE COMPLICATED, AND I DON'T EVEN KNOW ALL THE RULES MYSELF...IT'S, UM, HARD TO EXPLAIN, BUT...
?

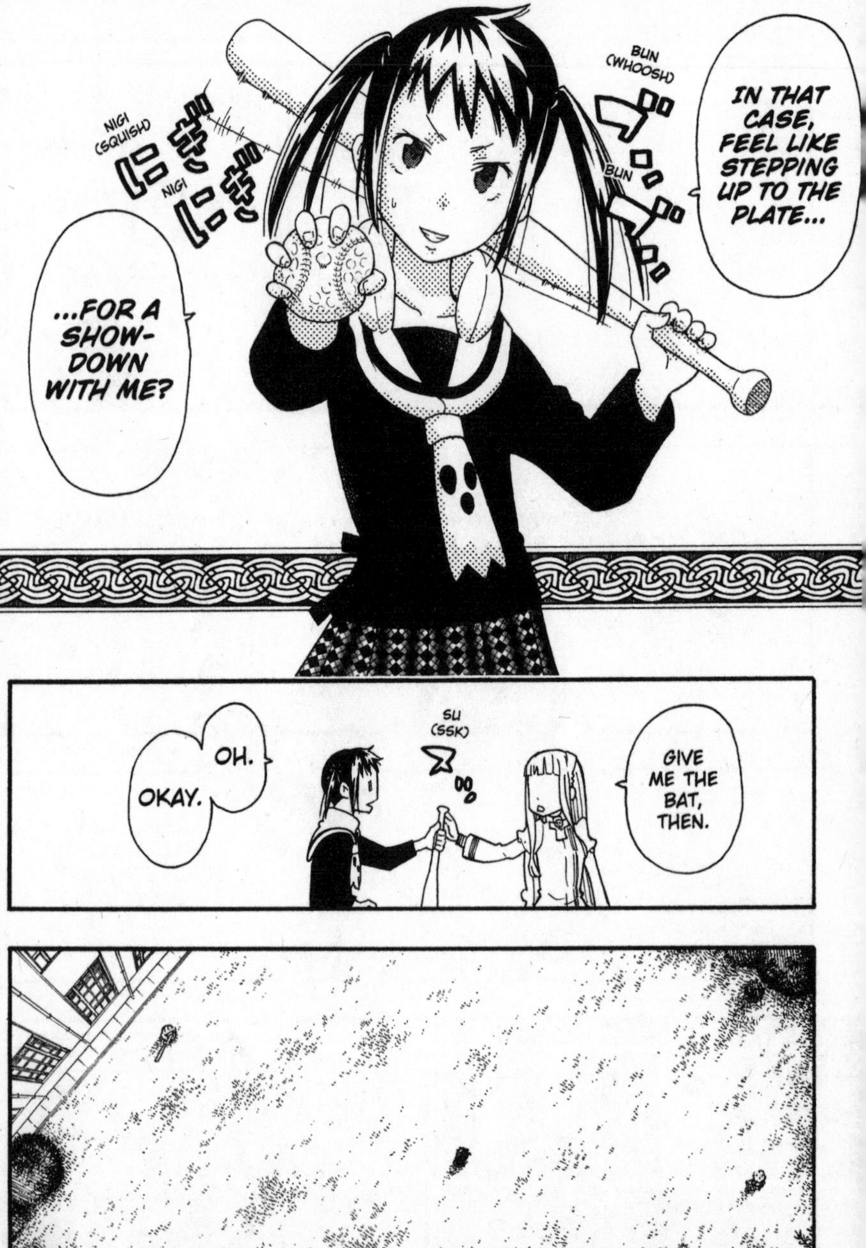
IN THAT CASE, FEEL LIKE STEPPING UP TO THE PLATE...
BUN (WHOOSH)
BUN
NIGI (SQUISH)
NIGI
...FOR A SHOW-DOWN WITH ME?
GIVE ME THE BAT, THEN.
SU (SSK)
OH.
OKAY.

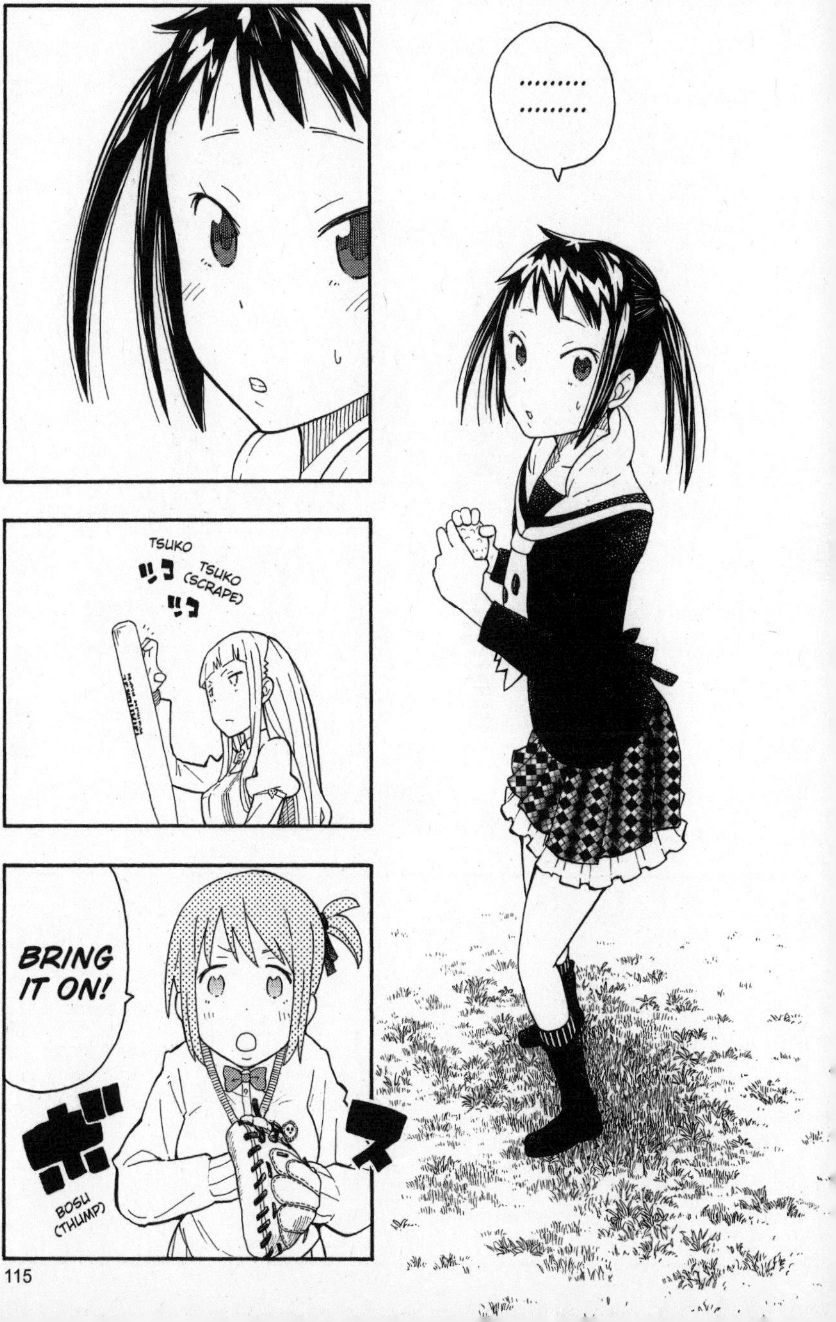

....
....
TSUKO
ツコ
TSUKO (SCRAPE)
ツコ
BRING IT ON!
ボス
BOSU (THUMP)

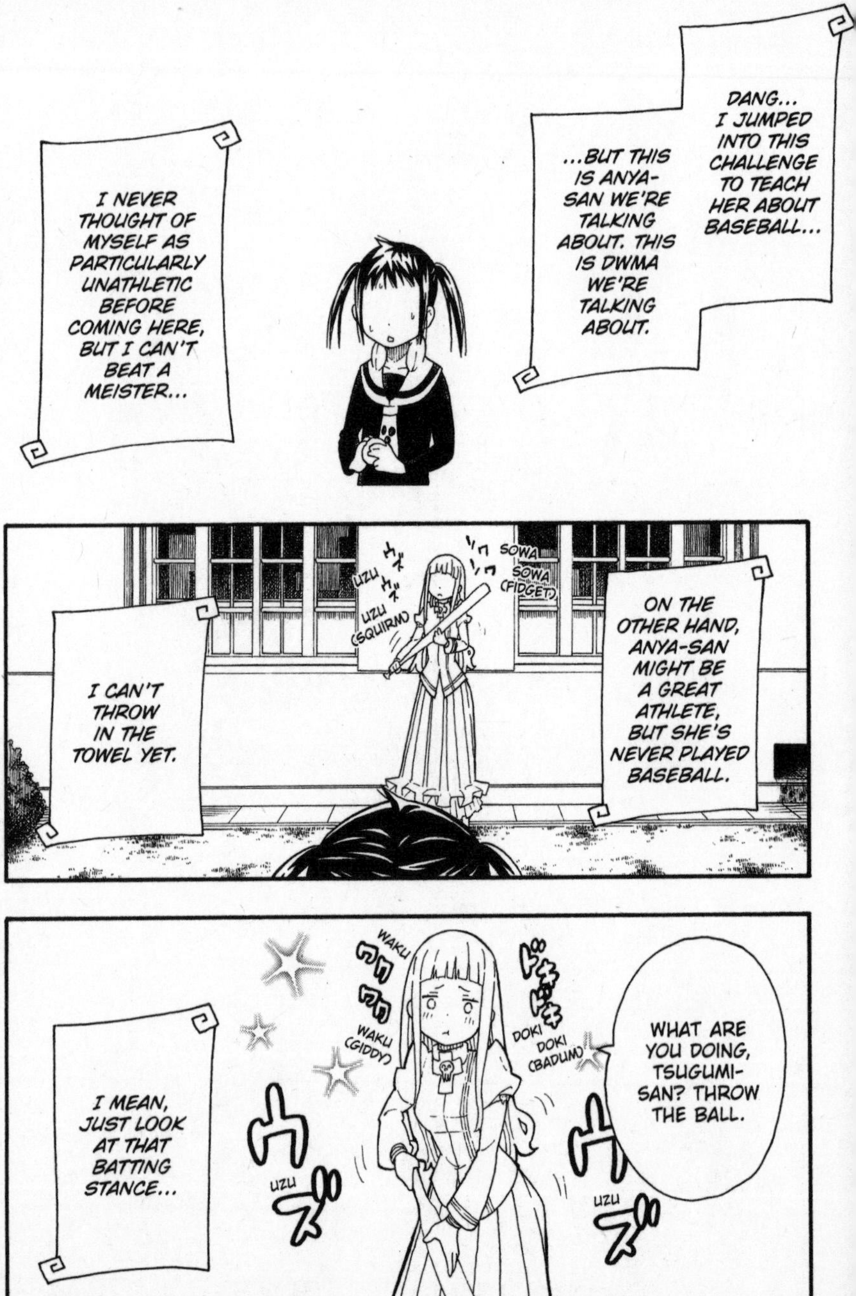
DANG... I JUMPED INTO THIS CHALLENGE TO TEACH HER ABOUT BASEBALL...
...BUT THIS IS ANYA-SAN WE'RE TALKING ABOUT. THIS IS DWMA WE'RE TALKING ABOUT.
I NEVER THOUGHT OF MYSELF AS PARTICULARLY UNATHLETIC BEFORE COMING HERE, BUT I CAN'T BEAT A MEISTER...
ON THE OTHER HAND, ANYA-SAN MIGHT BE A GREAT ATHLETE, BUT SHE'S NEVER PLAYED BASEBALL.
SOWA SOWA (FIDGET)
UZU UZU (SQUIRM)
I CAN'T THROW IN THE TOWEL YET.
WHAT ARE YOU DOING, TSUGUMI-SAN? THROW THE BALL.
DOKI DOKI (BADUM)
WAKU WAKU (GIDDY)
UZU
UZU
I MEAN, JUST LOOK AT THAT BATTING STANCE...

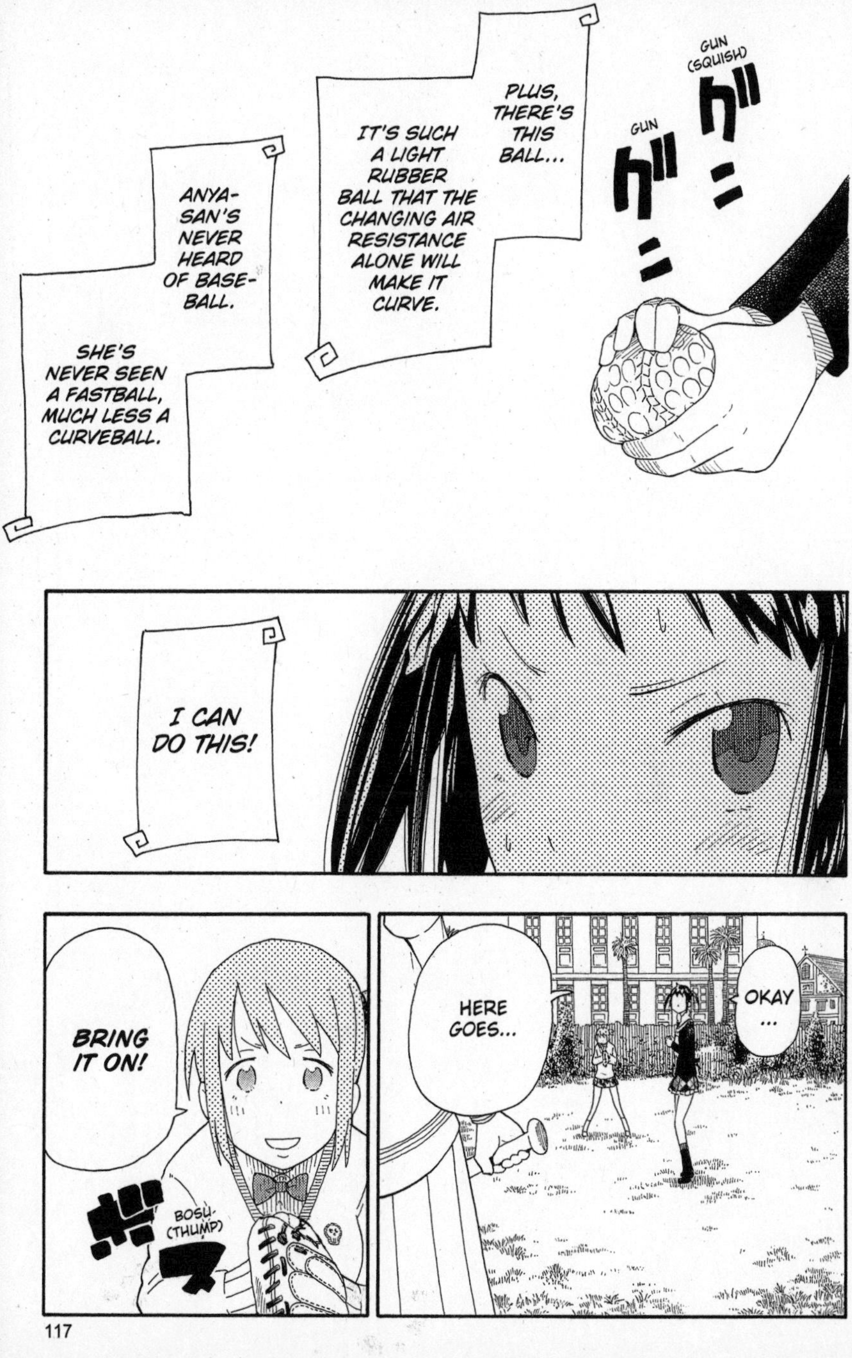
GUN (SQUISH)
GUN
PLUS, THERE'S THIS BALL...
IT'S SUCH A LIGHT RUBBER BALL THAT THE CHANGING AIR RESISTANCE ALONE WILL MAKE IT CURVE.
ANYA-SAN'S NEVER HEARD OF BASE-BALL.
SHE'S NEVER SEEN A FASTBALL, MUCH LESS A CURVEBALL.
I CAN DO THIS!
OKAY ...
HERE GOES...
BRING IT ON!
BOSU (THUMP)

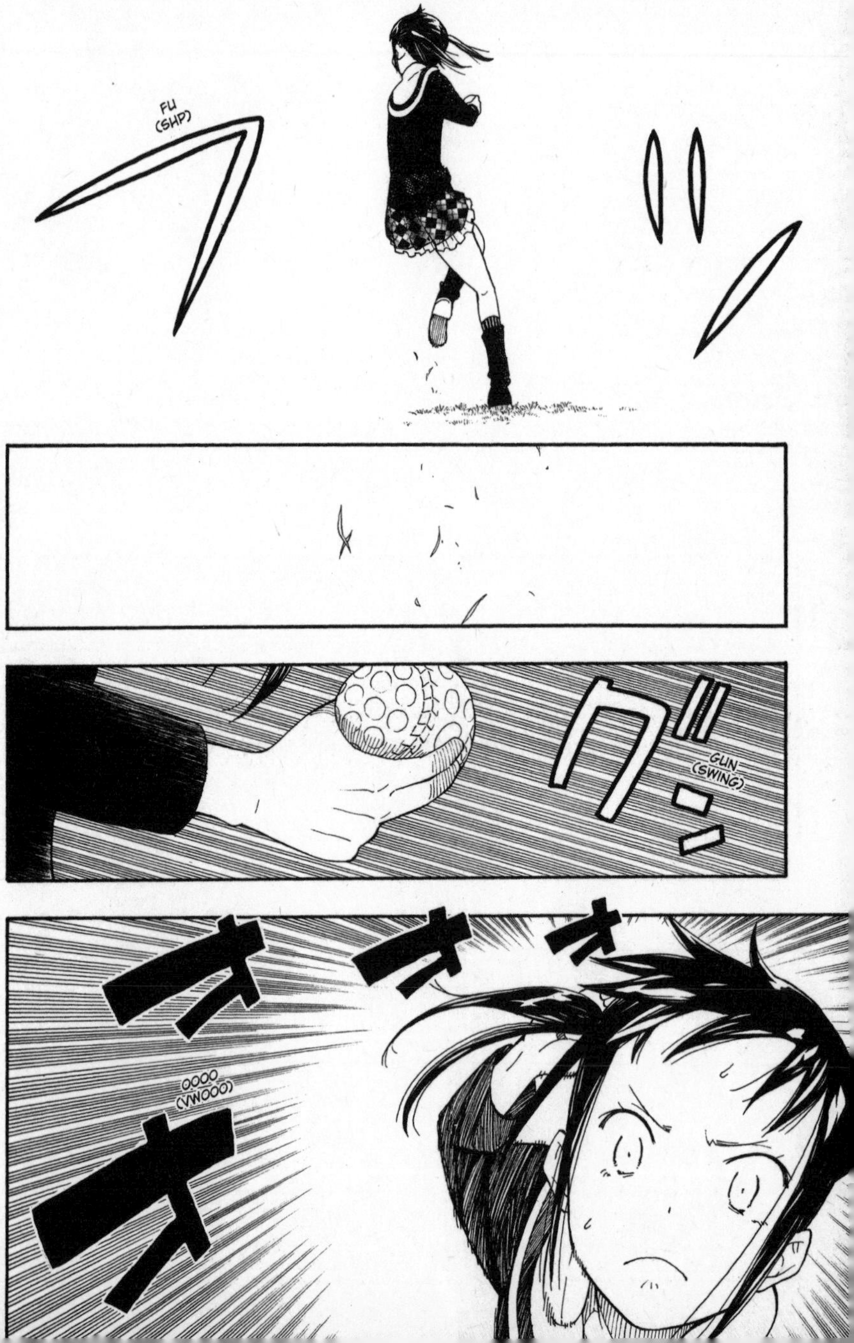
FU
(SHP)
GUN
(SWING)
OOOO
(VWOOO)

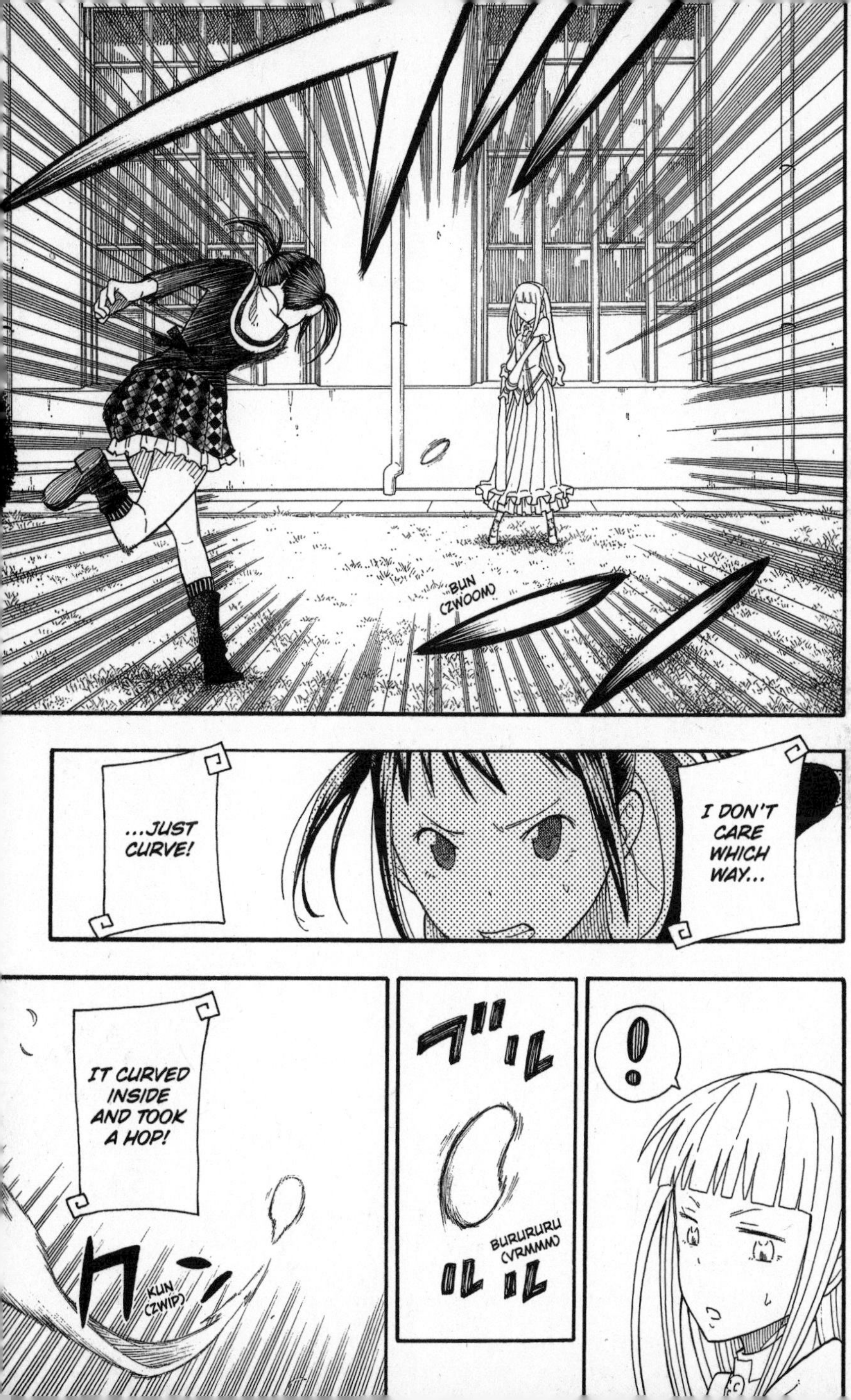

BUN (ZWOOM)
I DON'T CARE WHICH WAY...
...JUST CURVE!
!
BURURURU (VRMMM)
IT CURVED INSIDE AND TOOK A HOP!
KUN (ZWIP)

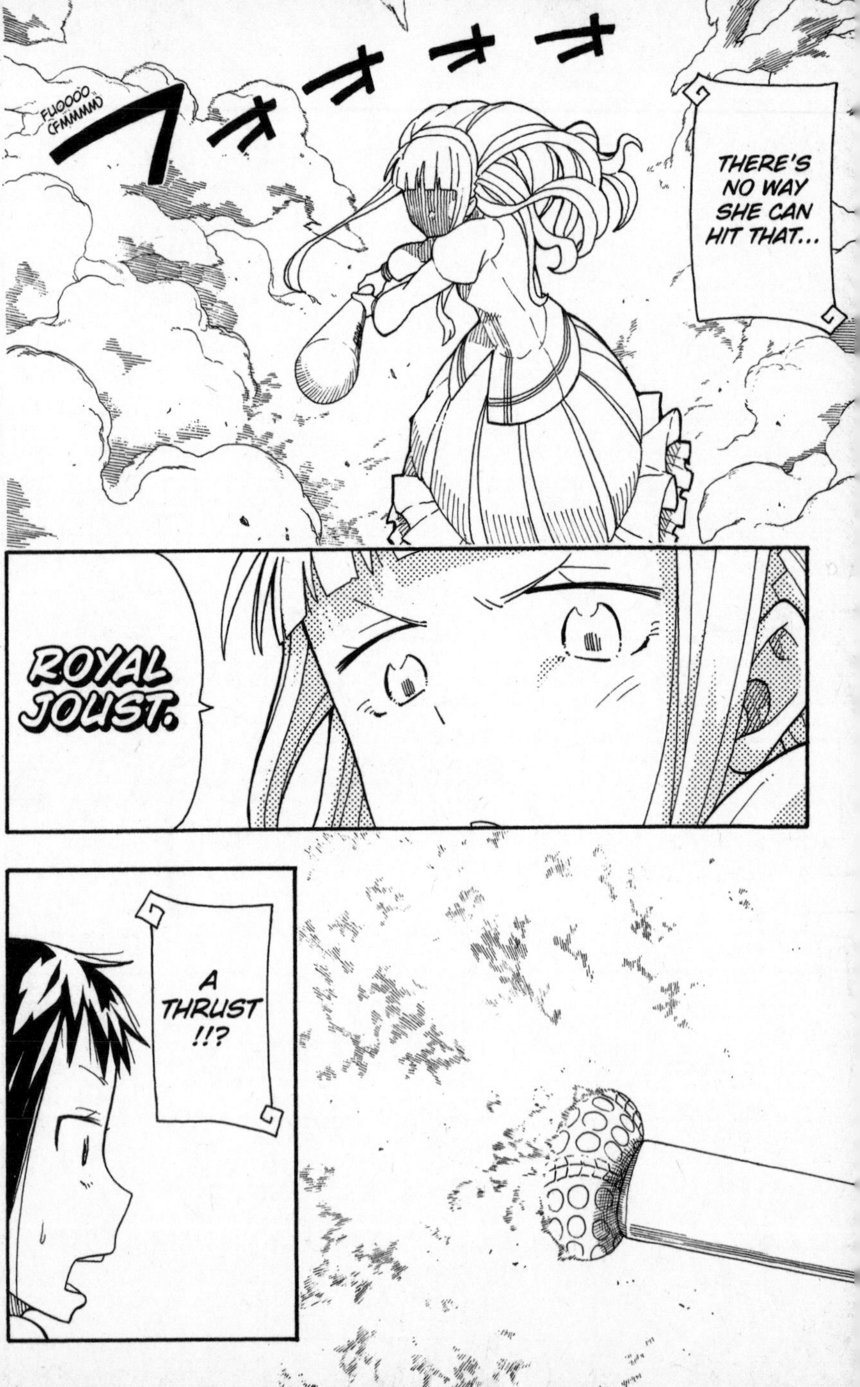
THERE'S NO WAY SHE CAN HIT THAT...
フォォォォ
FUOOOO (FMMMM)
ROYAL JOUST.
A THRUST !!?

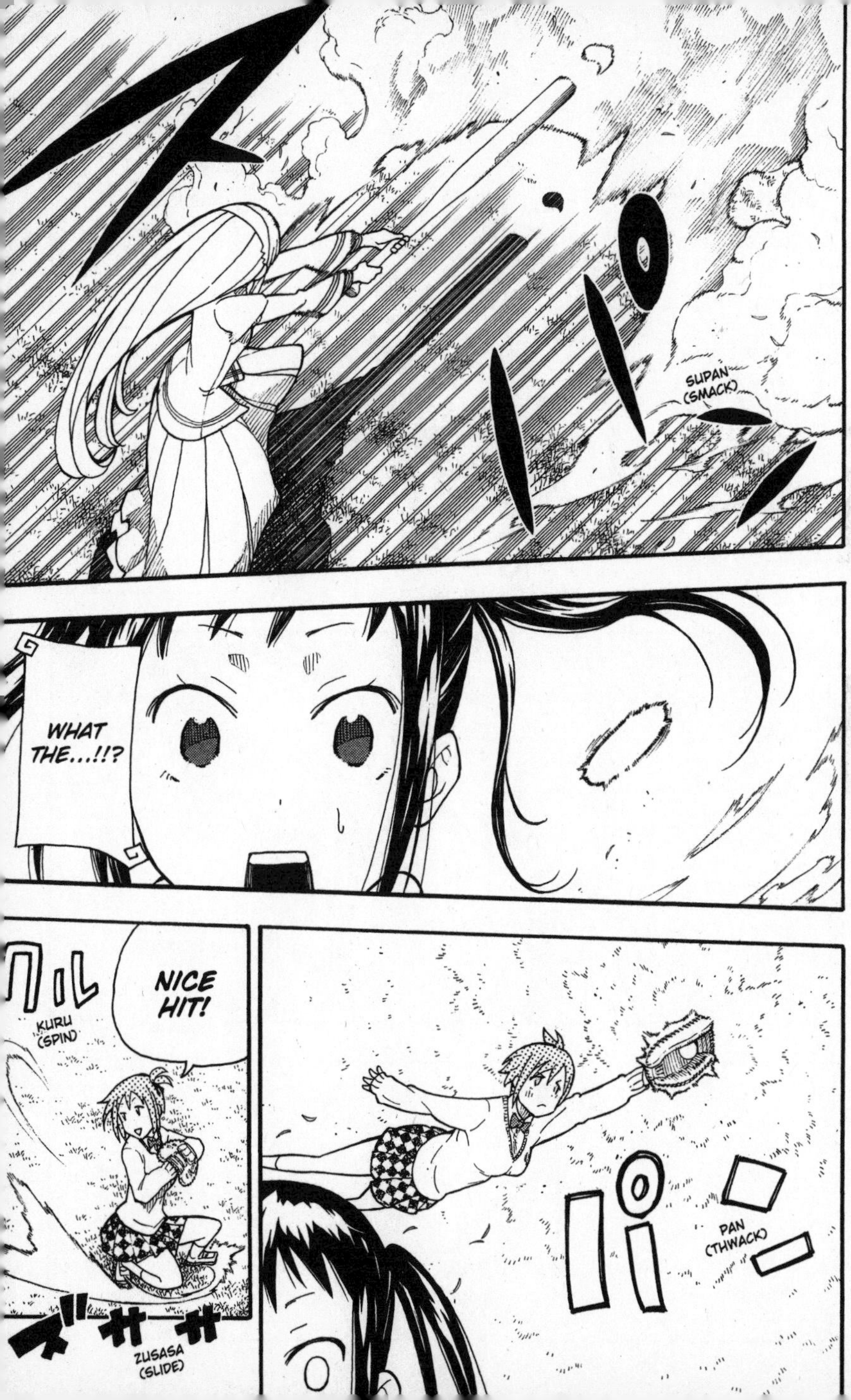
SUPAN
(SMACK)
WHAT THE...!!?
PAN
(THWACK)
NICE HIT!
KURU
(SPIN)
ZUSASA
(SLIDE)

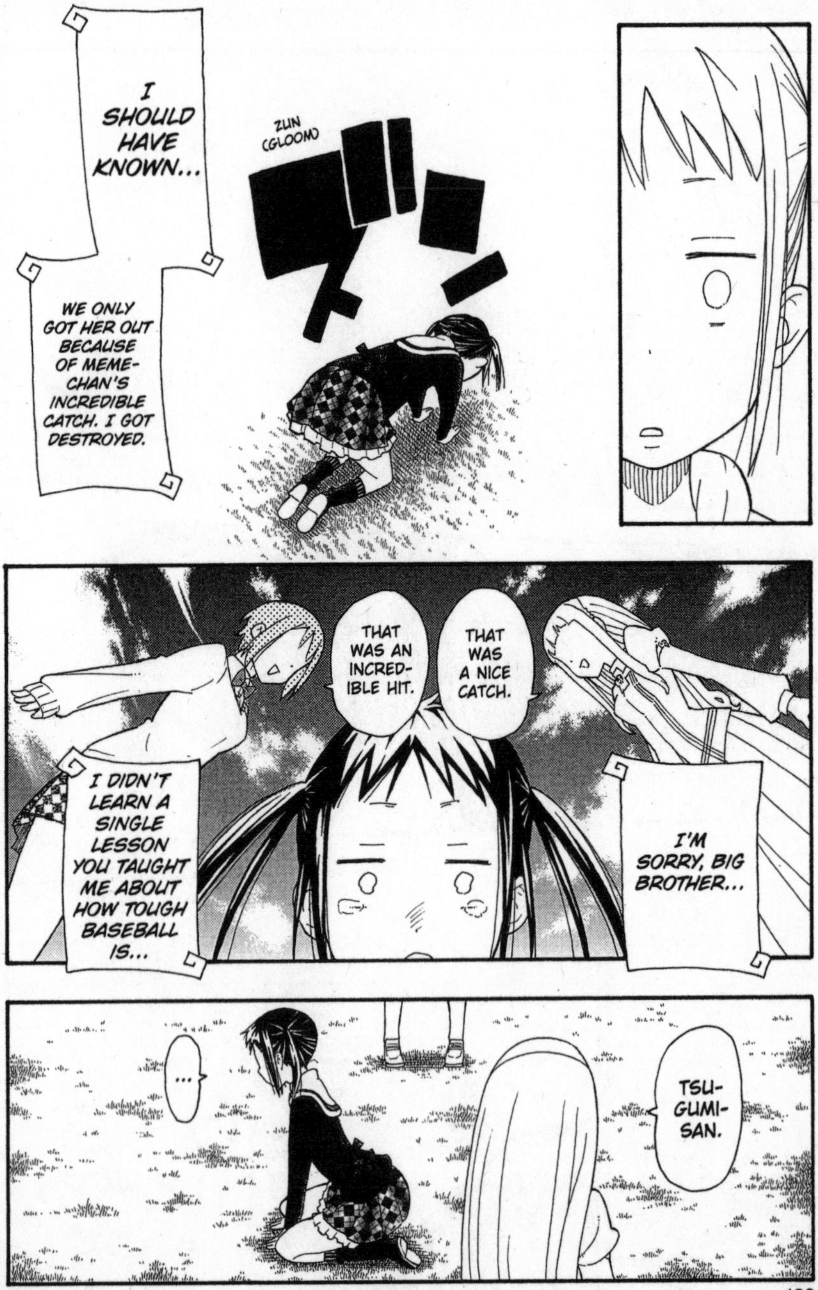
ZUN (GLOOM)
I SHOULD HAVE KNOWN...
WE ONLY GOT HER OUT BECAUSE OF MEME-CHAN'S INCREDIBLE CATCH. I GOT DESTROYED.
THAT WAS A NICE CATCH.
THAT WAS AN INCRED-IBLE HIT.
I'M SORRY, BIG BROTHER...
I DIDN'T LEARN A SINGLE LESSON YOU TAUGHT ME ABOUT HOW TOUGH BASEBALL IS...
TSU-GUMI-SAN.
...

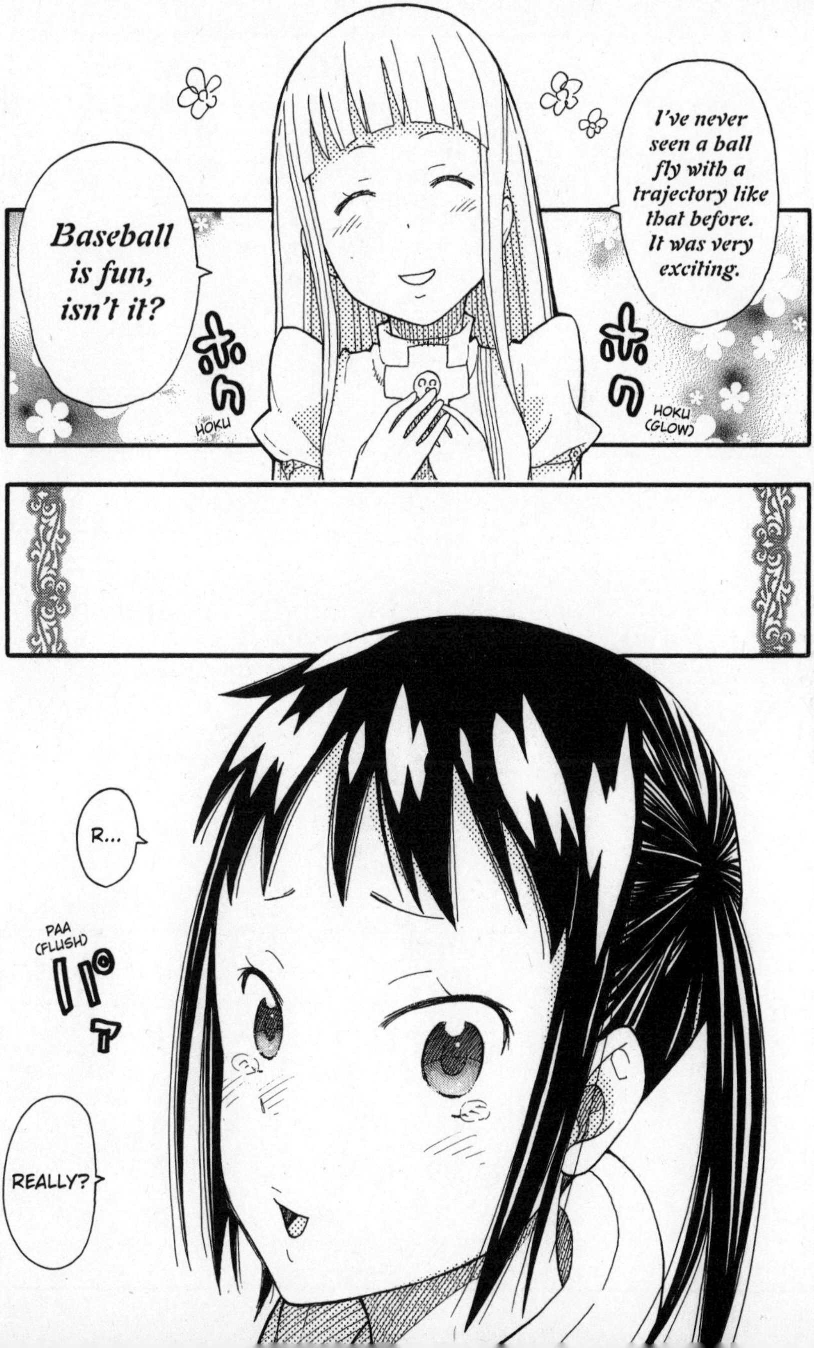
I've never seen a ball fly with a trajectory like that before. It was very exciting.
HOKU (GLOW)
Baseball is fun, isn't it?
HOKU
R...
PAA (FLUSH)
REALLY?

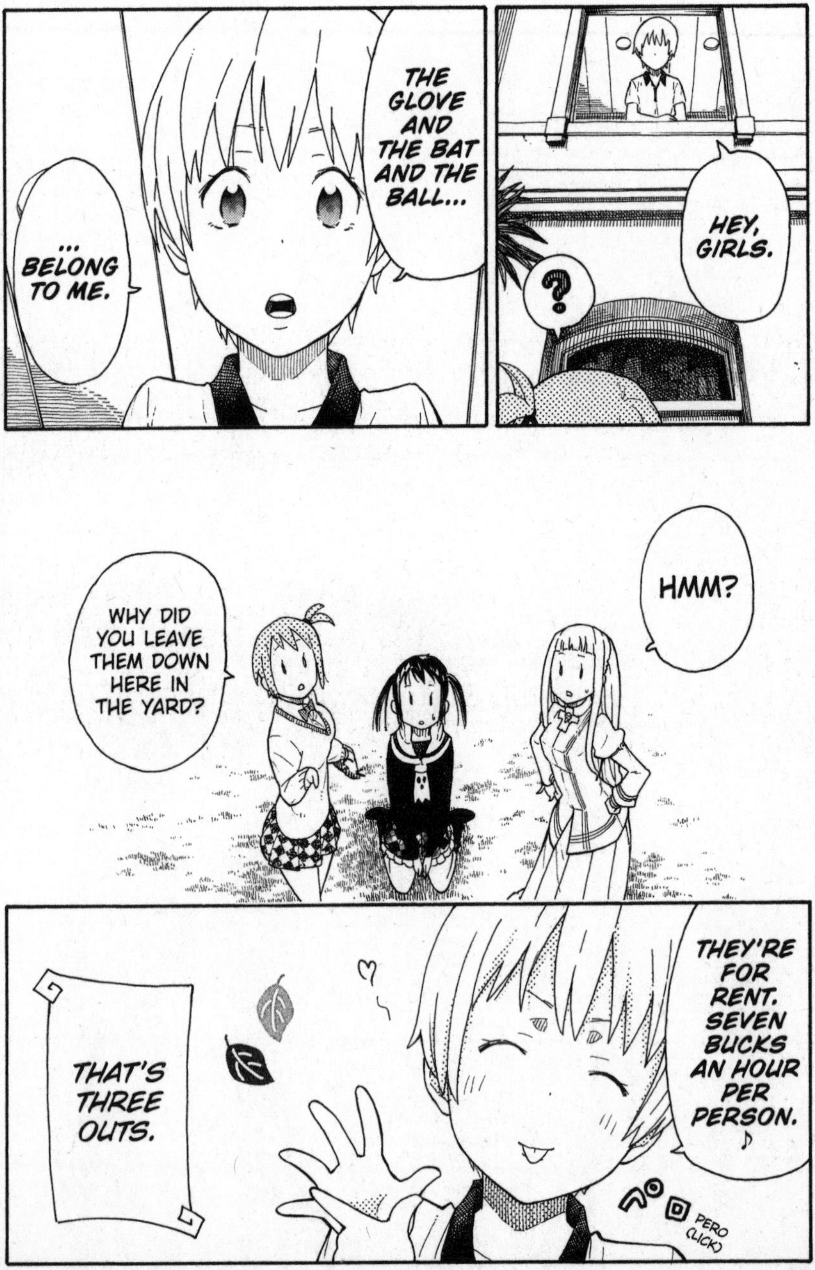
HEY, GIRLS.
?
THE GLOVE AND THE BAT AND THE BALL...
...BELONG TO ME.
HMM?
WHY DID YOU LEAVE THEM DOWN HERE IN THE YARD?
THEY'RE FOR RENT. SEVEN BUCKS AN HOUR PER PERSON. ♪
PERO (LICK)
THAT'S THREE OUTS.

SOUL EATER NOT!

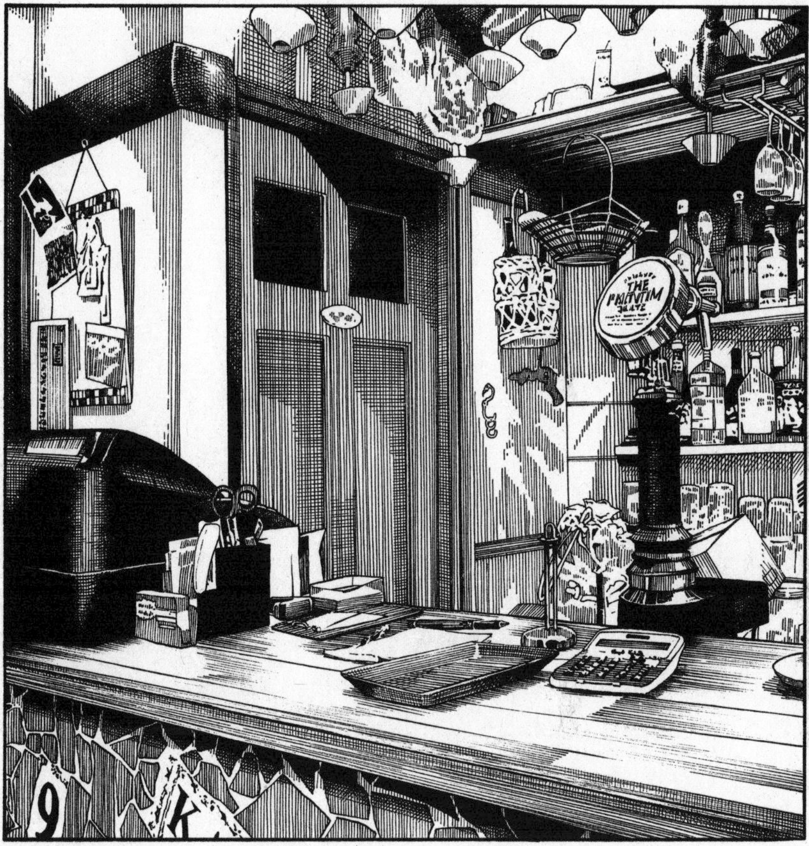

SOUL EATER

JOT

PART 5

BORED

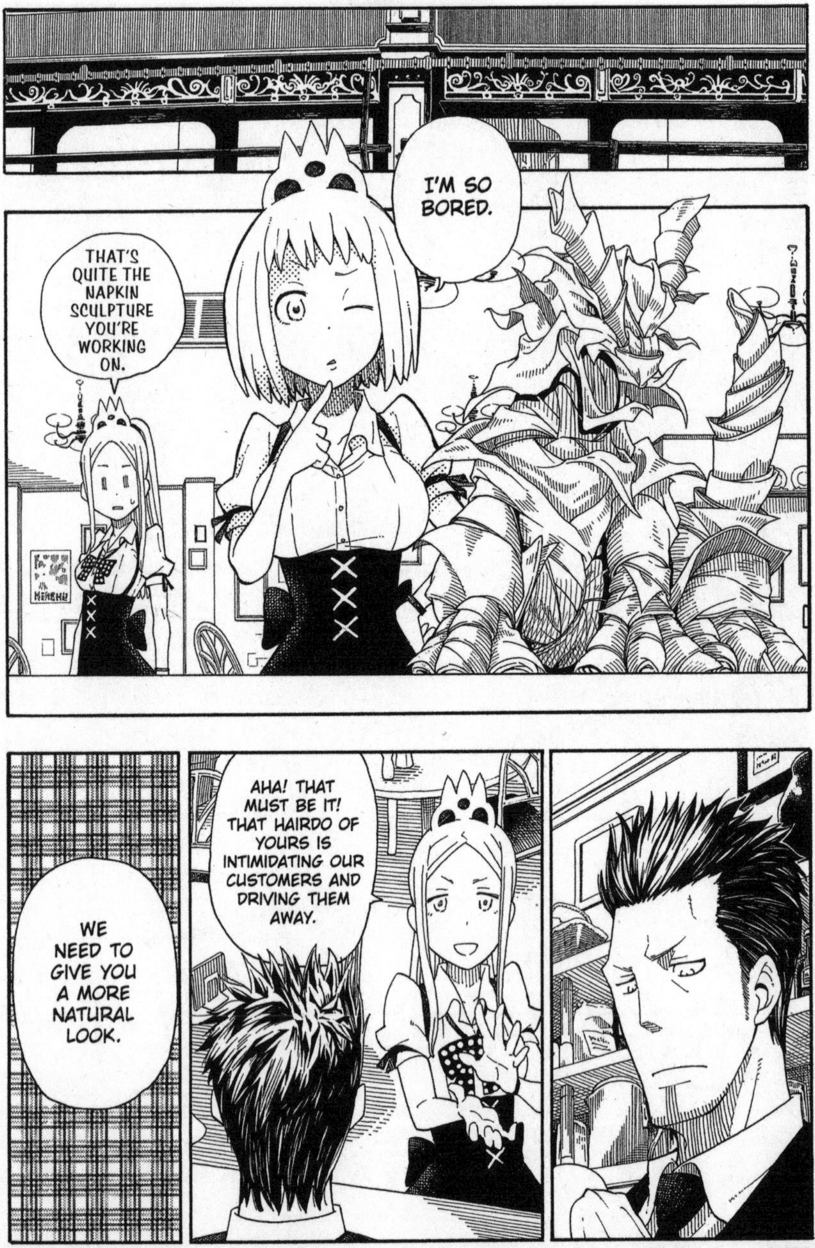

I'M SO BORED.
THAT'S QUITE THE NAPKIN SCULPTURE YOU'RE WORKING ON.
AHA! THAT MUST BE IT! THAT HAIRDO OF YOURS IS INTIMIDATING OUR CUSTOMERS AND DRIVING THEM AWAY.
WE NEED TO GIVE YOU A MORE NATURAL LOOK.

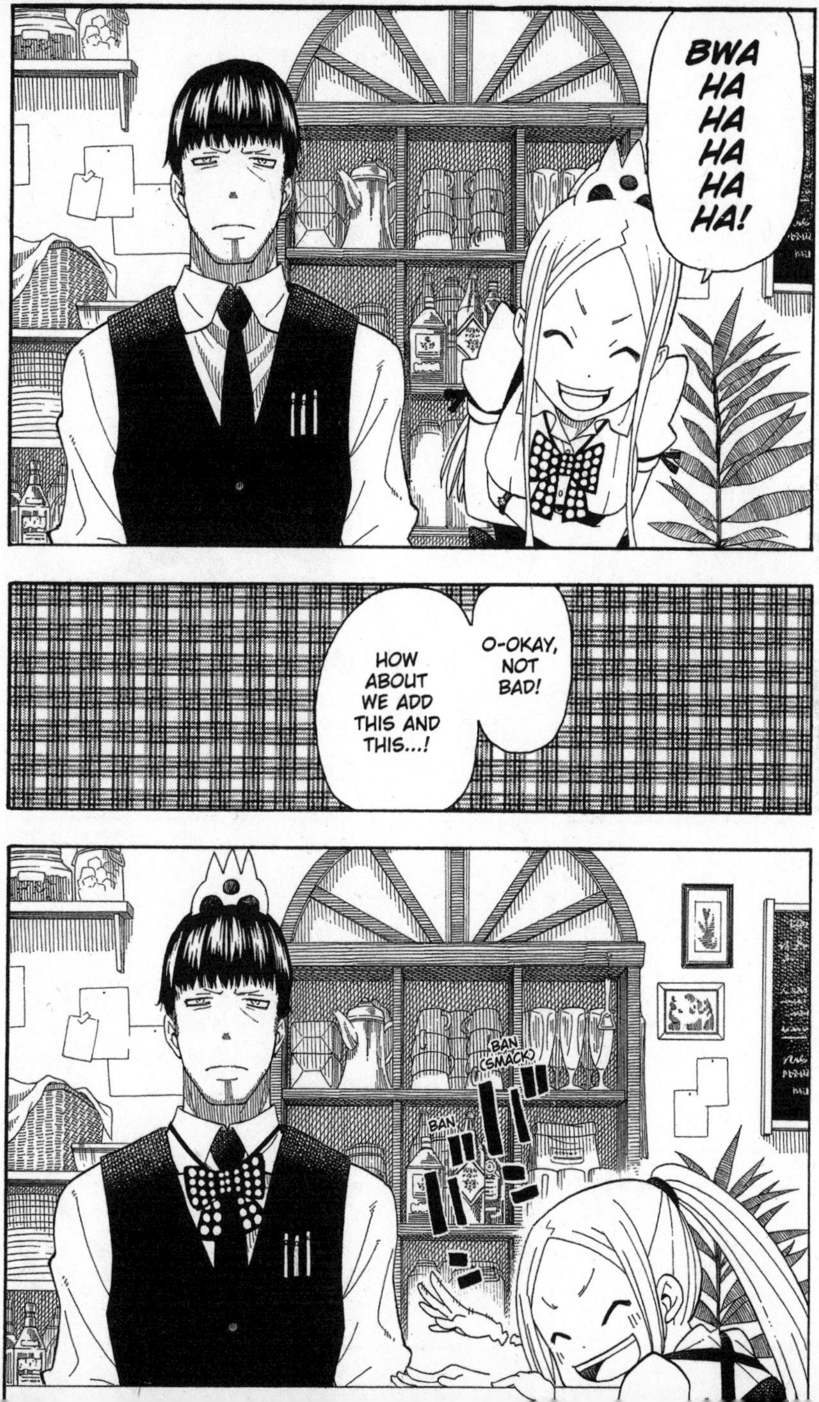
BWA HA HA HA HA HA!
O-OKAY, NOT BAD!
HOW ABOUT WE ADD THIS AND THIS...!
BAN (SMACK)
BAN

FINGER WHISTLING

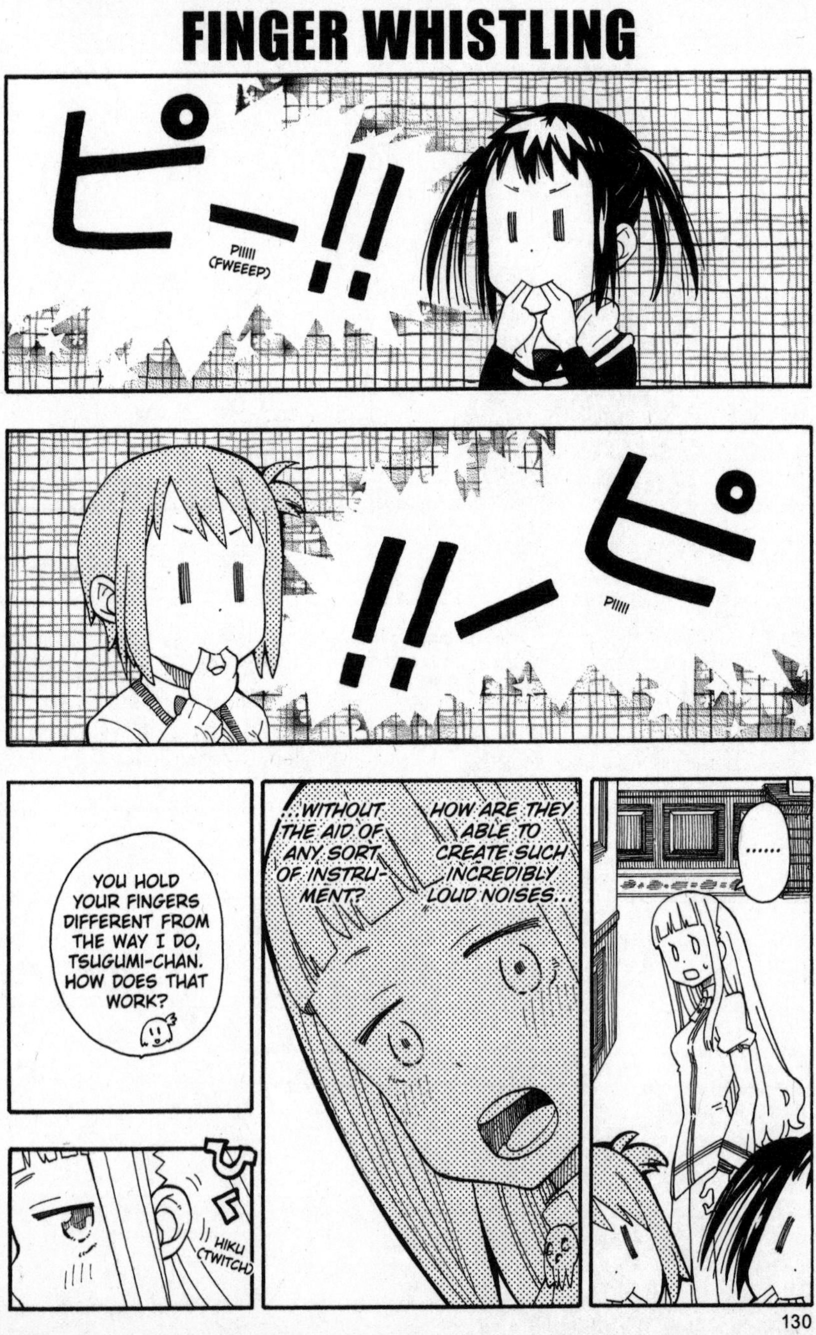
ピー!!
PIIII (FWEEEP)
ピー!!
PIIII
......
HOW ARE THEY ABLE TO CREATE SUCH INCREDIBLY LOUD NOISES...
...WITHOUT THE AID OF ANY SORT OF INSTRUMENT?
YOU HOLD YOUR FINGERS DIFFERENT FROM THE WAY I DO, TSUGUMI-CHAN. HOW DOES THAT WORK?
HIKU (TWITCH)

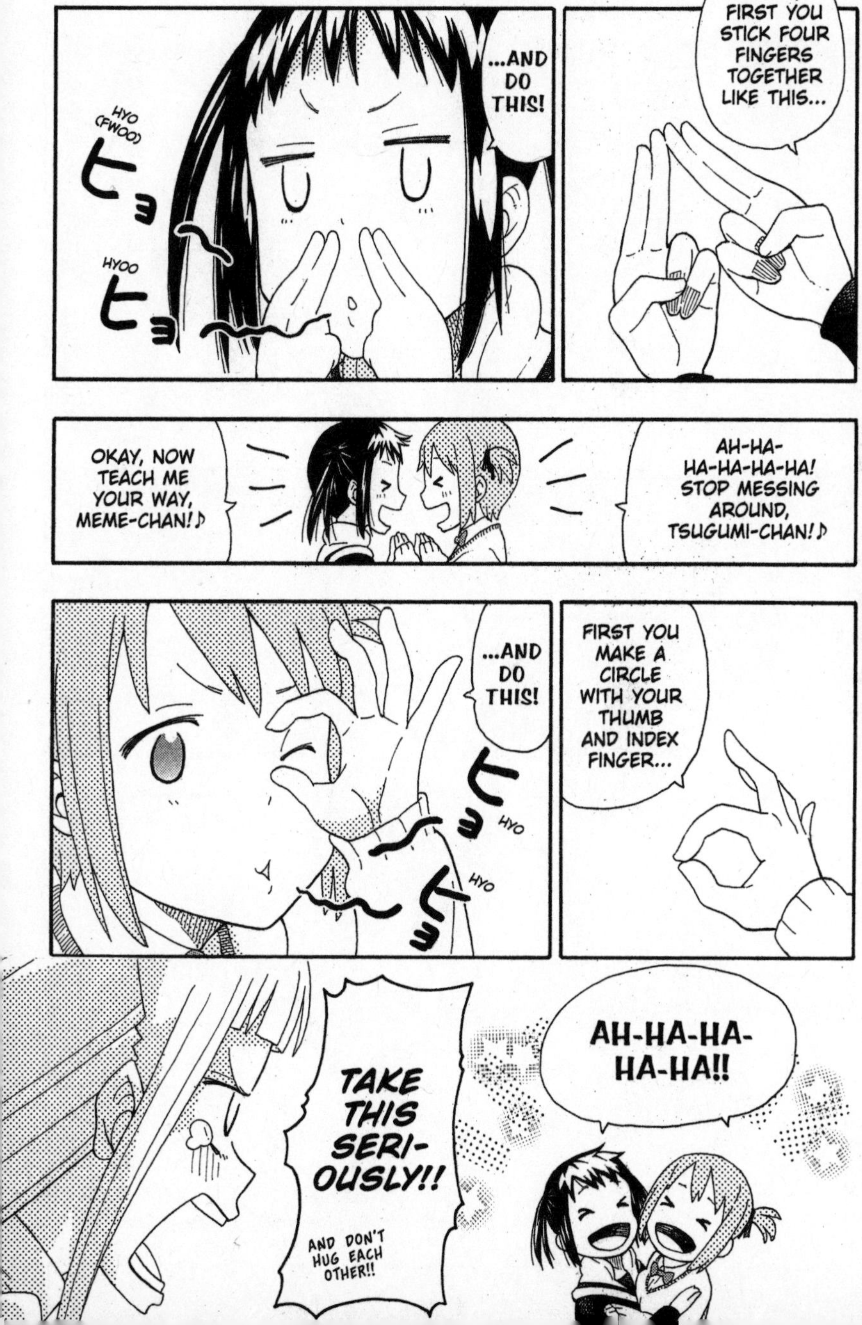
WELL, FIRST YOU STICK FOUR FINGERS TOGETHER LIKE THIS...
...AND DO THIS!
HYO (FWOO)
HYOO
AH-HA-HA-HA-HA-HA! STOP MESSING AROUND, TSUGUMI-CHAN!♪
OKAY, NOW TEACH ME YOUR WAY, MEME-CHAN!♪
FIRST YOU MAKE A CIRCLE WITH YOUR THUMB AND INDEX FINGER...
...AND DO THIS!
HYO
HYO
AH-HA-HA-HA-HA!!
TAKE THIS SERI-OUSLY!!
AND DON'T HUG EACH OTHER!!

TEXAS MASK

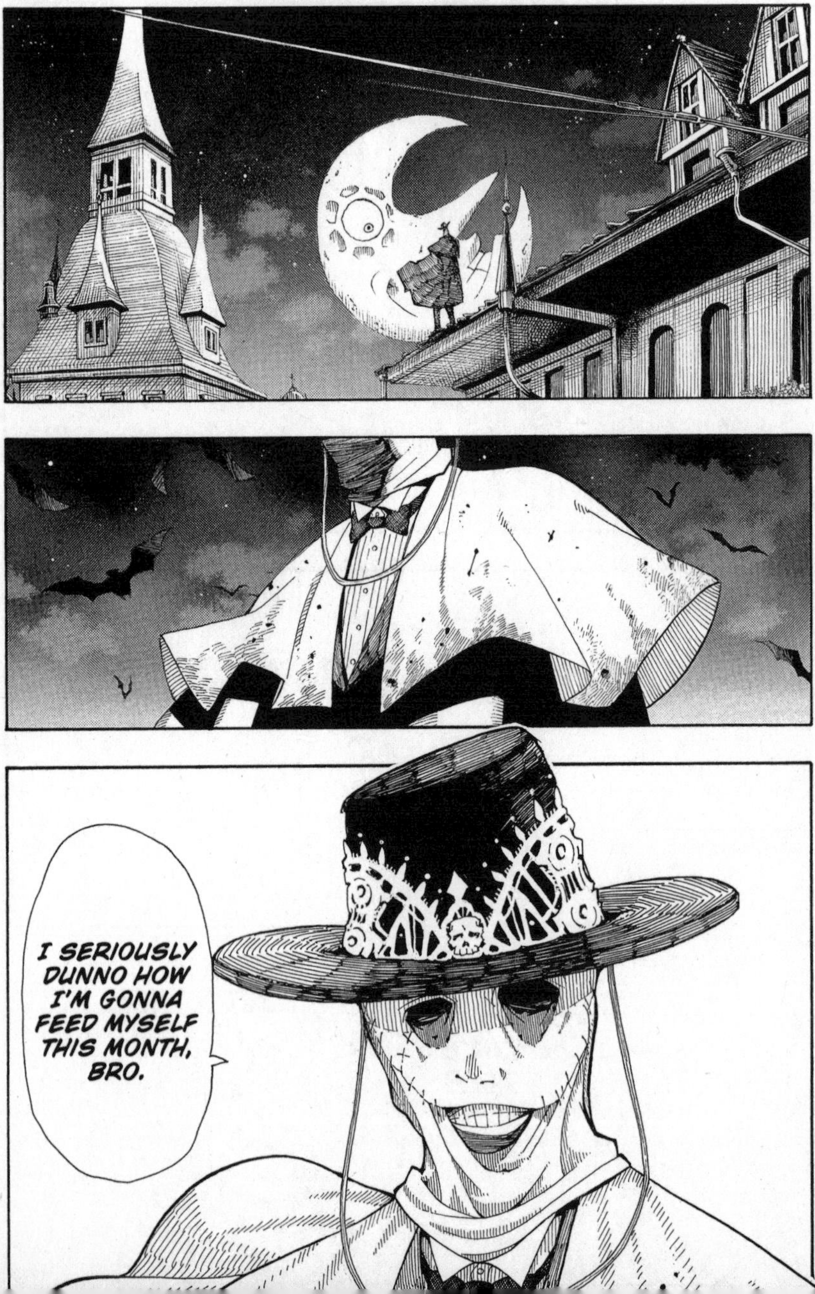
I SERIOUSLY DUNNO HOW I'M GONNA FEED MYSELF THIS MONTH, BRO.

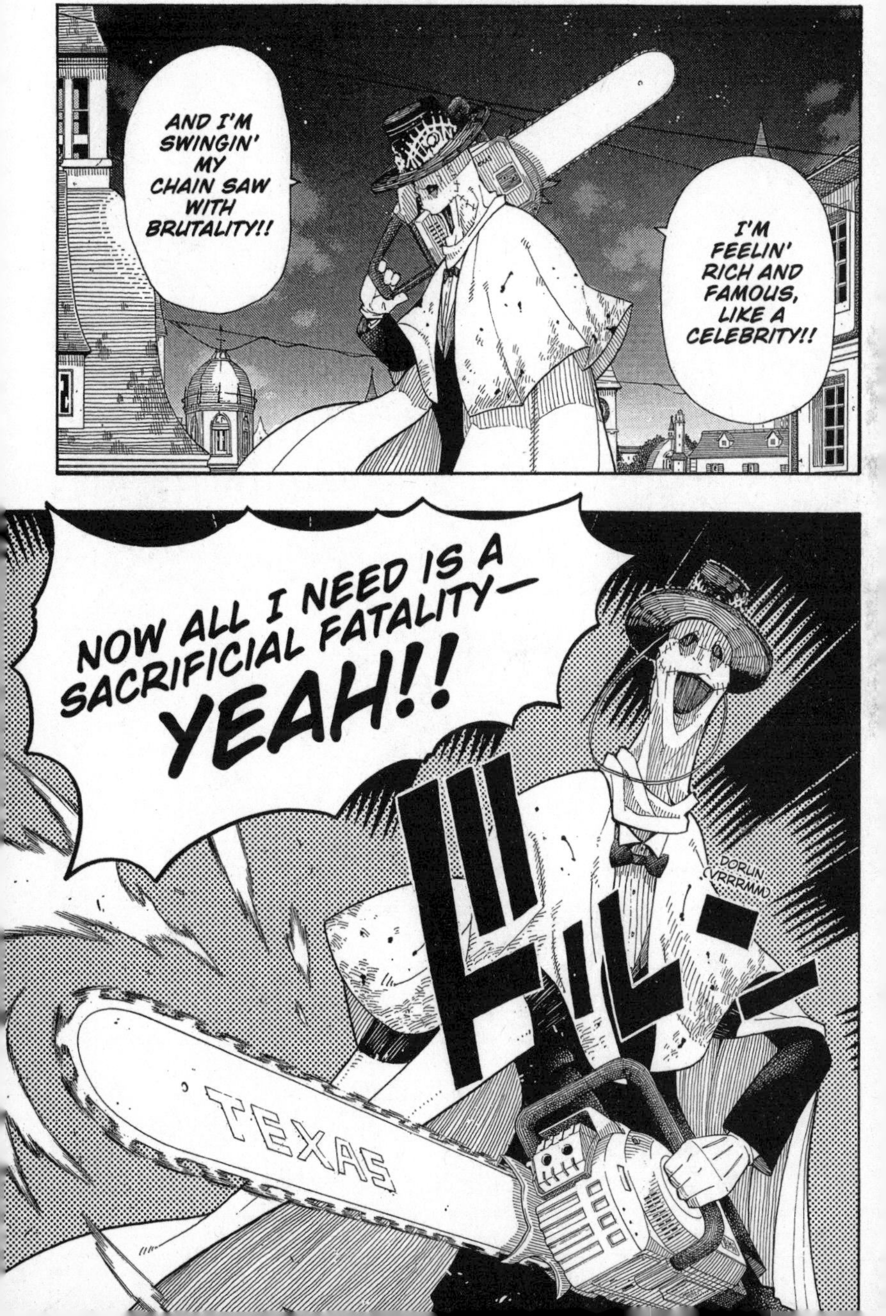
I'M FEELIN' RICH AND FAMOUS, LIKE A CELEBRITY!!
AND I'M SWINGIN' MY CHAIN SAW WITH BRUTALITY!!
NOW ALL I NEED IS A SACRIFICIAL FATALITY—YEAH!!
DORUN (VRRRMM)
TEXAS

READY FOR BUSINESS

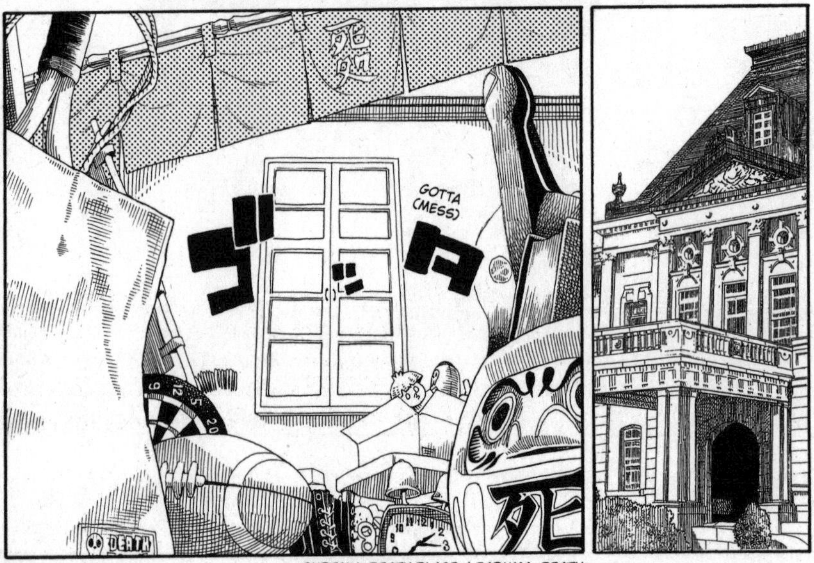
ゴタ
GOTTA (MESS)

CURTAIN: DEATH PLACE / DARUMA: DEATH

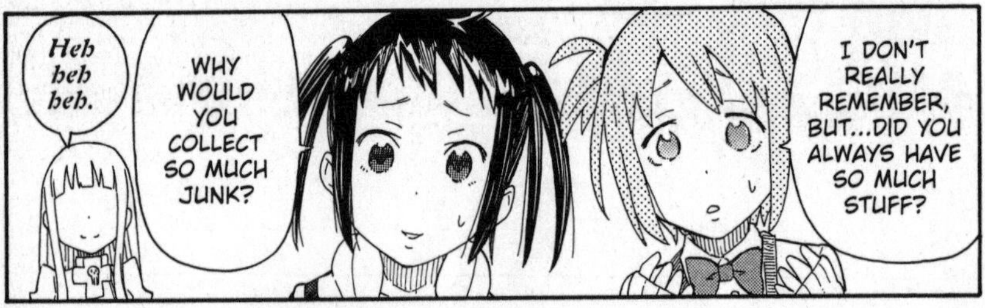
I DON'T REALLY REMEMBER, BUT...DID YOU ALWAYS HAVE SO MUCH STUFF?
WHY WOULD YOU COLLECT SO MUCH JUNK?
Heh heh heh.

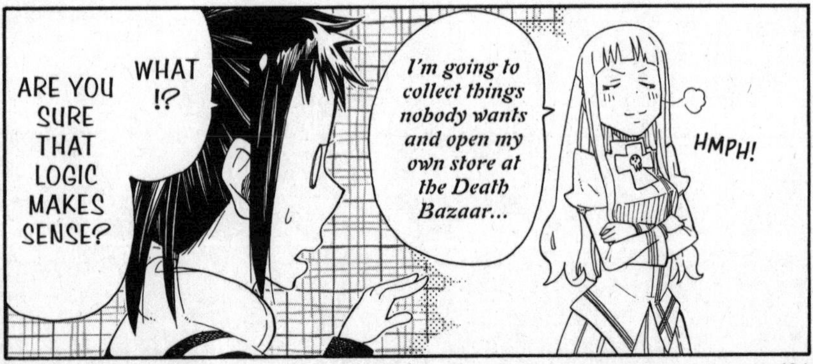
HMPH!
I'm going to collect things nobody wants and open my own store at the Death Bazaar...
WHAT!?
ARE YOU SURE THAT LOGIC MAKES SENSE?

SOUL EATER NOT!

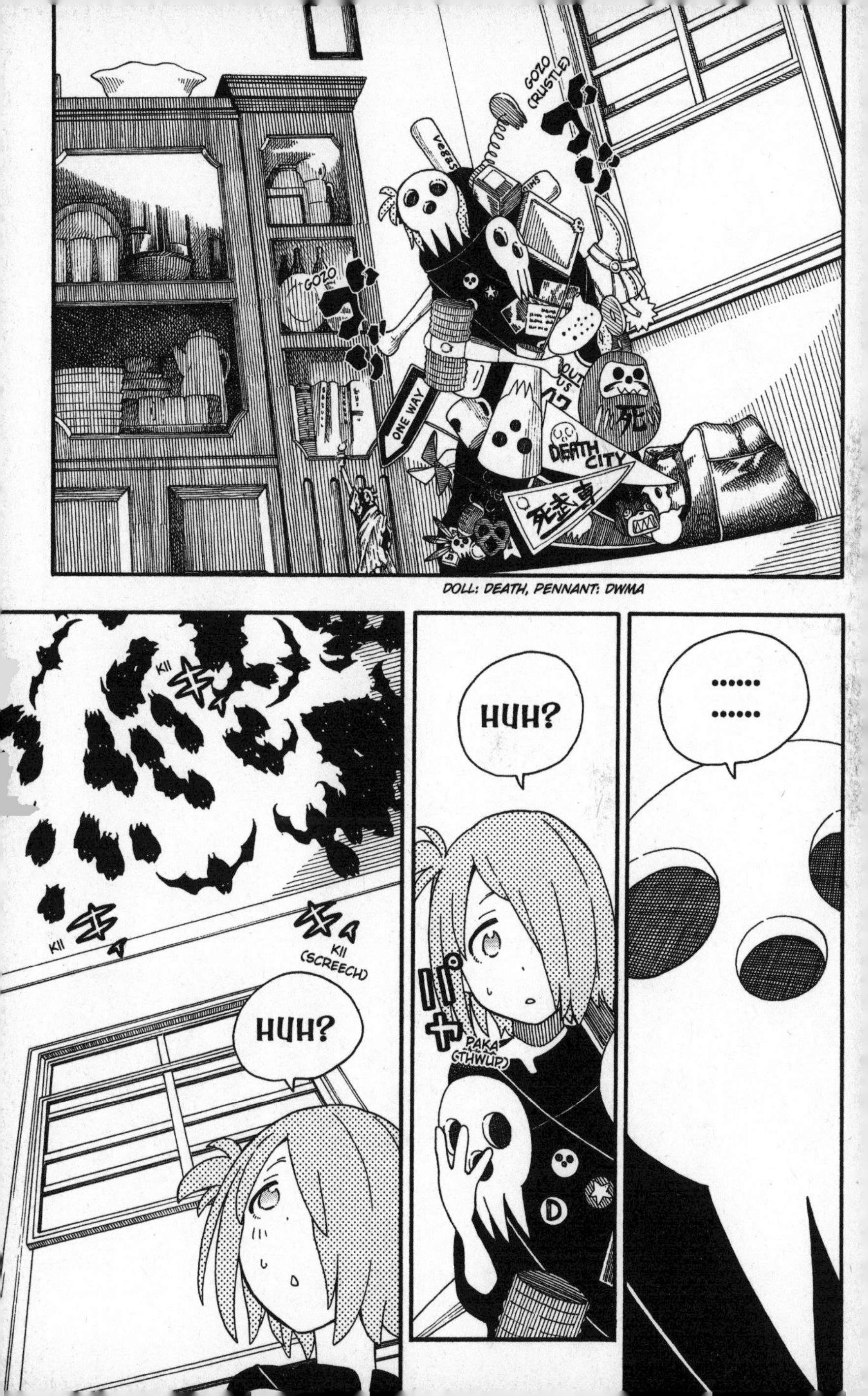
GOZO (RUSTLE)
VEGAS
GOZO
ONE WAY
DEATH CITY
DOLL: DEATH, PENNANT: DWMA
……
……
HUH?
PAKA (THWUP)
KII
KII
KII (SCREECH)
HUH?

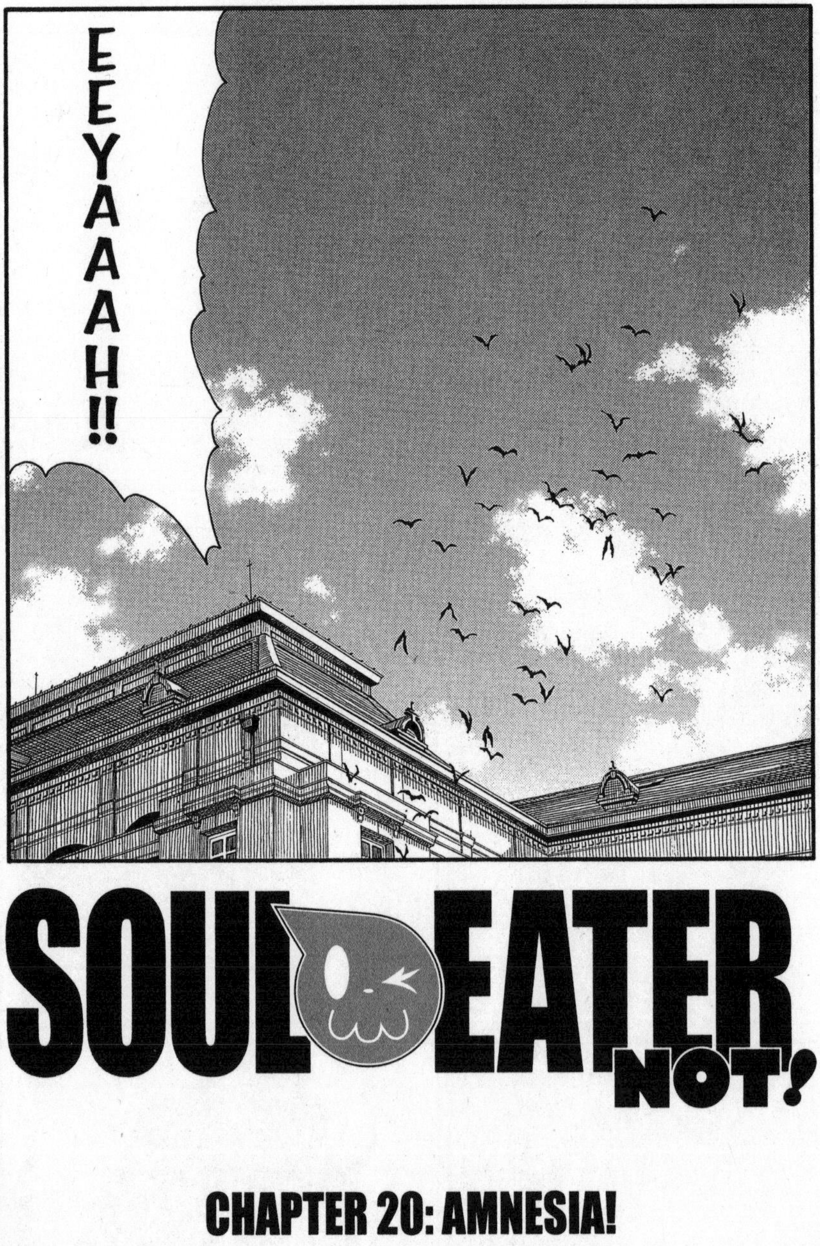
EEYAAAH!!

SOUL EATER NOT!

CHAPTER 20: AMNESIA!

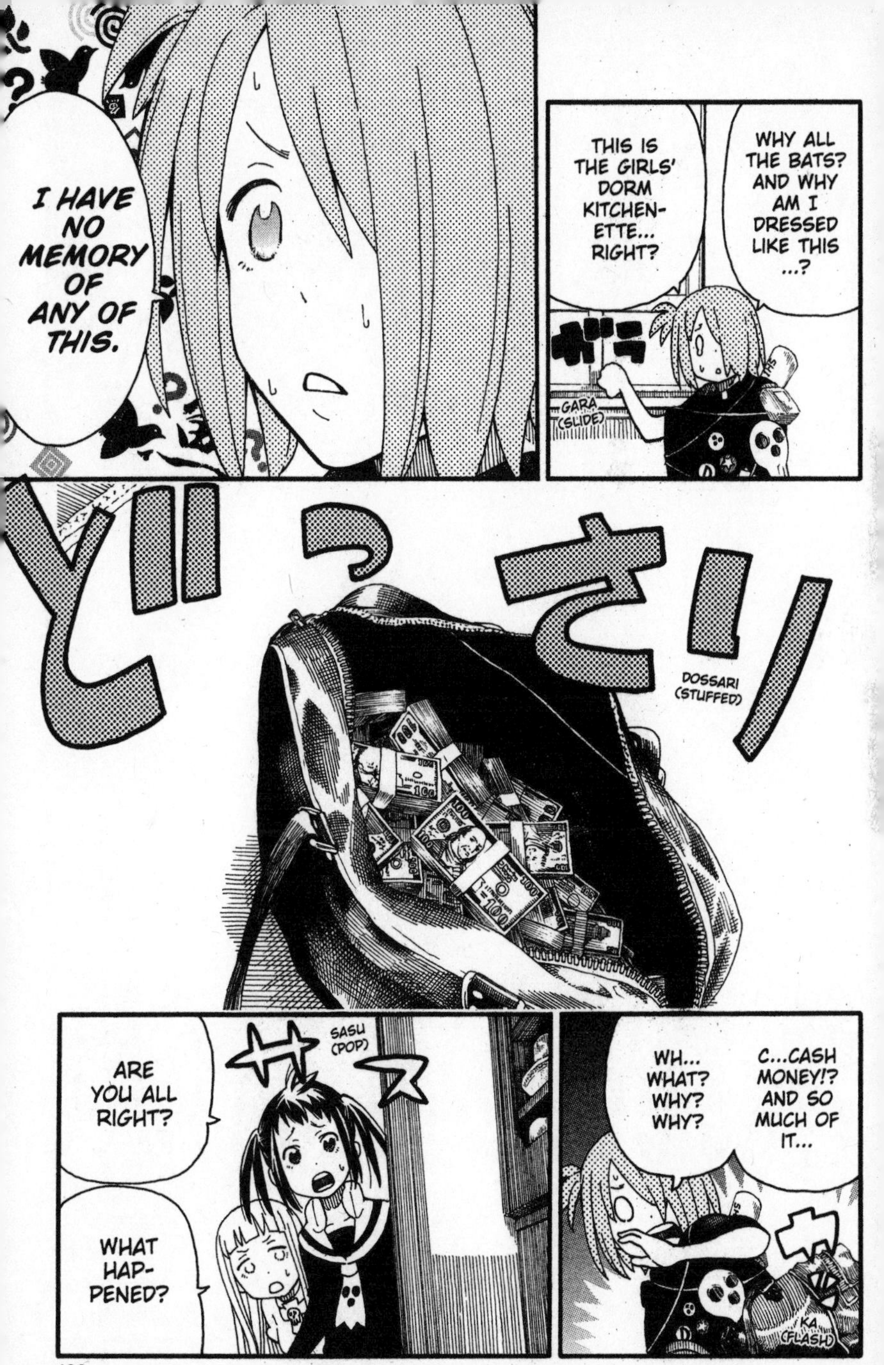
WHY ALL THE BATS? AND WHY AM I DRESSED LIKE THIS ...?
THIS IS THE GIRLS' DORM KITCHEN-ETTE... RIGHT?
GARA (SLIDE)
I HAVE NO MEMORY OF ANY OF THIS.
どっさり
DOSSARI (STUFFED)
C...CASH MONEY!? AND SO MUCH OF IT...
WH... WHAT? WHY? WHY?
KA (FLASH)
SASU (POP)
ARE YOU ALL RIGHT?
WHAT HAP-PENED?

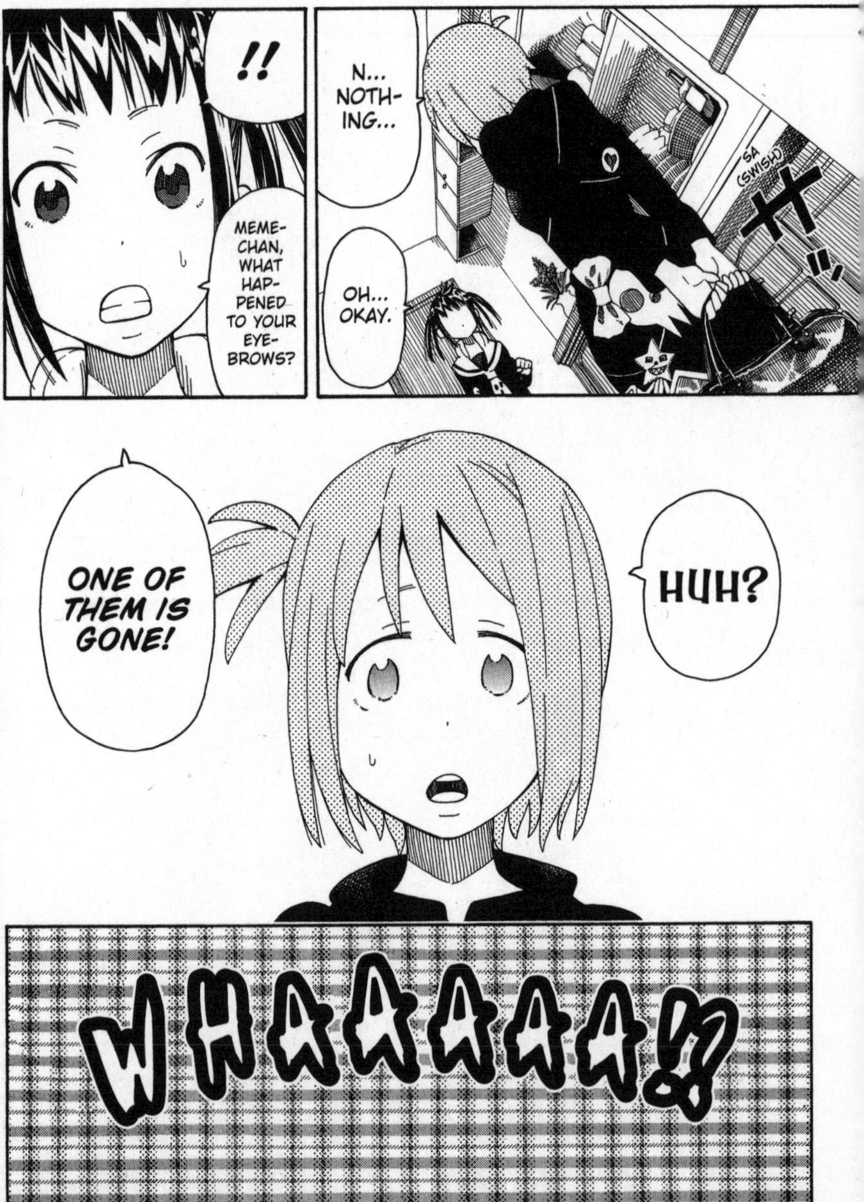
SA (SWISH)
N... NOTHING...
OH... OKAY.
!!
MEME-CHAN, WHAT HAPPENED TO YOUR EYE-BROWS?
HUH?
ONE OF THEM IS GONE!
WHAAAAAA!!

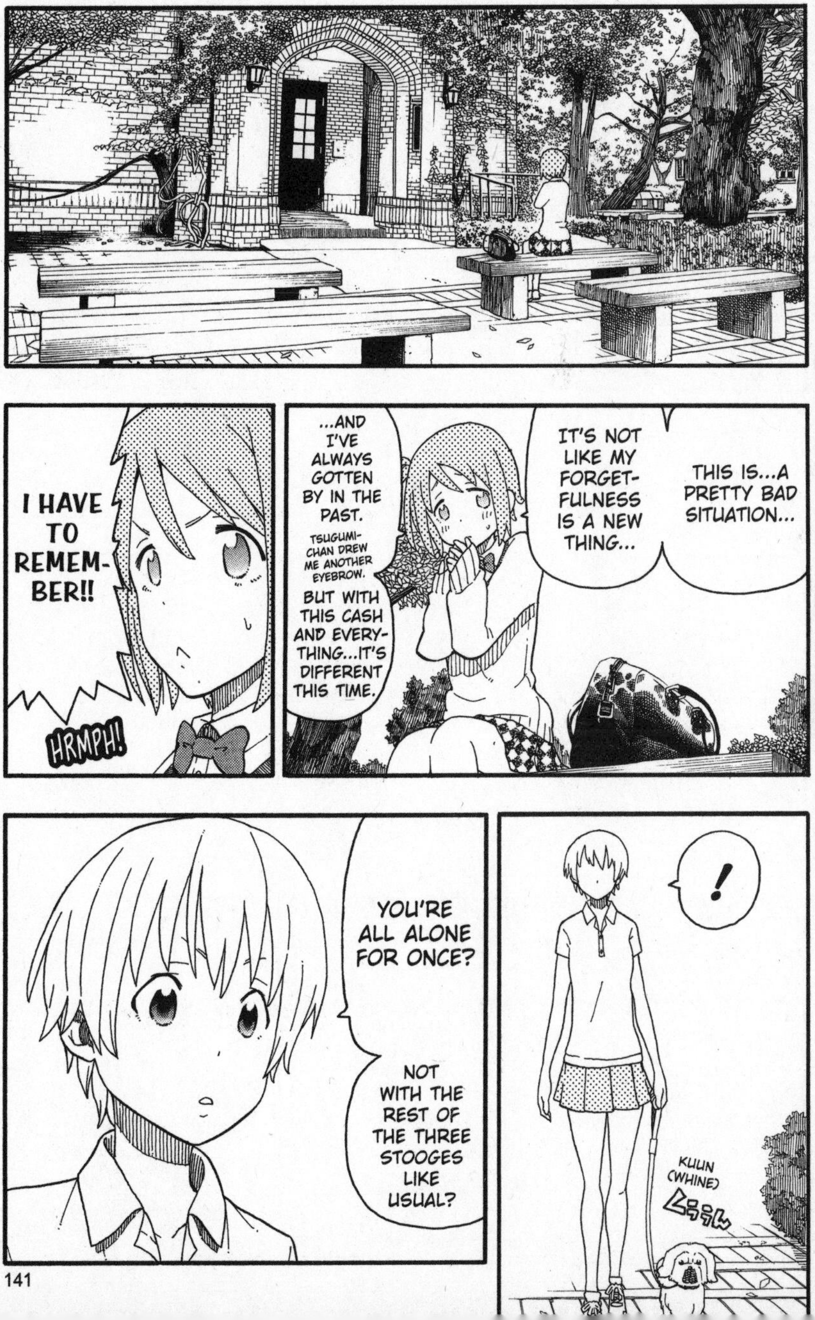

THIS IS...A PRETTY BAD SITUATION...
IT'S NOT LIKE MY FORGET-FULNESS IS A NEW THING...
...AND I'VE ALWAYS GOTTEN BY IN THE PAST.
TSUGUMI-CHAN DREW ME ANOTHER EYEBROW.
BUT WITH THIS CASH AND EVERY-THING...IT'S DIFFERENT THIS TIME.
I HAVE TO REMEM-BER!!
HRMPH!
!
KUUN (WHINE)
YOU'RE ALL ALONE FOR ONCE?
NOT WITH THE REST OF THE THREE STOOGES LIKE USUAL?

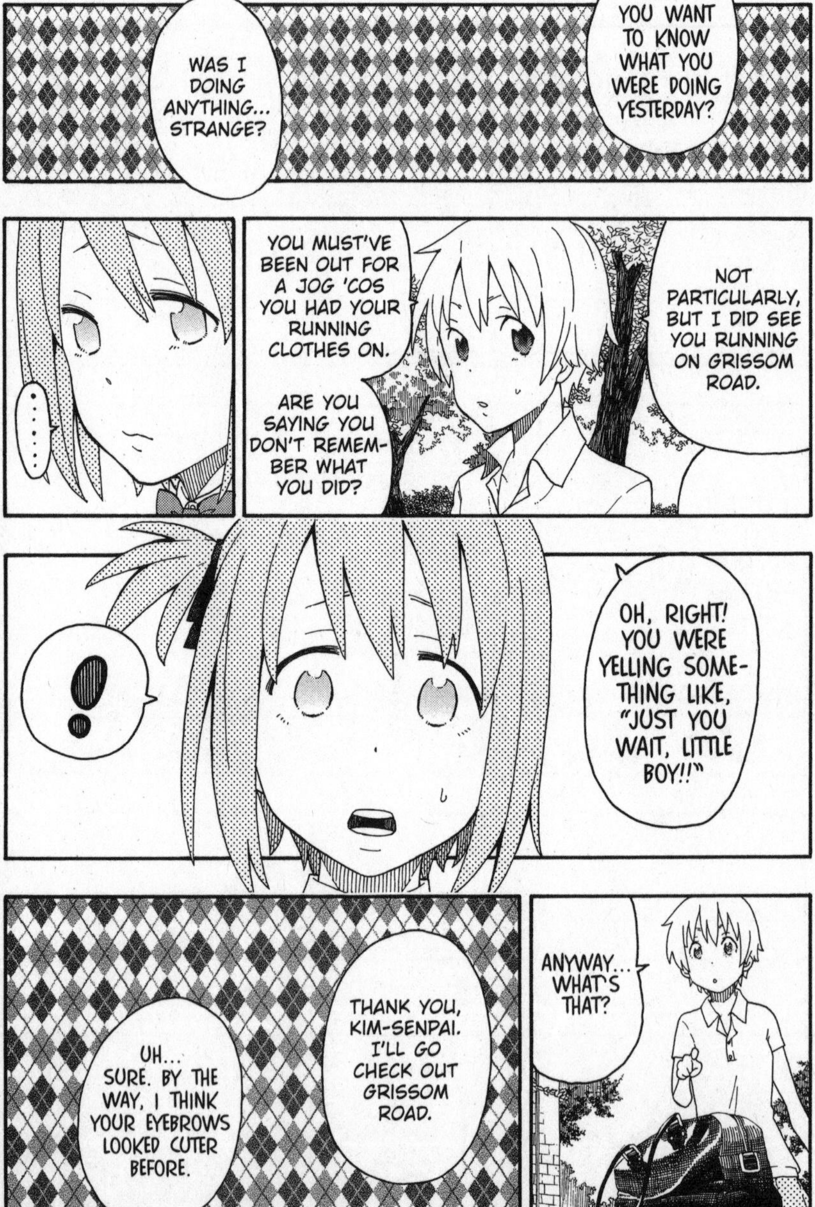
HUH!? YOU WANT TO KNOW WHAT YOU WERE DOING YESTERDAY?
WAS I DOING ANYTHING... STRANGE?
NOT PARTICULARLY, BUT I DID SEE YOU RUNNING ON GRISSOM ROAD.
YOU MUST'VE BEEN OUT FOR A JOG 'COS YOU HAD YOUR RUNNING CLOTHES ON.
ARE YOU SAYING YOU DON'T REMEMBER WHAT YOU DID?
......
OH, RIGHT! YOU WERE YELLING SOMETHING LIKE, "JUST YOU WAIT, LITTLE BOY!!"
!
ANYWAY... WHAT'S THAT?
THANK YOU, KIM-SENPAI. I'LL GO CHECK OUT GRISSOM ROAD.
UH... SURE. BY THE WAY, I THINK YOUR EYEBROWS LOOKED CUTER BEFORE.

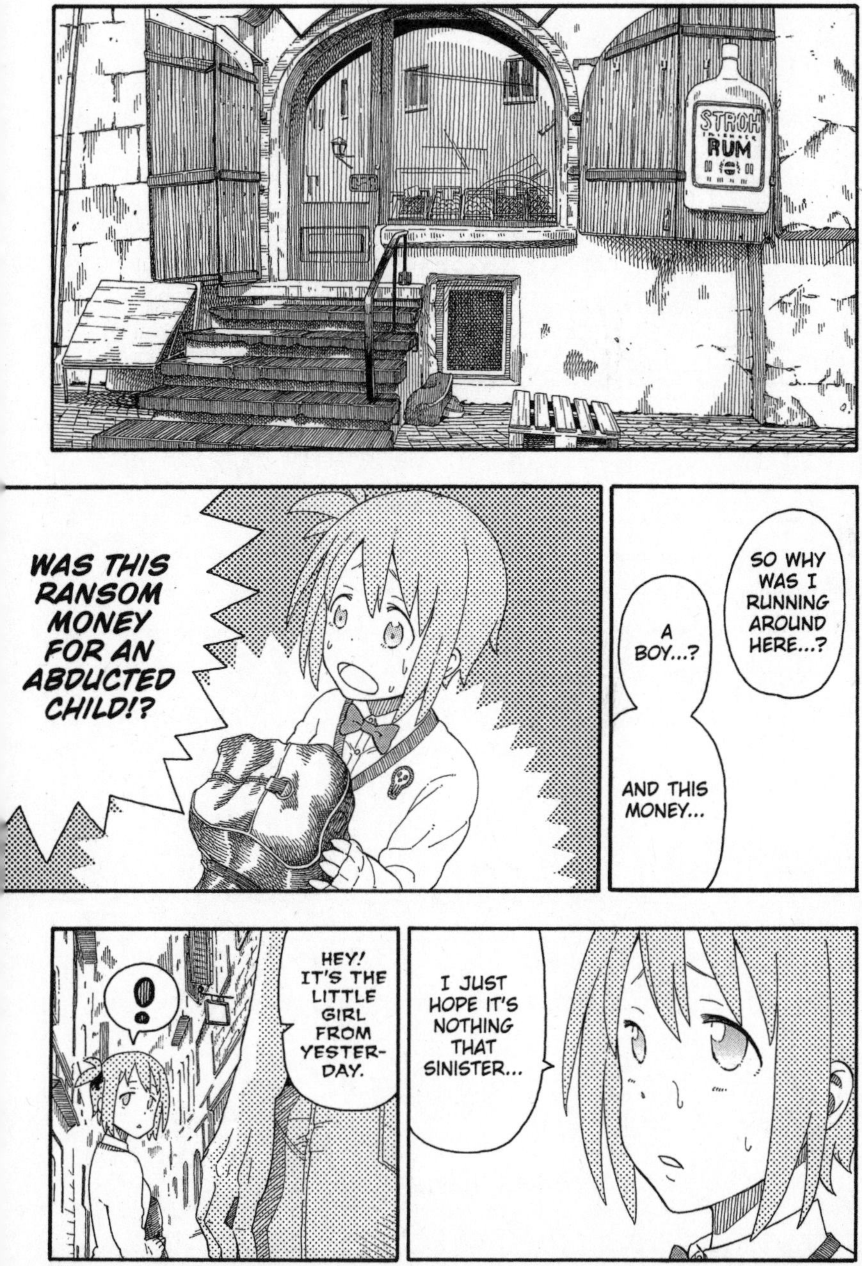
STROH
RUM
SO WHY WAS I RUNNING AROUND HERE...?
A BOY...?
AND THIS MONEY...
WAS THIS RANSOM MONEY FOR AN ABDUCTED CHILD!?
I JUST HOPE IT'S NOTHING THAT SINISTER...
HEY! IT'S THE LITTLE GIRL FROM YESTER-DAY.
!

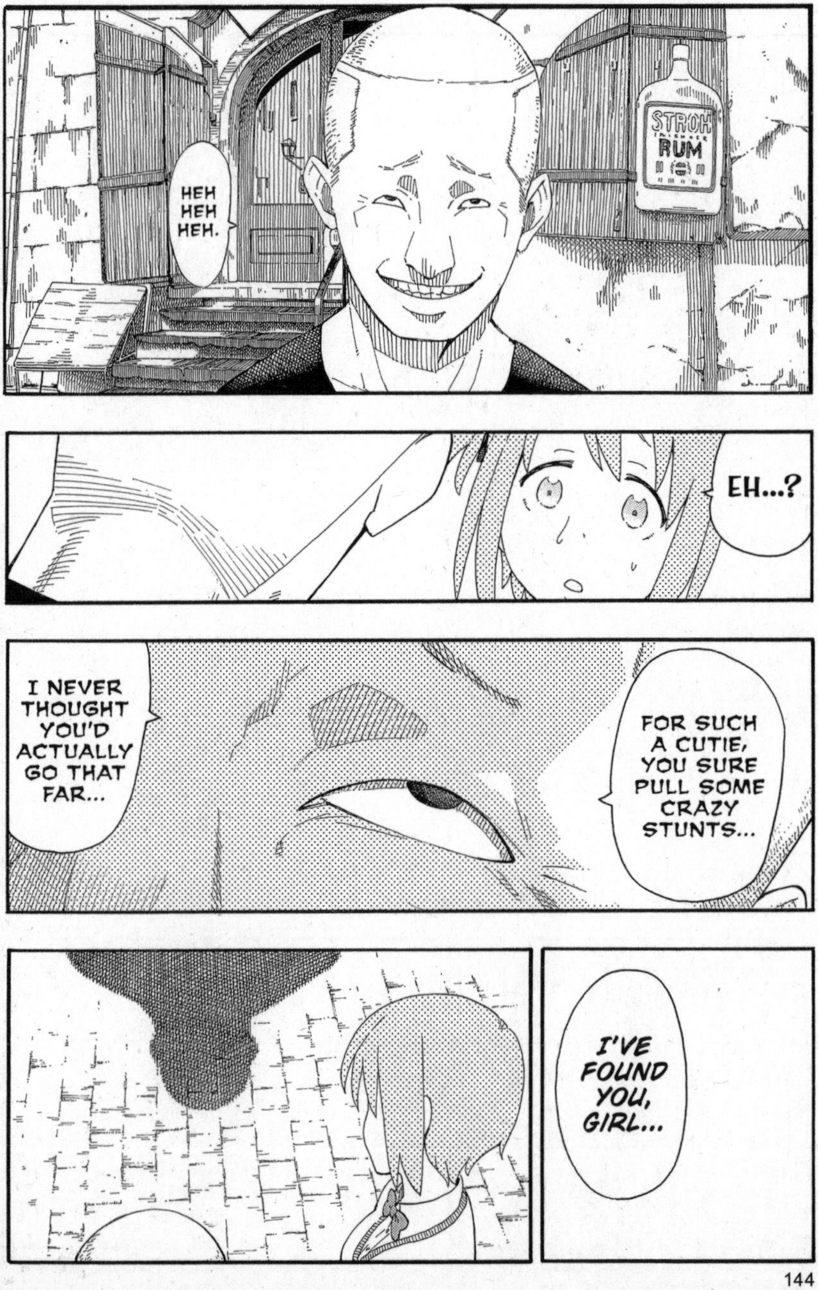
HEH HEH HEH.
STROH
RUM
EH...?
FOR SUCH A CUTIE, YOU SURE PULL SOME CRAZY STUNTS...
I NEVER THOUGHT YOU'D ACTUALLY GO THAT FAR...
I'VE FOUND YOU, GIRL...

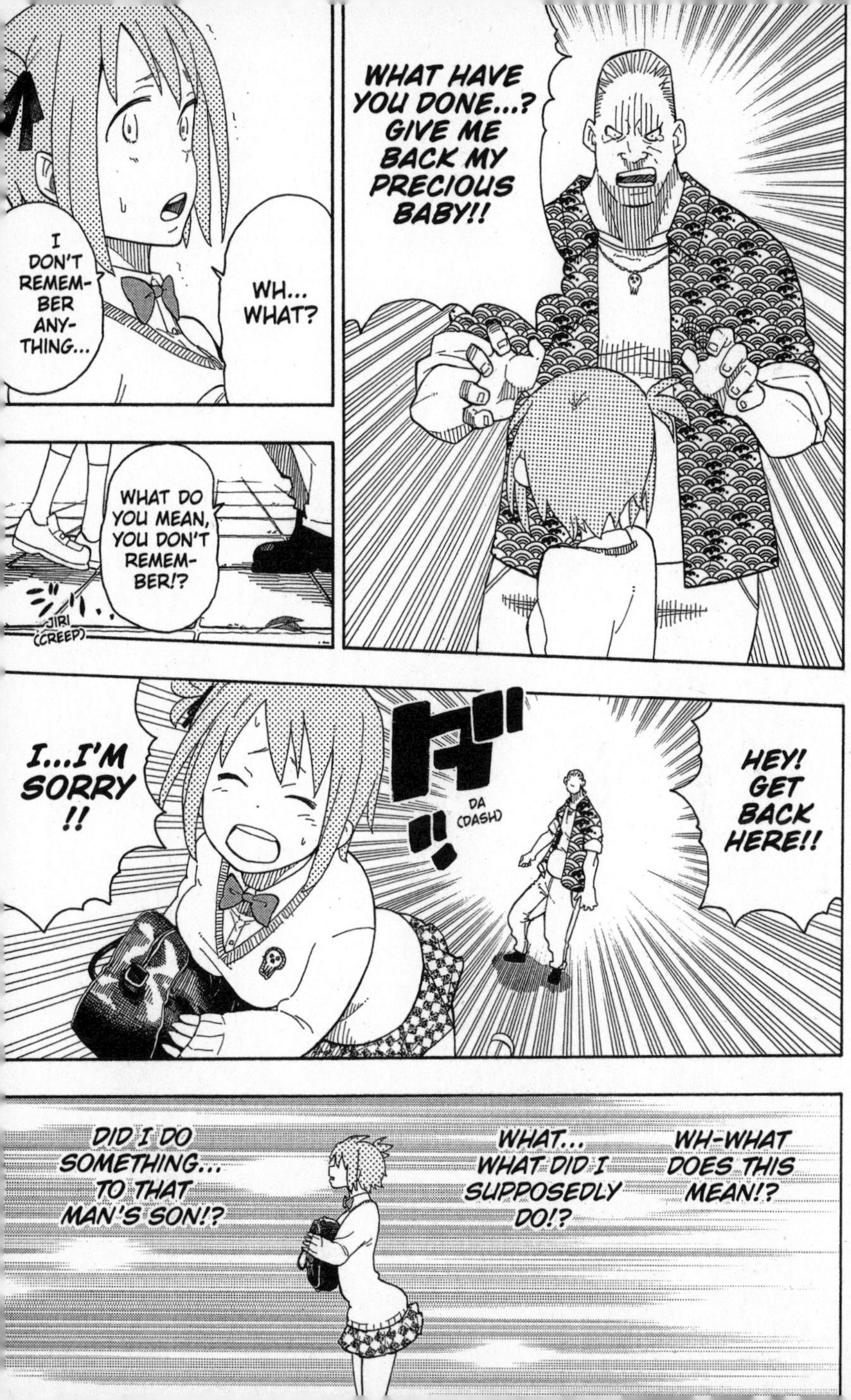
WHAT HAVE YOU DONE...? GIVE ME BACK MY PRECIOUS BABY!!
WH... WHAT?
I DON'T REMEMBER ANYTHING...
WHAT DO YOU MEAN, YOU DON'T REMEMBER!?
JIRI (CREEP)
HEY! GET BACK HERE!!
DA (DASH)
I...I'M SORRY!!
WH-WHAT DOES THIS MEAN!?
WHAT... WHAT DID I SUPPOSEDLY DO!?
DID I DO SOMETHING... TO THAT MAN'S SON!?

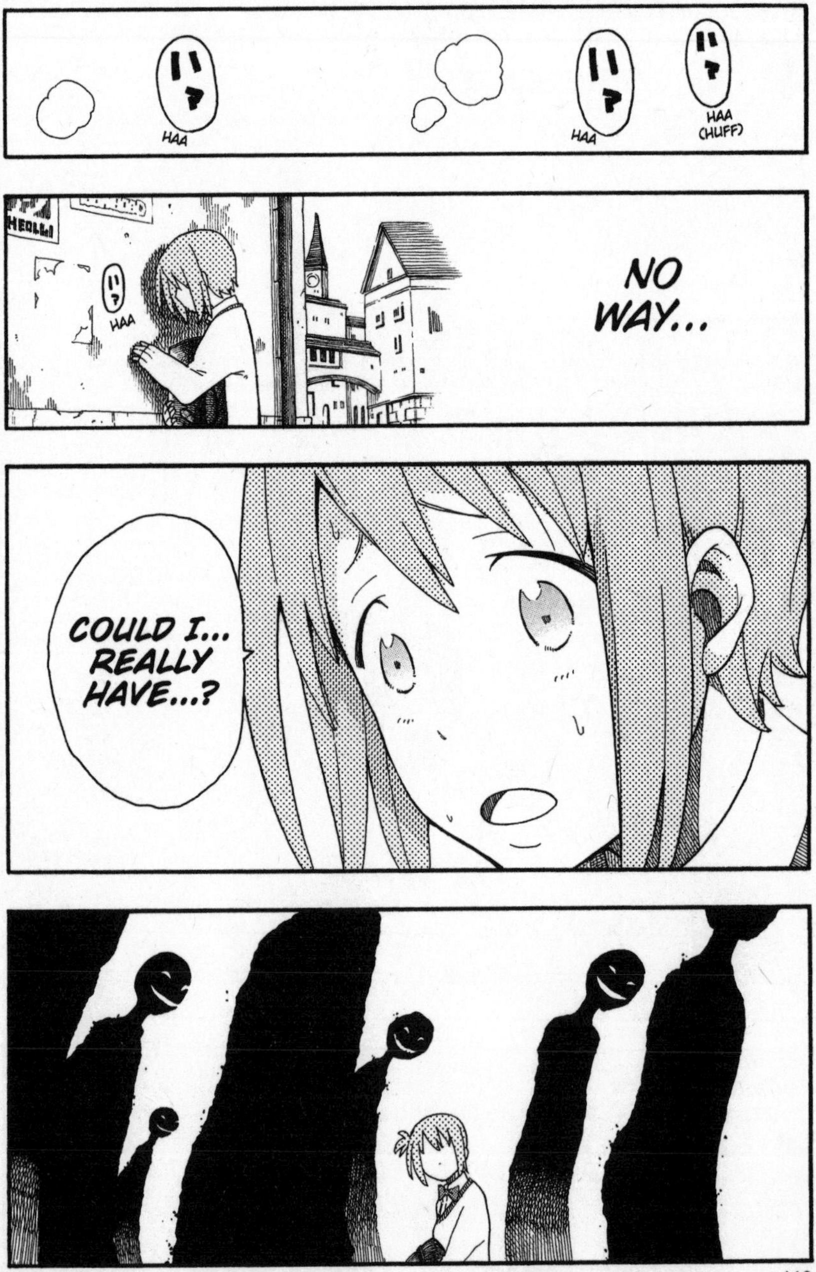
ハァ
HAA (HUFF)
ハァ
HAA
ハァ
HAA
NO WAY...
ハァ
HAA
COULD I... REALLY HAVE...?

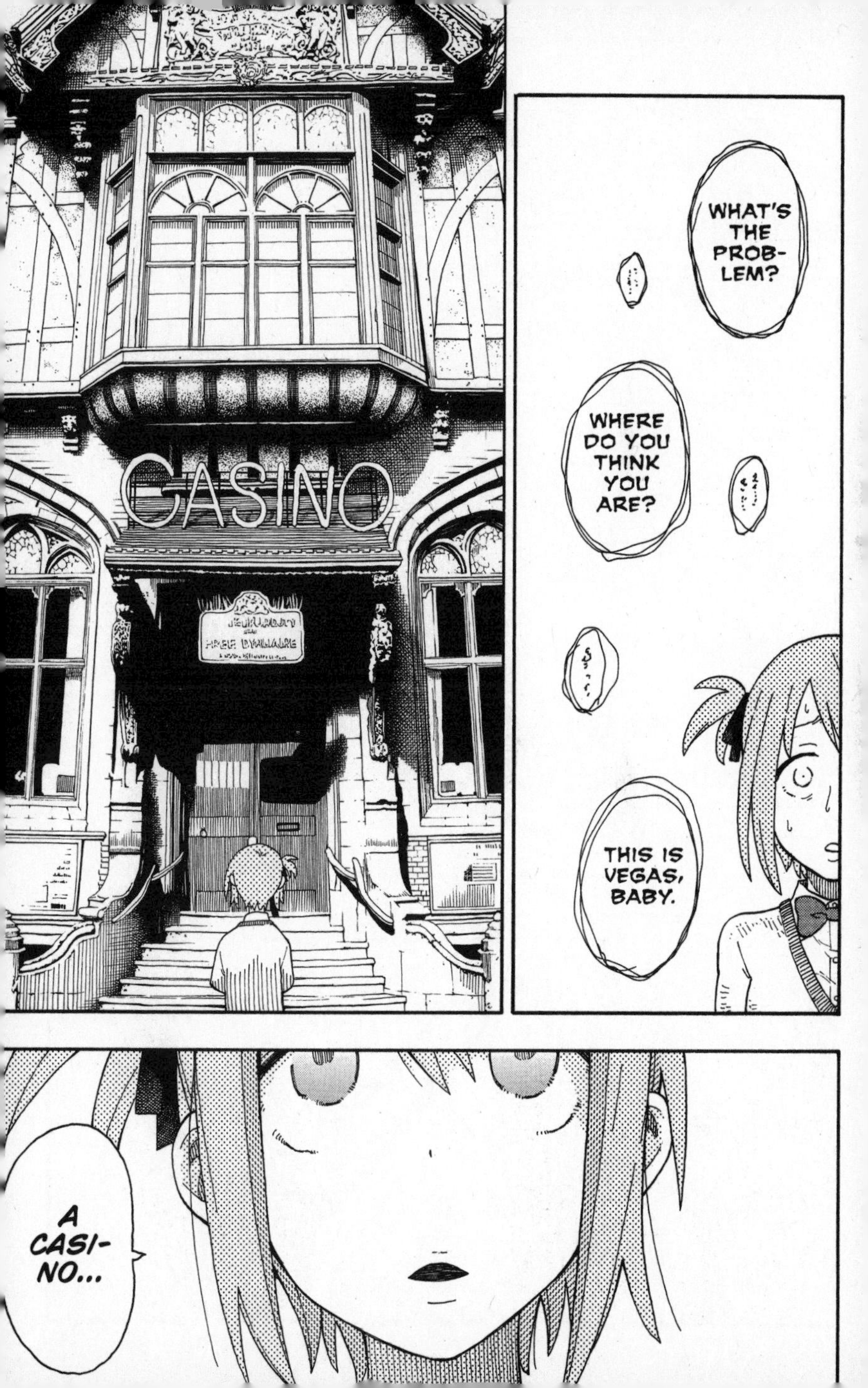
WHAT'S THE PROB-LEM?
WHERE DO YOU THINK YOU ARE?
THIS IS VEGAS, BABY.
CASINO
A CASI-NO...

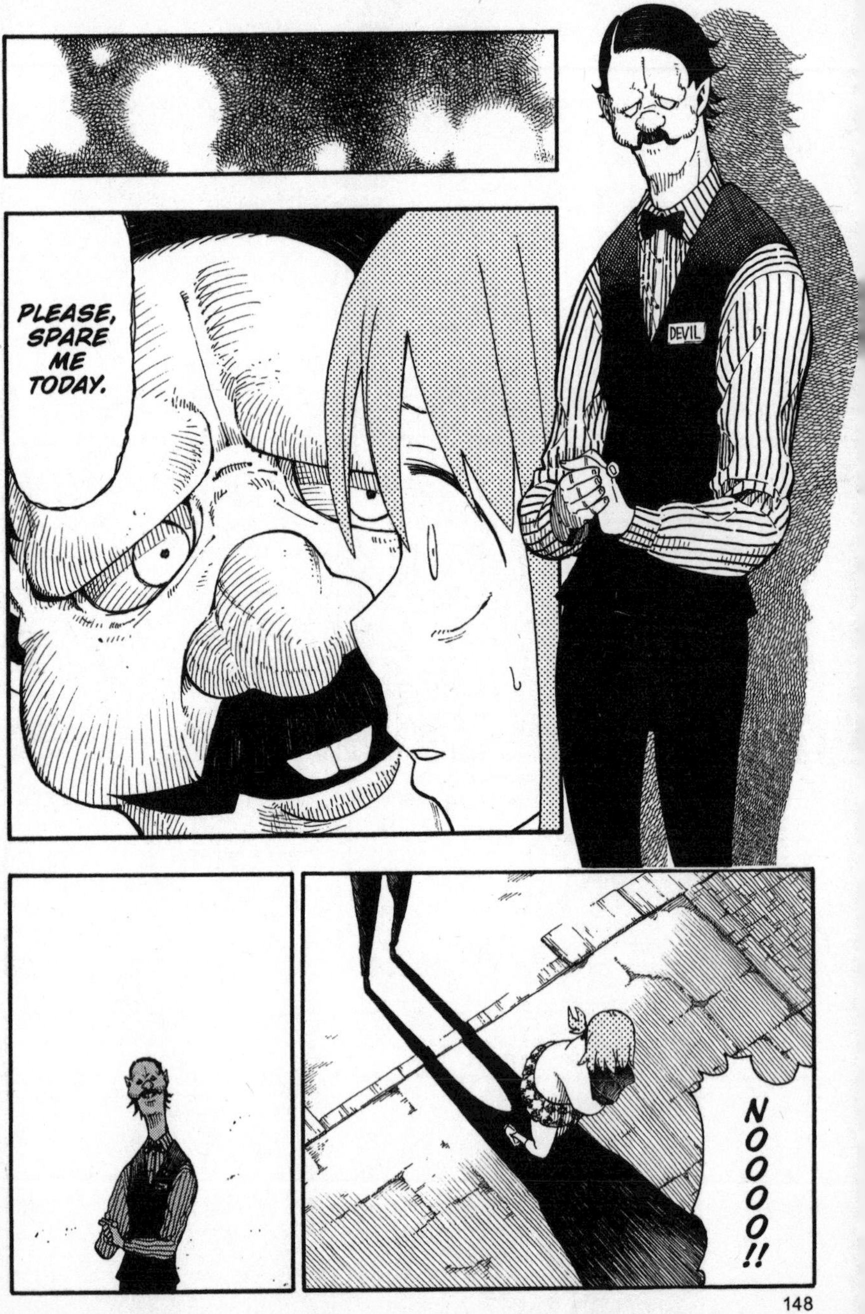
DEVIL
PLEASE, SPARE ME TODAY.
NOOOOO!!

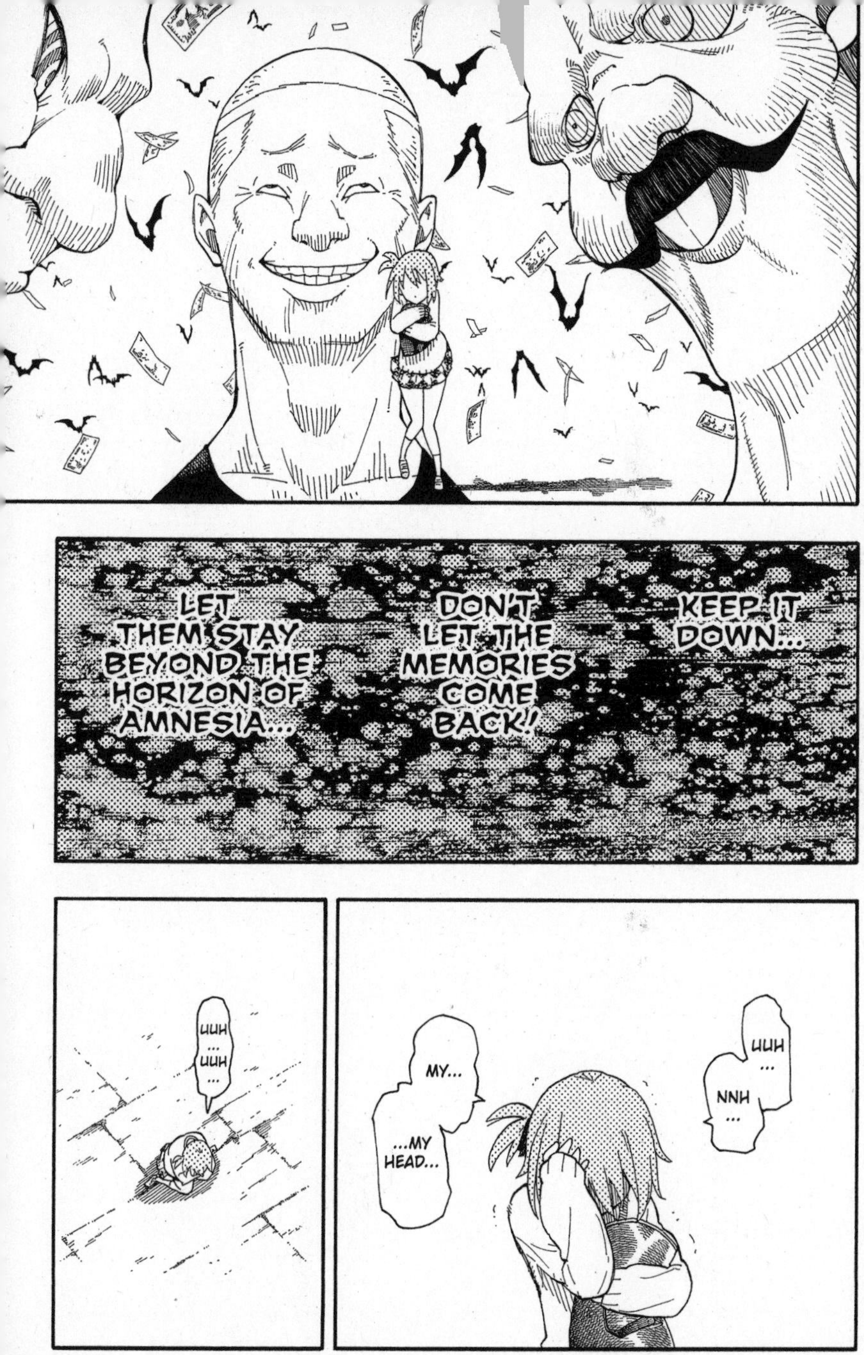
KEEP IT DOWN...
DON'T LET THE MEMORIES COME BACK!
LET THEM STAY BEYOND THE HORIZON OF AMNESIA...
UUH... NNH...
MY... ...MY HEAD...
UUH... UUH...

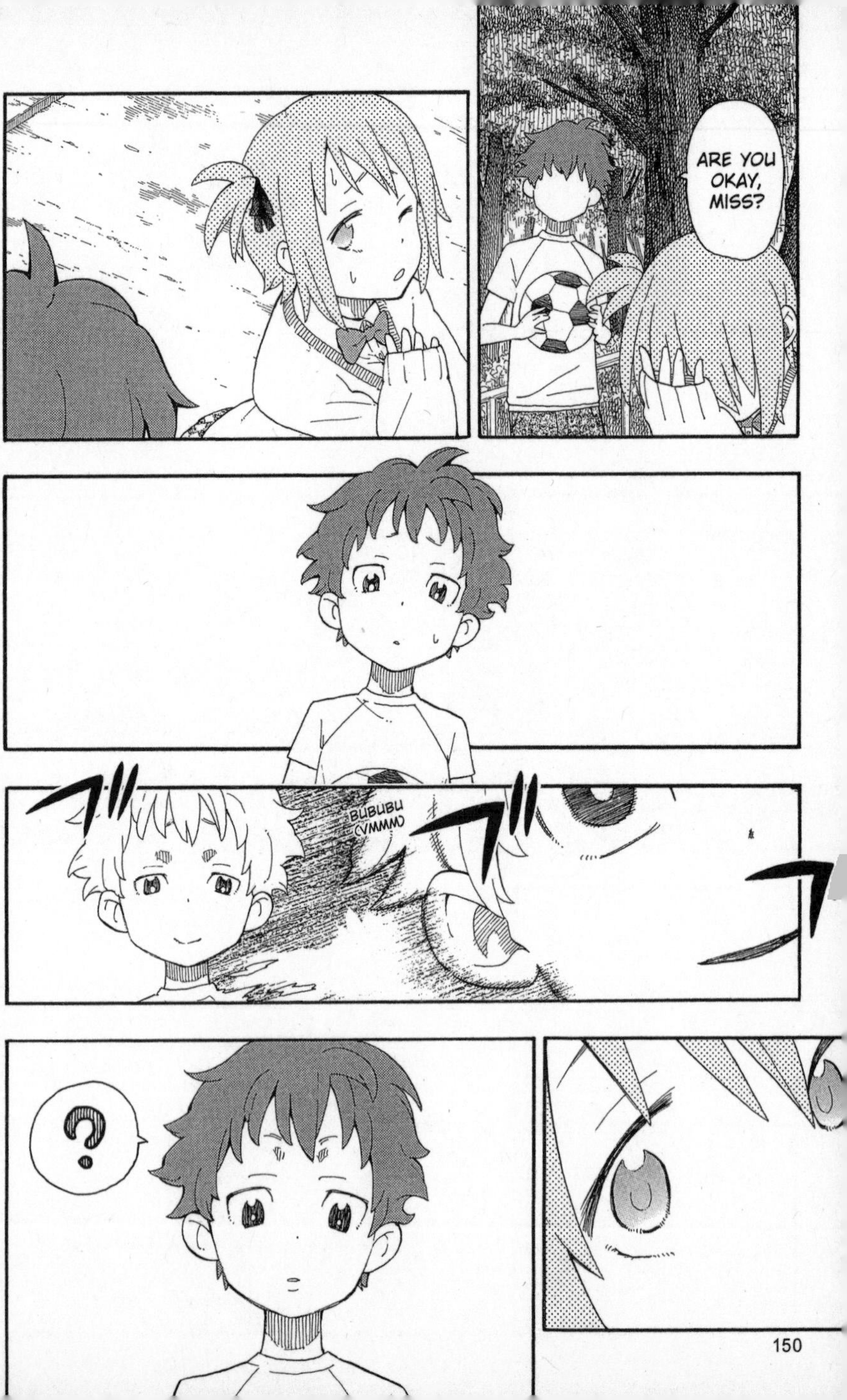
ARE YOU OKAY, MISS?
BUBUBU (VMMM)
?

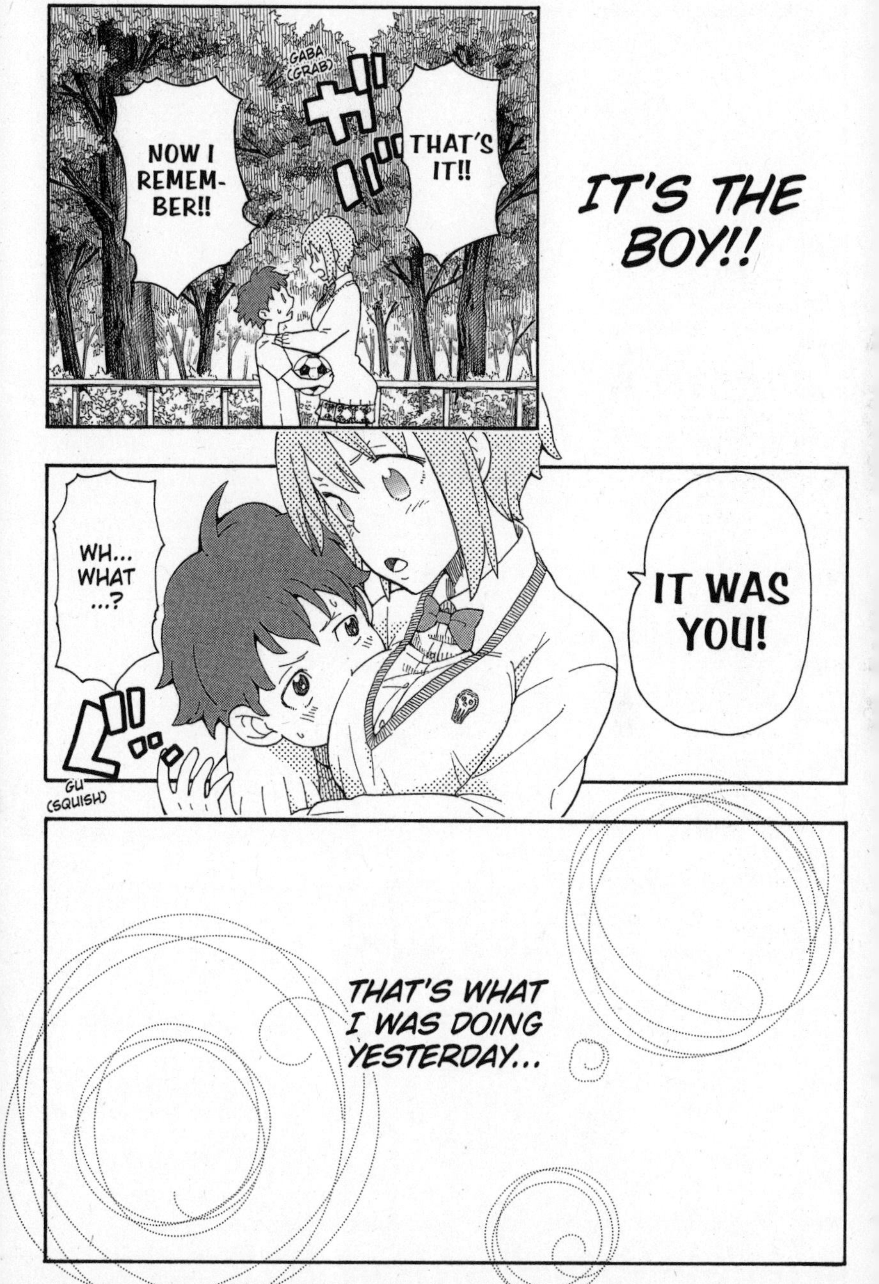
IT'S THE BOY!!
THAT'S IT!!
GABA (GRAB)
NOW I REMEMBER!!
IT WAS YOU!
WH... WHAT ...?
GU (SQUISH)
THAT'S WHAT I WAS DOING YESTERDAY...

FOR SOME REASON, I WAS JOGGING DOWN GRISSOM ROAD...

THEN, THE GUY WITH THE CREW CUT TOLD ME THAT PULLING THAT CART WHILE JOGGING WOULD BE BETTER EXERCISE.

I TOOK HIS SUGGESTION AND STARTED RUNNING OFF WITH THE SOUVENIR CART.

I PICKED UP TOO MUCH SPEED AND CRASHED AROUND A CORNER, TOTALING THE CART...

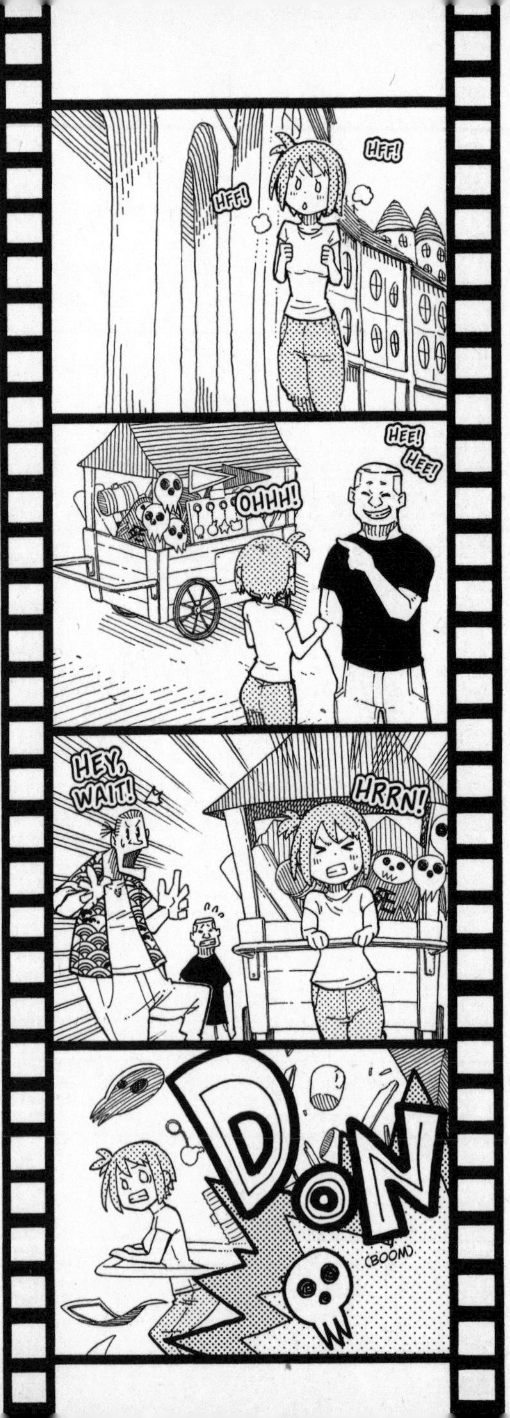
HFF!
HFF!
HEE! HEE!
OHHH!
HRRN!
HEY, WAIT!
DON
(BOOM)

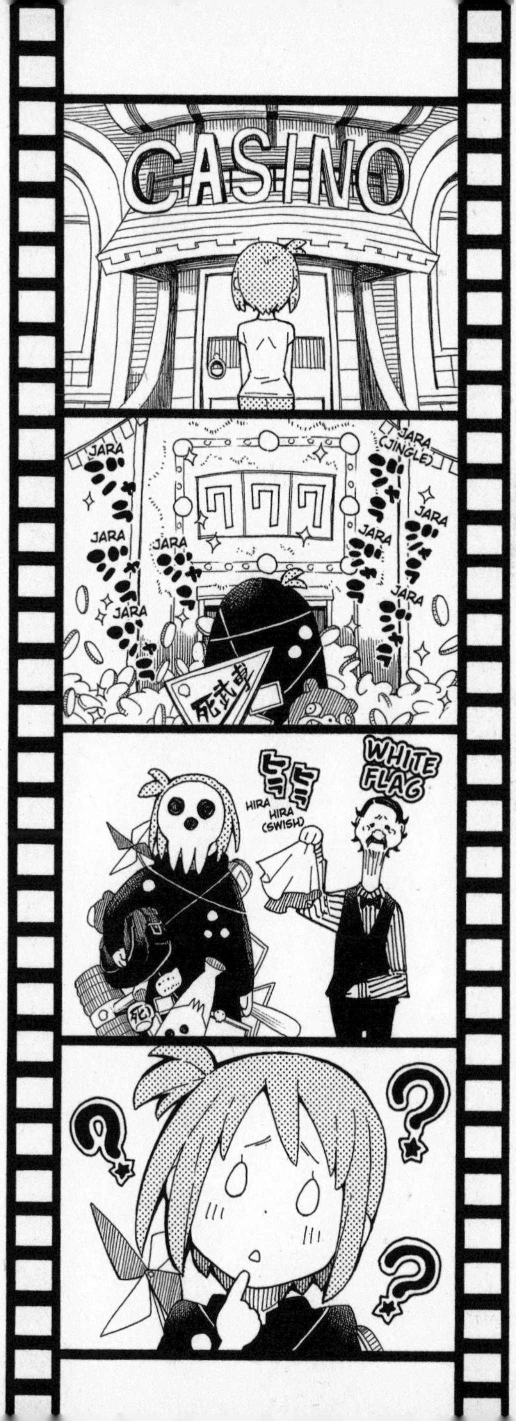
CASINO
JARA (JINGLE)
JARA
JARA
JARA
JARA
JARA
JARA
JARA
死武専
WHITE FLAG
HIRA HIRA (SWISH)

DEJECTED, I WANDERED AROUND UNTIL SOMEONE REMINDED ME, "THIS IS VEGAS"...

...SO I PUT ON THE SOUVENIR CART'S MERCHANDISE FOR GOOD LUCK AND HIT THE JACKPOT!

I MADE BACK THE REPAIR COSTS OF THE CART, BROUGHT THE CASINO MANAGER TO TEARS...

...AND THEN FORGOT EVERYTHING THAT HAD HAPPENED...

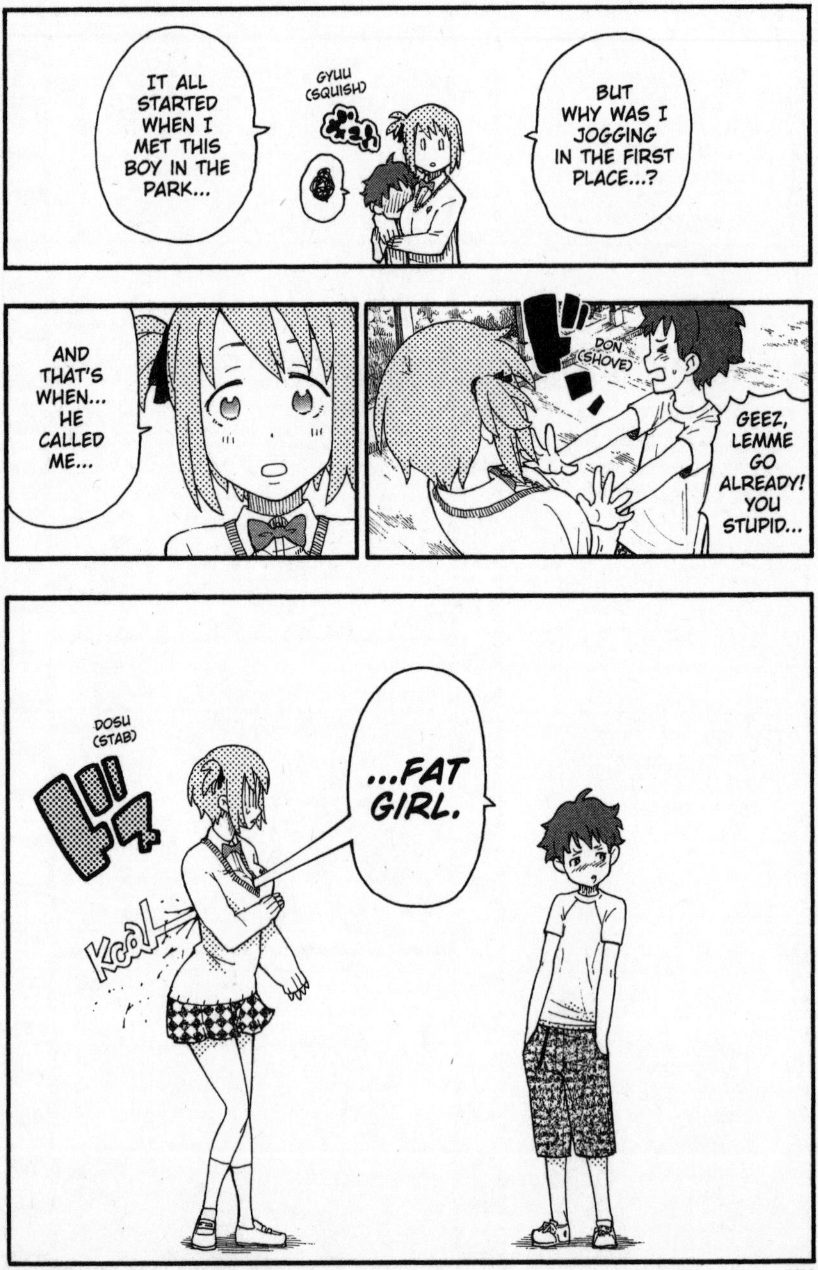
BUT WHY WAS I JOGGING IN THE FIRST PLACE...?
GYUU (SQUISH)
IT ALL STARTED WHEN I MET THIS BOY IN THE PARK...
DON (SHOVE)
GEEZ, LEMME GO ALREADY! YOU STUPID...
AND THAT'S WHEN... HE CALLED ME...
...FAT GIRL.
DOSU (STAB)
Kcal

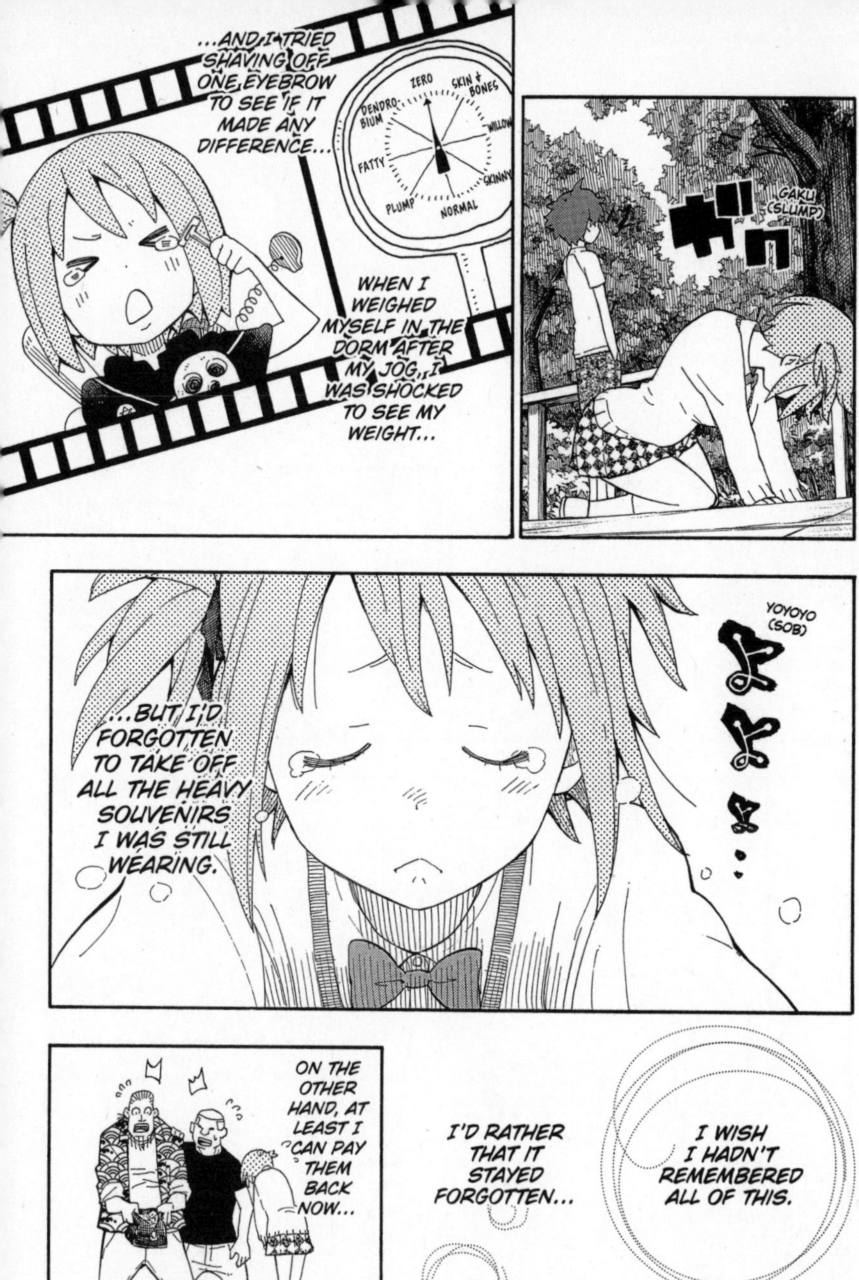
GAKU (SLUMP)
WHEN I WEIGHED MYSELF IN THE DORM AFTER MY JOG, I WAS SHOCKED TO SEE MY WEIGHT...
ZERO
SKIN & BONES
WILLOW
SKINNY
NORMAL
PLUMP
FATTY
DENDROBIUM
...AND I TRIED SHAVING OFF ONE EYEBROW TO SEE IF IT MADE ANY DIFFERENCE...
YOYOYO (SOB)
...BUT I'D FORGOTTEN TO TAKE OFF ALL THE HEAVY SOUVENIRS I WAS STILL WEARING.
I WISH I HADN'T REMEMBERED ALL OF THIS.
I'D RATHER THAT IT STAYED FORGOTTEN...
ON THE OTHER HAND, AT LEAST I CAN PAY THEM BACK NOW...

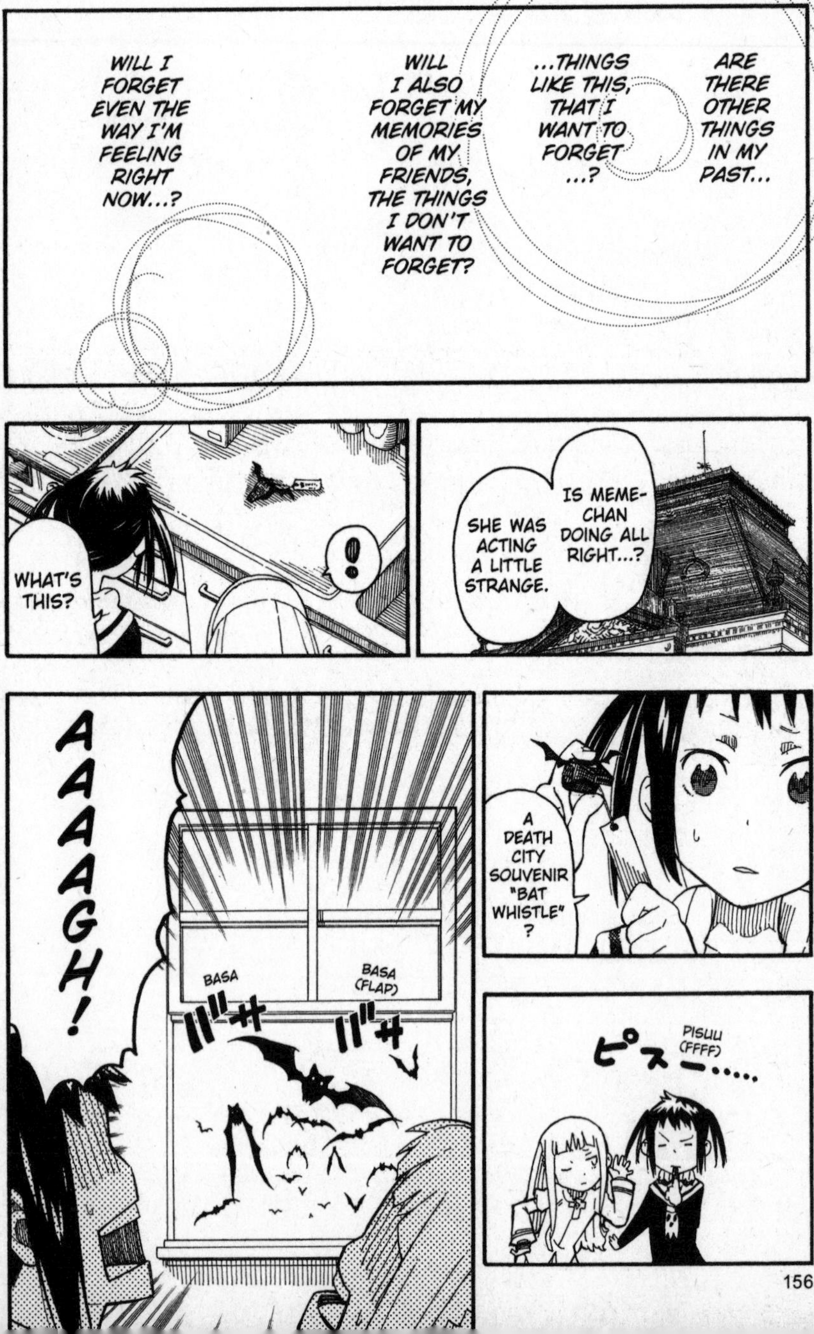
ARE THERE OTHER THINGS IN MY PAST...
...THINGS LIKE THIS, THAT I WANT TO FORGET ...?
WILL I ALSO FORGET MY MEMORIES OF MY FRIENDS, THE THINGS I DON'T WANT TO FORGET?
WILL I FORGET EVEN THE WAY I'M FEELING RIGHT NOW...?
IS MEME-CHAN DOING ALL RIGHT...?
SHE WAS ACTING A LITTLE STRANGE.
!
WHAT'S THIS?
A DEATH CITY SOUVENIR "BAT WHISTLE"?
ピスー.....
PISUU (FFFF)
AAAAAGH!
バサ
BASA
バサ
BASA (FLAP)

SOUL EATER NOT!

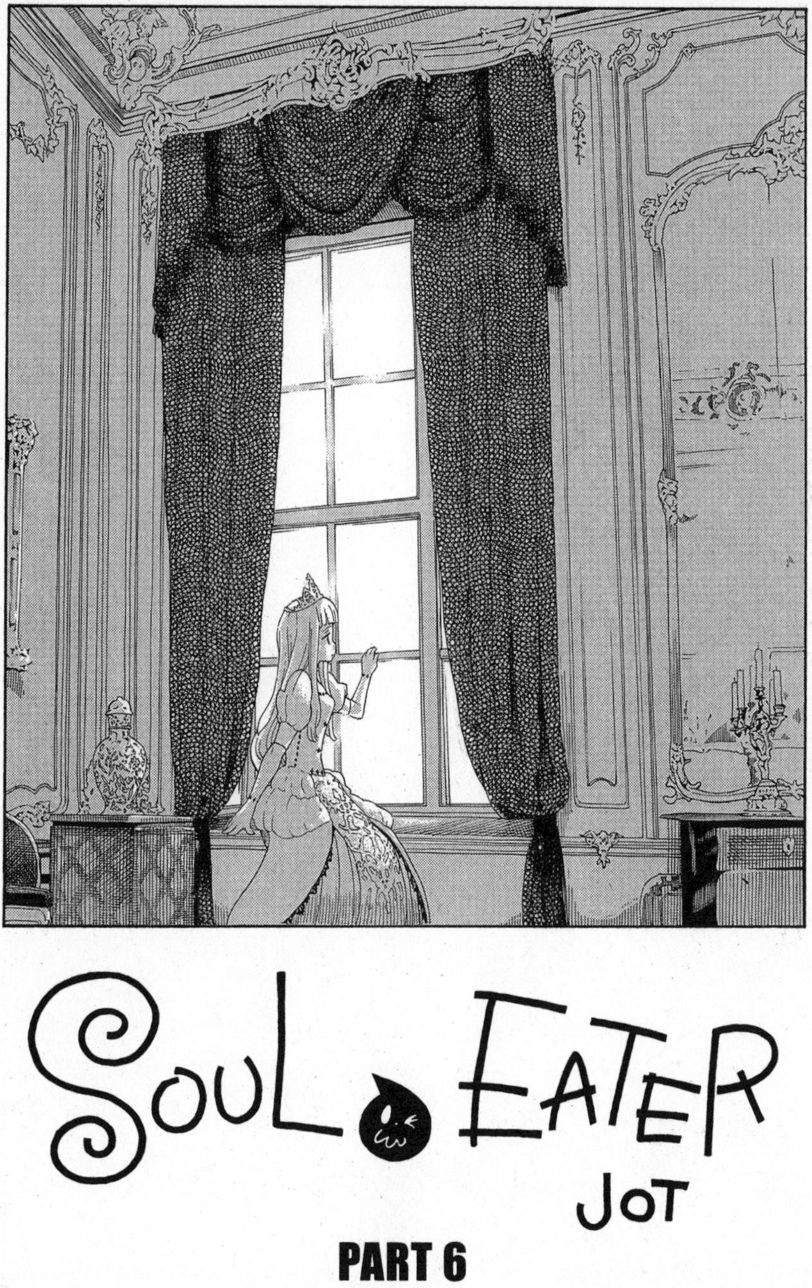

SOUL EATER
JOT

PART 6

DESIRE

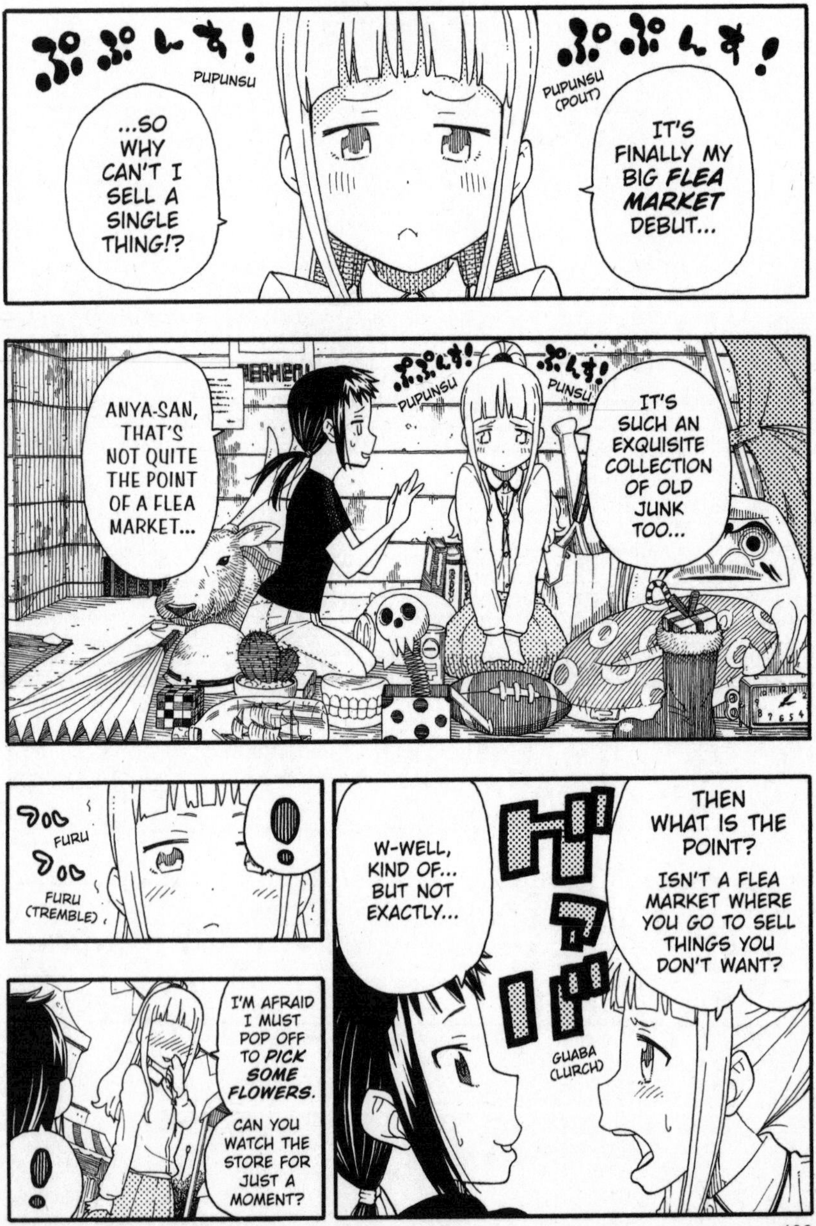

ぷぷんす!
PUPUNSU (POUT)
IT'S FINALLY MY BIG FLEA MARKET DEBUT...
ぷぷんす!
PUPUNSU
...SO WHY CAN'T I SELL A SINGLE THING!?
ぷんす!
PUNSU
IT'S SUCH AN EXQUISITE COLLECTION OF OLD JUNK TOO...
ぷぷんす!
PUPUNSU
ANYA-SAN, THAT'S NOT QUITE THE POINT OF A FLEA MARKET...
THEN WHAT IS THE POINT?
ISN'T A FLEA MARKET WHERE YOU GO TO SELL THINGS YOU DON'T WANT?
GUABA (LURCH)
W-WELL, KIND OF... BUT NOT EXACTLY...
!
FURU
FURU (TREMBLE)
I'M AFRAID I MUST POP OFF TO PICK SOME FLOWERS.
CAN YOU WATCH THE STORE FOR JUST A MOMENT?
!

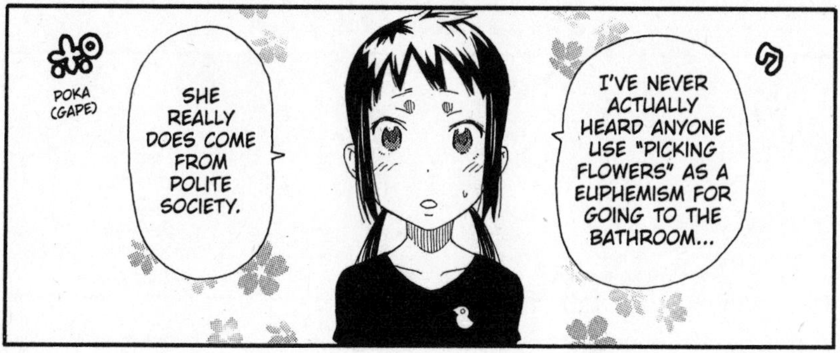
I'VE NEVER ACTUALLY HEARD ANYONE USE "PICKING FLOWERS" AS A EUPHEMISM FOR GOING TO THE BATHROOM...
SHE REALLY DOES COME FROM POLITE SOCIETY.
POKA (GAPE)

TEN MINUTES LATER...

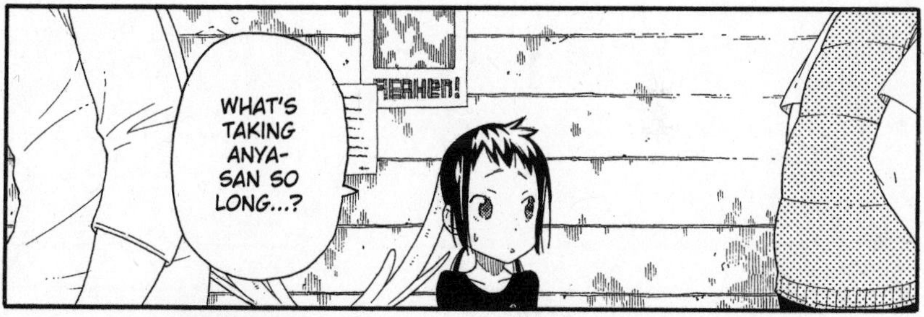
WHAT'S TAKING ANYA-SAN SO LONG...?

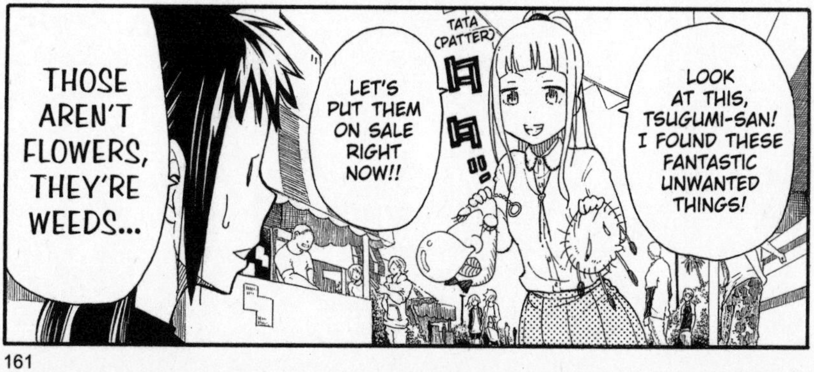
LOOK AT THIS, TSUGUMI-SAN! I FOUND THESE FANTASTIC UNWANTED THINGS!
TATA (PATTER)
LET'S PUT THEM ON SALE RIGHT NOW!!
THOSE AREN'T FLOWERS, THEY'RE WEEDS...

TATANE STYLE

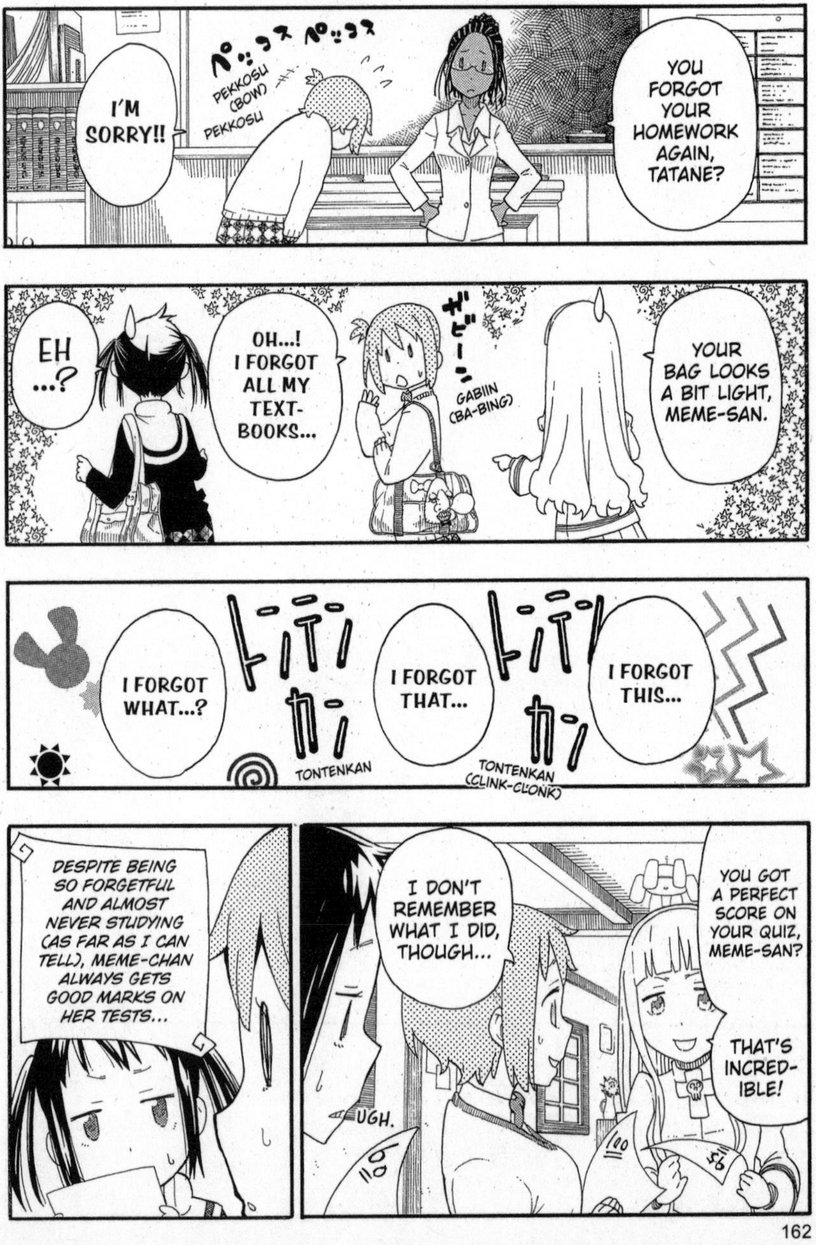
YOU FORGOT YOUR HOMEWORK AGAIN, TATANE?
PEKKOSU (BOW) PEKKOSU
I'M SORRY!!
YOUR BAG LOOKS A BIT LIGHT, MEME-SAN.
GABIIN (BA-BING)
OH...! I FORGOT ALL MY TEXTBOOKS...
EH ...?
I FORGOT THIS...
TONTENKAN (CLINK-CLONK)
I FORGOT THAT...
TONTENKAN
I FORGOT WHAT...?
YOU GOT A PERFECT SCORE ON YOUR QUIZ, MEME-SAN?
THAT'S INCREDIBLE!
I DON'T REMEMBER WHAT I DID, THOUGH...
UGH.
DESPITE BEING SO FORGETFUL AND ALMOST NEVER STUDYING (AS FAR AS I CAN TELL), MEME-CHAN ALWAYS GETS GOOD MARKS ON HER TESTS...

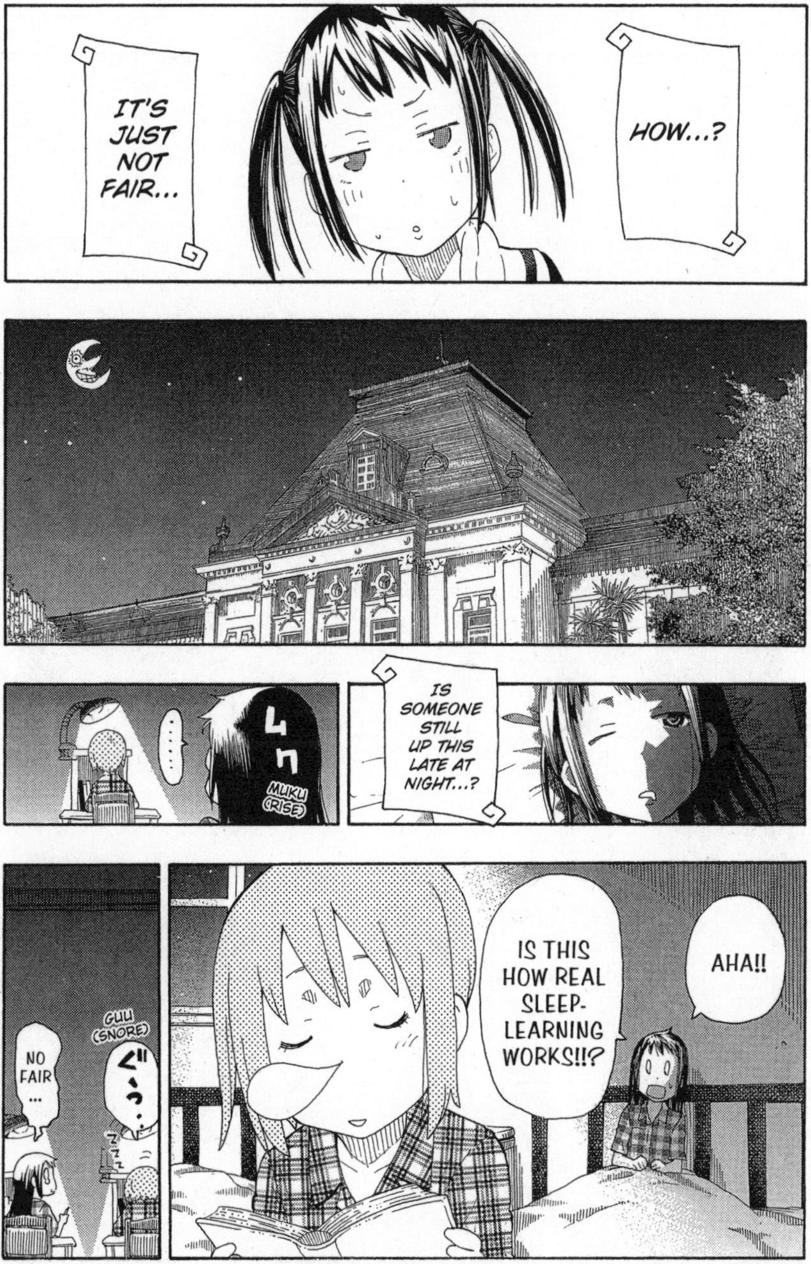
HOW...?
IT'S JUST NOT FAIR...
IS SOMEONE STILL UP THIS LATE AT NIGHT...?
......
ムク
MUKU (RISE)
AHA!!
IS THIS HOW REAL SLEEP-LEARNING WORKS!!?
GUU (SNORE)
NO FAIR ...

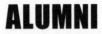

ALUMNI

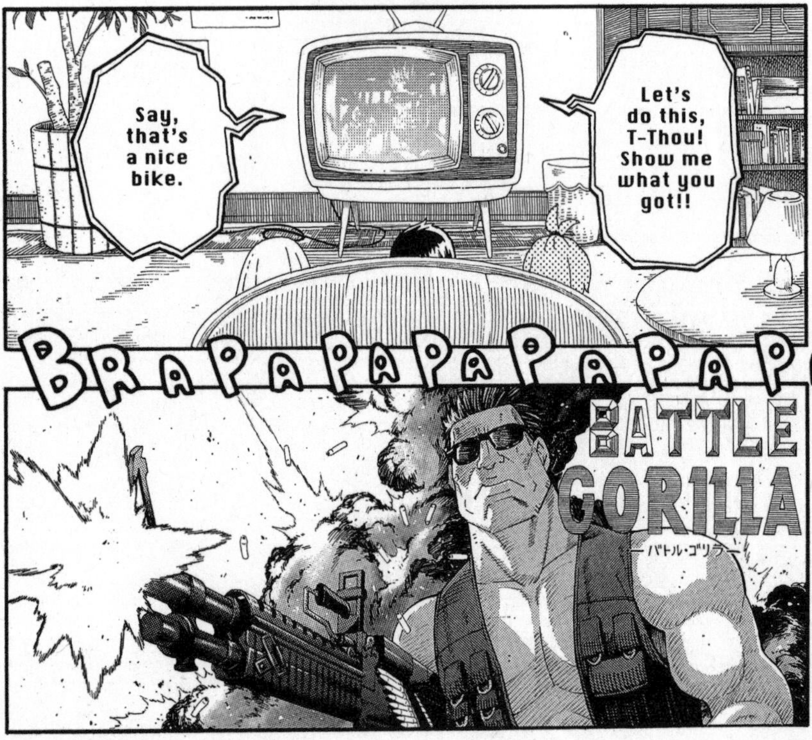
Let's do this, T-Thou! Show me what you got!!
Say, that's a nice bike.
BRAPAPAPAPAPAPAPA
BATTLE GORILLA
バトル・ゴリラ

SFX: UIIIN (VWRRR)

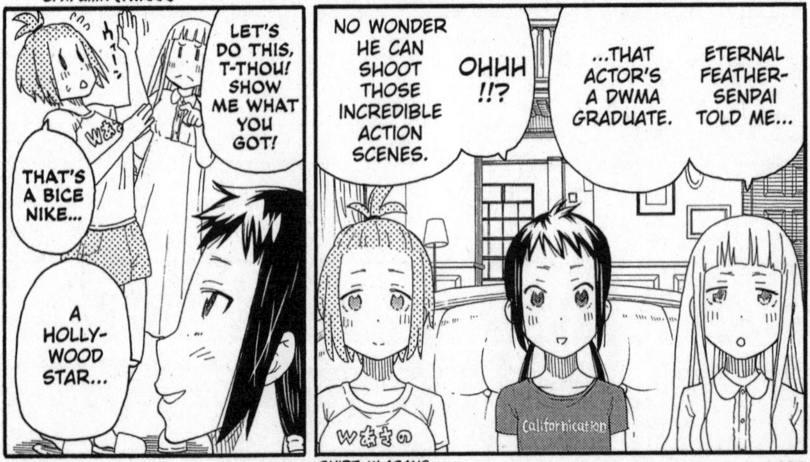
ETERNAL FEATHER-SENPAI TOLD ME...
...THAT ACTOR'S A DWMA GRADUATE.
OHHH !!?
NO WONDER HE CAN SHOOT THOSE INCREDIBLE ACTION SCENES.
Californication
LET'S DO THIS, T-THOU! SHOW ME WHAT YOU GOT!
THAT'S A BICE NIKE...
A HOLLY-WOOD STAR...

SHIRT: W ASANO

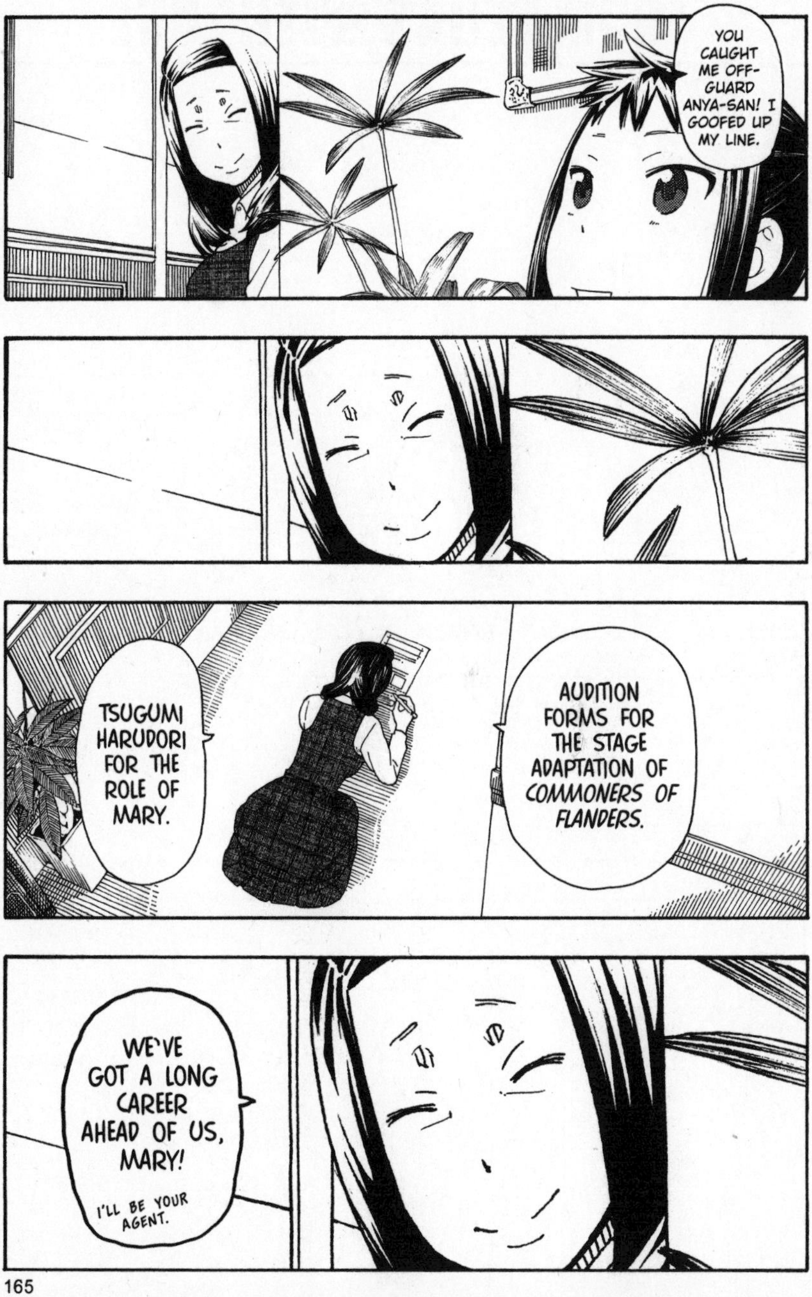
YOU CAUGHT ME OFF-GUARD ANYA-SAN! I GOOFED UP MY LINE.
AUDITION FORMS FOR THE STAGE ADAPTATION OF COMMONERS OF FLANDERS.
TSUGUMI HARUDORI FOR THE ROLE OF MARY.
WE'VE GOT A LONG CAREER AHEAD OF US, MARY!
I'LL BE YOUR AGENT.

FROM VEGAS WITH LOVE

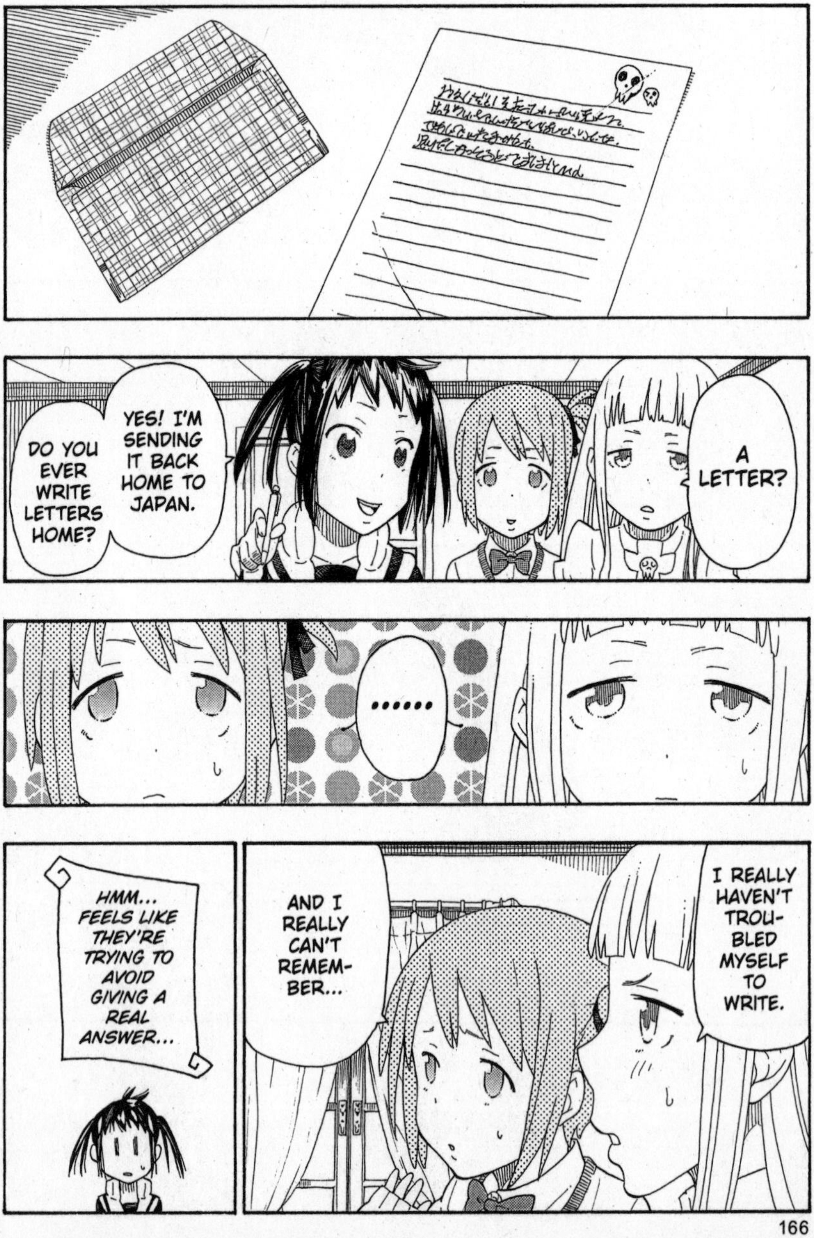
A LETTER?
YES! I'M SENDING IT BACK HOME TO JAPAN.
DO YOU EVER WRITE LETTERS HOME?
......
I REALLY HAVEN'T TROUBLED MYSELF TO WRITE.
AND I REALLY CAN'T REMEMBER...
HMM... FEELS LIKE THEY'RE TRYING TO AVOID GIVING A REAL ANSWER...

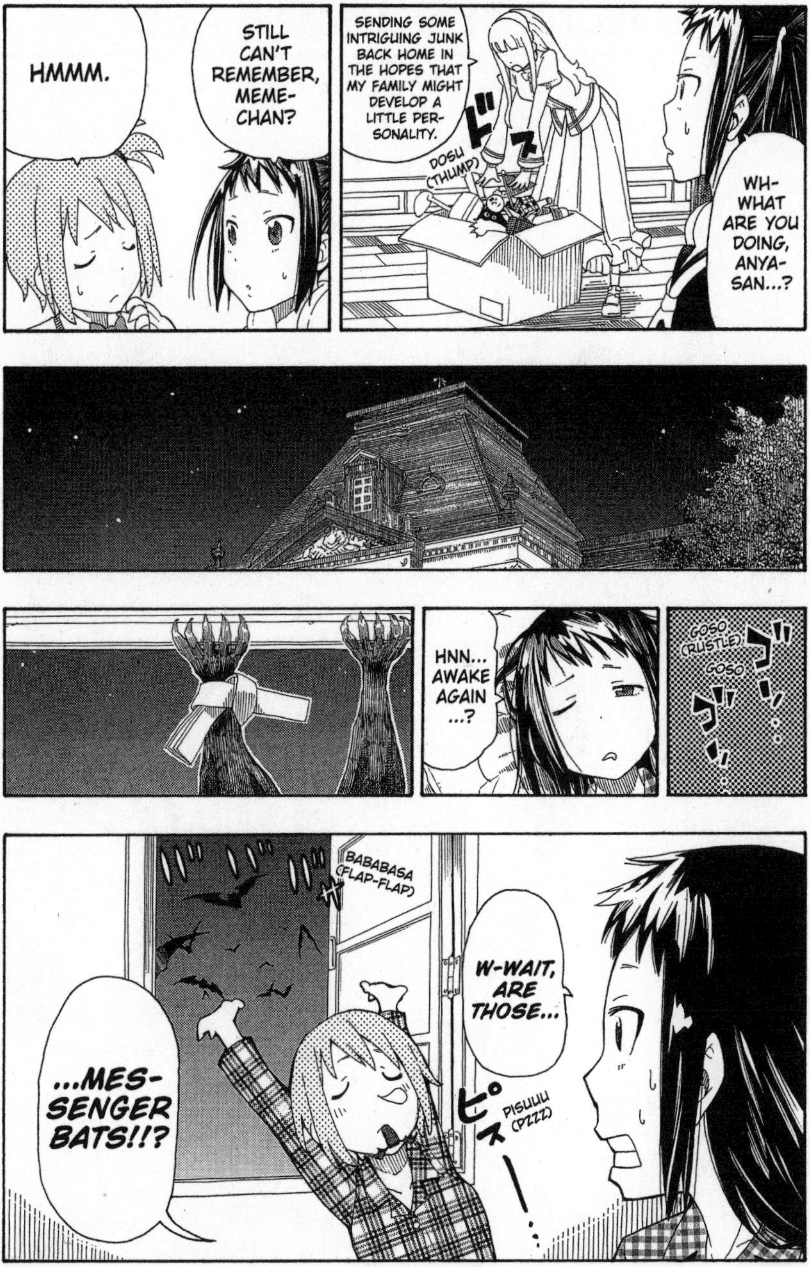
WH- WHAT ARE YOU DOING, ANYA-SAN...?
SENDING SOME INTRIGUING JUNK BACK HOME IN THE HOPES THAT MY FAMILY MIGHT DEVELOP A LITTLE PER-SONALITY.
DOSU (THUMP)
STILL CAN'T REMEMBER, MEME-CHAN?
HMMM.
GOSO (RUSTLE) GOSO
HNN... AWAKE AGAIN ...?
W-WAIT, ARE THOSE...
PISUUU (PZZZ)
BABABASA (FLAP-FLAP)
...MES-SENGER BATS!!?

RESPONSE

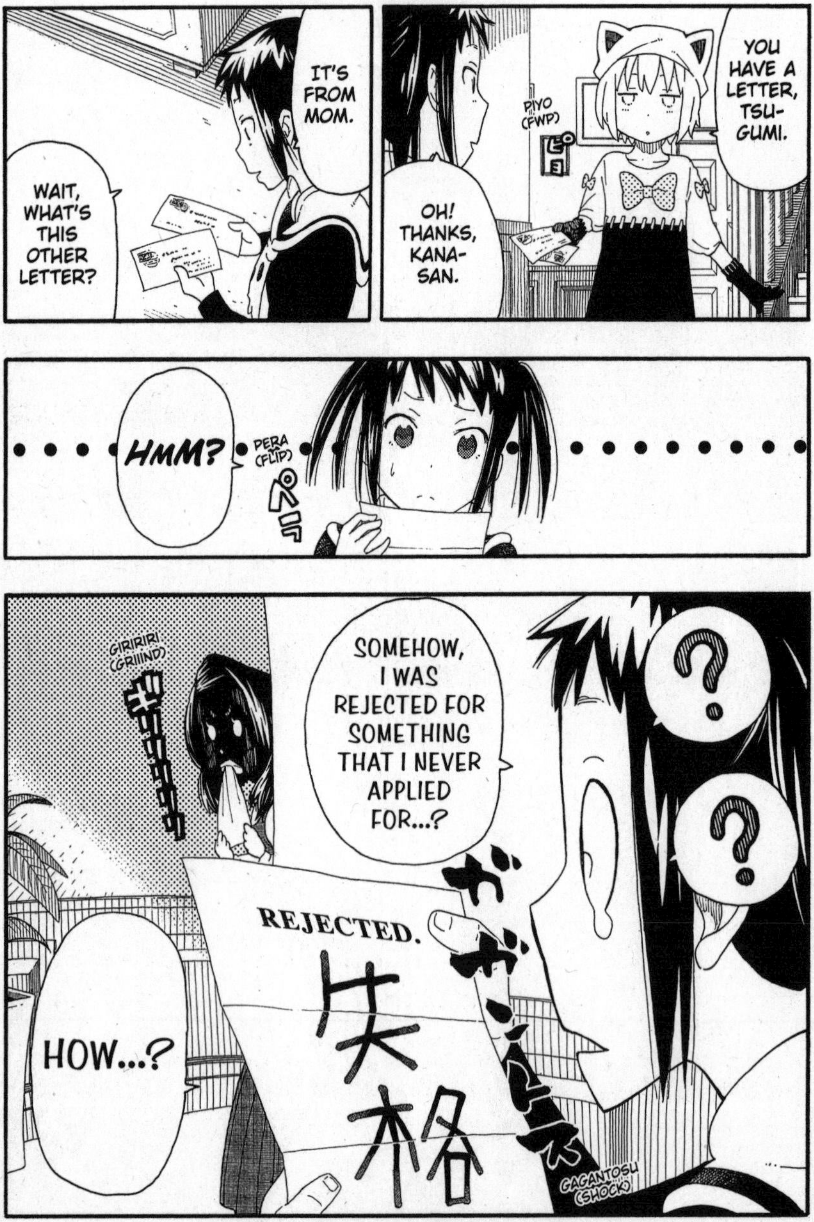

YOU HAVE A LETTER, TSUGUMI.
PIYO (FWP)
OH! THANKS, KANA-SAN.
IT'S FROM MOM.
WAIT, WHAT'S THIS OTHER LETTER?
HMM?
PERA (FLIP)
SOMEHOW, I WAS REJECTED FOR SOMETHING THAT I NEVER APPLIED FOR...?
REJECTED.
失格
GAGANTOSU (SHOCK)
GIRIRIRI (GRIIIND)
HOW...?

SOUL EATER NOT! 3 END

SOUL EATER NOT!

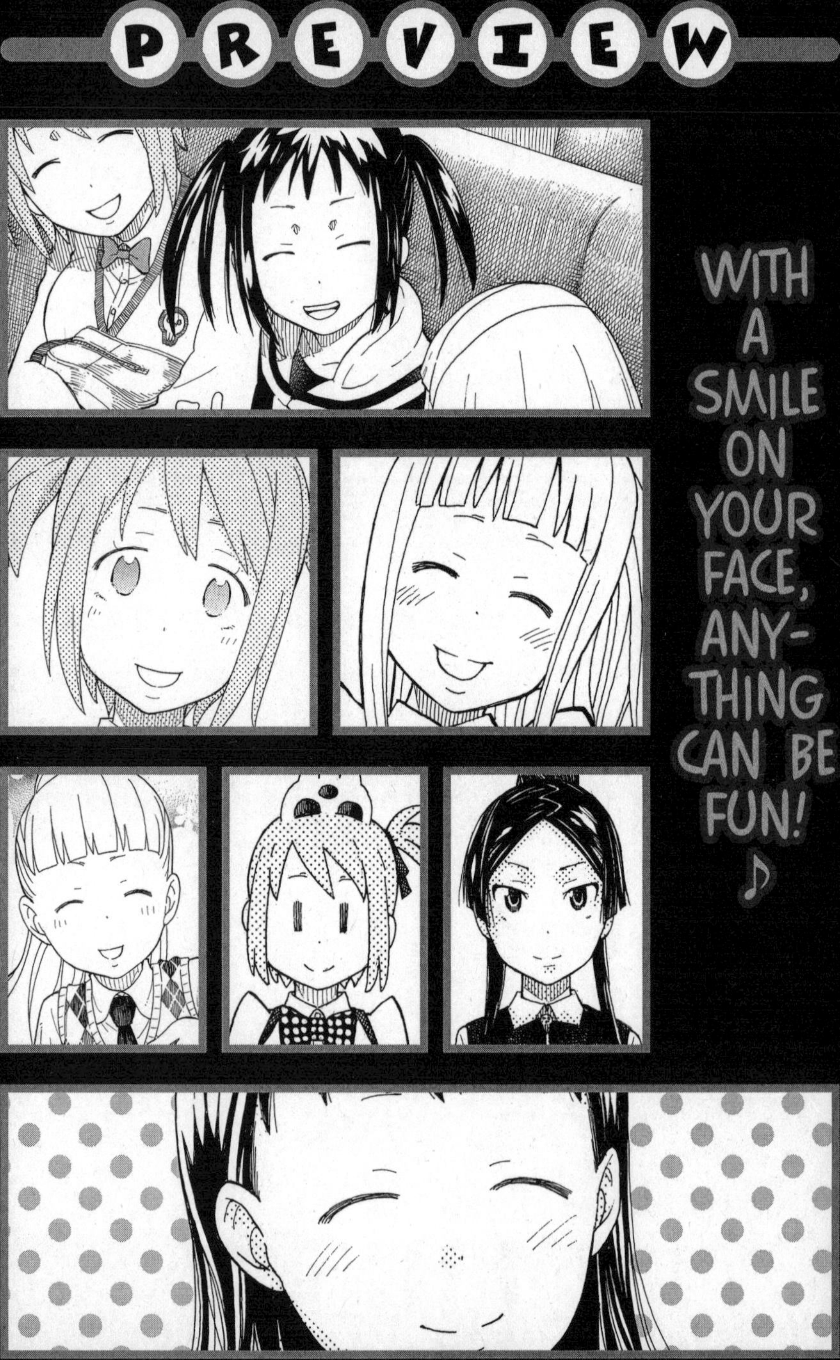
PREVIEW
WITH A SMILE ON YOUR FACE, ANY-THING CAN BE FUN! ♪

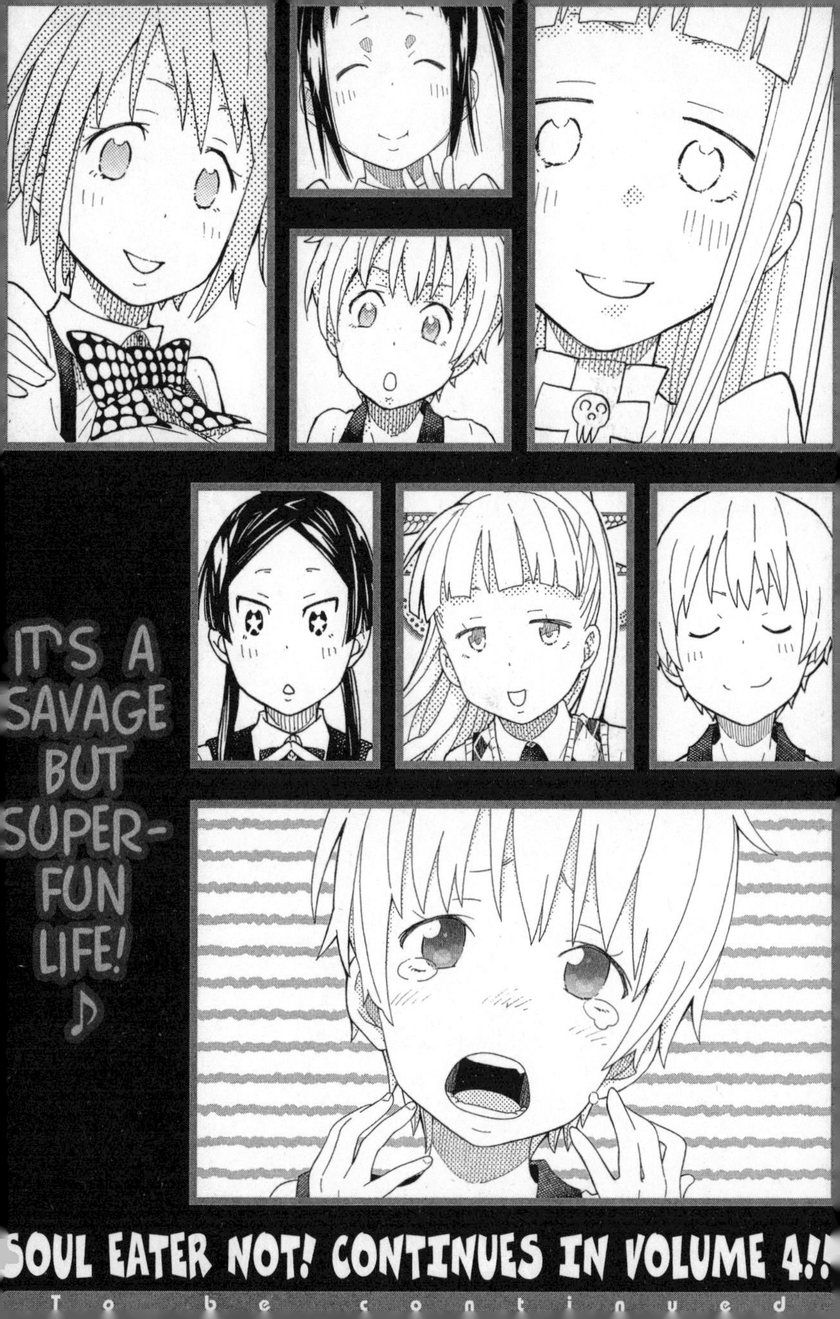
IT'S A SAVAGE BUT SUPER-FUN LIFE! ♪
SOUL EATER NOT! CONTINUES IN VOLUME 4!!
To be continued

Atsushiya
Not! Location

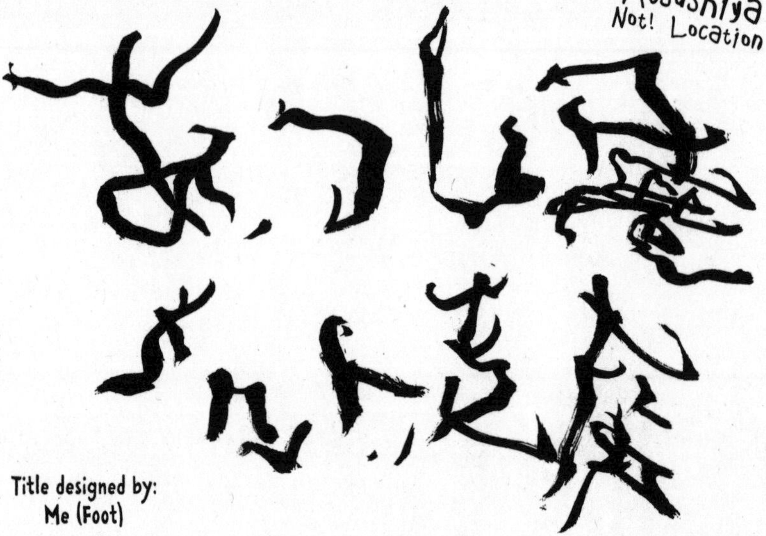

Title designed by:
Me (Foot)

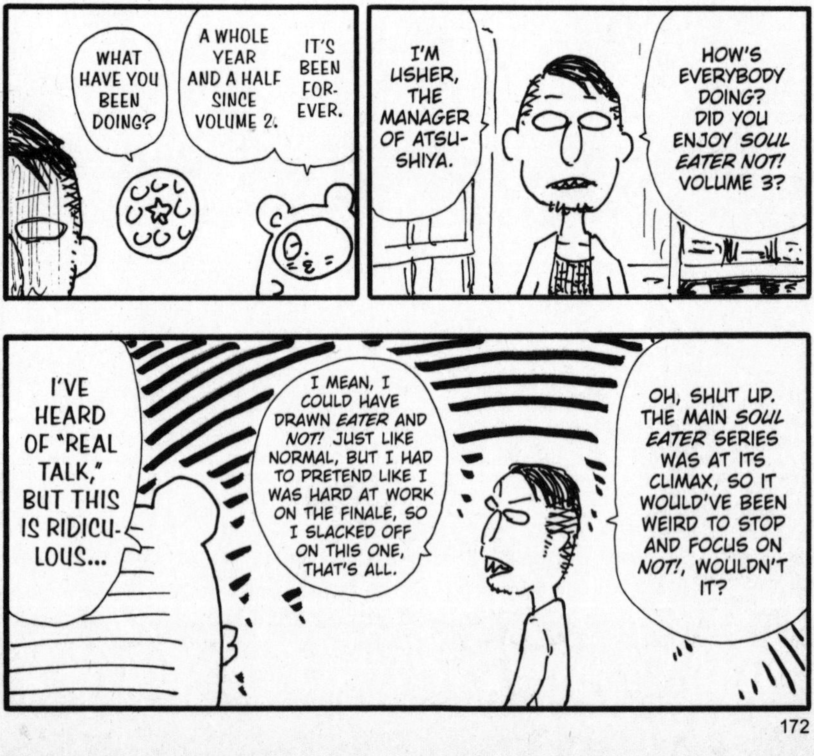

I'M USHER, THE MANAGER OF ATSU-SHIYA.
HOW'S EVERYBODY DOING? DID YOU ENJOY *SOUL EATER NOT!* VOLUME 3?
IT'S BEEN FOR-EVER.
A WHOLE YEAR AND A HALF SINCE VOLUME 2.
WHAT HAVE YOU BEEN DOING?
OH, SHUT UP. THE MAIN *SOUL EATER* SERIES WAS AT ITS CLIMAX, SO IT WOULD'VE BEEN WEIRD TO STOP AND FOCUS ON *NOT!*, WOULDN'T IT?
I MEAN, I COULD HAVE DRAWN *EATER* AND *NOT!* JUST LIKE NORMAL, BUT I HAD TO PRETEND LIKE I WAS HARD AT WORK ON THE FINALE, SO I SLACKED OFF ON THIS ONE, THAT'S ALL.
I'VE HEARD OF "REAL TALK," BUT THIS IS RIDICU-LOUS...

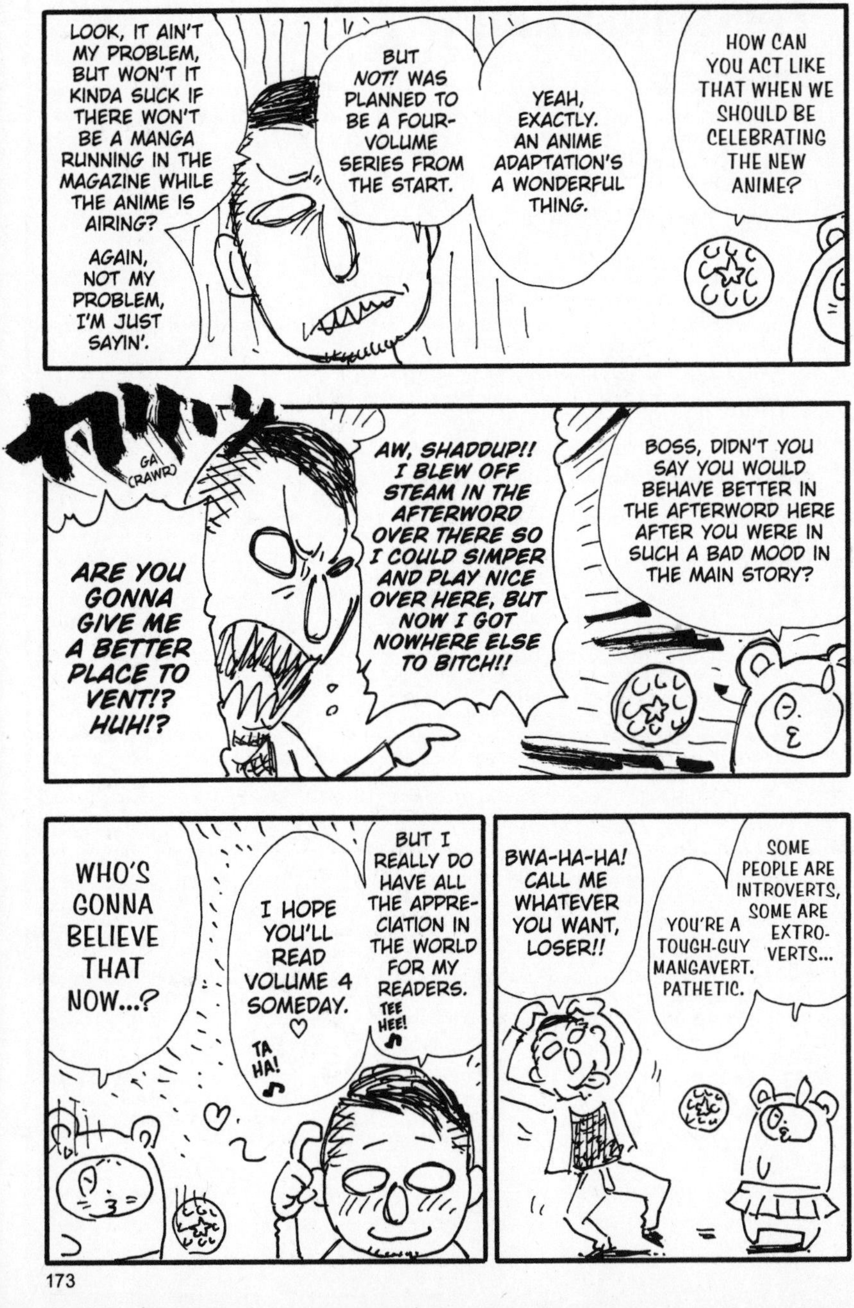
HOW CAN YOU ACT LIKE THAT WHEN WE SHOULD BE CELEBRATING THE NEW ANIME?
YEAH, EXACTLY. AN ANIME ADAPTATION'S A WONDERFUL THING.
BUT NOT! WAS PLANNED TO BE A FOUR-VOLUME SERIES FROM THE START.
LOOK, IT AIN'T MY PROBLEM, BUT WON'T IT KINDA SUCK IF THERE WON'T BE A MANGA RUNNING IN THE MAGAZINE WHILE THE ANIME IS AIRING?
AGAIN, NOT MY PROBLEM, I'M JUST SAYIN'.
BOSS, DIDN'T YOU SAY YOU WOULD BEHAVE BETTER IN THE AFTERWORD HERE AFTER YOU WERE IN SUCH A BAD MOOD IN THE MAIN STORY?
AW, SHADDUP!! I BLEW OFF STEAM IN THE AFTERWORD OVER THERE SO I COULD SIMPER AND PLAY NICE OVER HERE, BUT NOW I GOT NOWHERE ELSE TO BITCH!!
GA (RAWR)
ARE YOU GONNA GIVE ME A BETTER PLACE TO VENT!? HUH!?
SOME PEOPLE ARE INTROVERTS, SOME ARE EXTRO-VERTS...
YOU'RE A TOUGH-GUY MANGAVERT. PATHETIC.
BWA-HA-HA! CALL ME WHATEVER YOU WANT, LOSER!!
BUT I REALLY DO HAVE ALL THE APPRE-CIATION IN THE WORLD FOR MY READERS.
TEE HEE!
I HOPE YOU'LL READ VOLUME 4 SOMEDAY. ♡
TA HA!
WHO'S GONNA BELIEVE THAT NOW...?

Translation Notes

Common Honorifics

no honorific: Indicates familiarity or closeness; if used without permission or reason, addressing someone in this manner would constitute an insult.

-san: The Japanese equivalent of Mr./Mrs./Miss. If a situation calls for politeness, this is the fail-safe honorific.

-sama: Conveys great respect; may also indicate that the social status of the speaker is lower than that of the addressee.

-kun: Used most often when referring to boys, this indicates affection or familiarity. Occasionally used by older men among their peers, but it may also be used by anyone referring to a person of lower standing.

-chan: An affectionate honorific indicating familiarity used mostly in reference to girls; also used in reference to cute persons or animals of either gender.

-senpai: A suffix used to address upperclassmen or more experienced coworkers.

-sensei: A respectful term for teachers, artists, or high-level professionals.

Page 12
Chinese zombie: Known as the *jiangshi*, this monster from Chinese folklore is also known as a "hopping zombie" for the way it moves by leaping around with its arms outstretched. Over time the *jiangshi* has taken on aspects of the Western vampire such as bloodsucking.

Page 20
Jesús Navas: A Spanish soccer player. He played right winger for Sevilla FC for a number of years before joining Premier League club Manchester City.

Page 60
Tsugumi, tsubame, suzume: *Tsugumi* is the Japanese name for the thrush and other birds in the thrush family. *Tsubame* is the word for a swallow, and *suzume* means "sparrow."

Page 87
Edokko, dosanko: the term *edokko* means "child of Edo" with Edo being the old name for Tokyo. The classical depiction of an Edokko is one who spends money freely and is stubborn and quick to argue, but also sympathetic and honest. *Dosanko*, meaning "child produced in Hokkaido," can both refer to residents of Hokkaido and a type of horse bred on the island.

Page 100
Sasumata: A law-enforcement tool from feudal Japan used to apprehend criminals without harming them. The double-pronged head was used to snag the target's neck or another joint and hold him still until the target could be securely apprehended.

Page 155
Dendrobium: In *Mobile Suit Gundam*, Dendrobium (named after the orchid) is an enormous mobile suit model whose massive support unit (the "orchis") swallows up the actual fighting humanoid model ("stamen") much like a real orchid.

Page 164
W Asano: Stands for "Double Asano" ("W" is Japanese shorthand for the word "double"). "W Asano" was a term referring to Atsuko Asano and Yuuko Asano (no family relation), a pair of actresses who were popular in the late 1980s. The W Asano phenomenon started when they were cast as dual leads in the TV drama *Dakishimetai!* in 1988.

SOUL ⊙ EATER NOT!

Can't wait for volume 4?

Read the latest installments simultaneously with its Japanese release!

New chapters available monthly from your favorite ebook retailer and in the Yen Press App!

SOUL EATER NOT! ❸

ATSUSHI OHKUBO

Translation: Stephen Paul

Lettering: Abigail Blackman

SOUL EATER NOT! Vol. 3 © 2013 Atsushi Ohkubo / SQUARE ENIX. First published in Japan in 2013 by SQUARE ENIX CO., LTD. English translation rights arranged with SQUARE ENIX CO., LTD. and Hachette Book Group through Tuttle-Mori Agency, Inc.

Translation © 2014 by SQUARE ENIX CO., LTD.

Yen Press
Hachette Book Group
1290 Avenue of the Americas, New York, NY 10104

www.HachetteBookGroup.com
www.YenPress.com

Yen Press is an imprint of Hachette Book Group, Inc. The Yen Press name and logo are trademarks of Hachette Book Group, Inc.

First Yen Press Edition: July 2014

ISBN: 978-0-316-37666-2

10 9 8 7 6 5 4 3 2

BVG

Printed in the United States of America